BASIC FR

Jean-Claude Arragon was born in France, and has degrees from the Universities of Bordeaux and Leeds. Before joining Huddersfield Polytechnic, where he is now Senior Lecturer in French, he was Head of Modern Languages in a secondary school. His teaching experience has brought him into contact with a wide variety of age groups and ability levels in part-time, full-time and intensive courses. He is author of *Teach Yourself French Grammar* and co-author of the BBC French series for beginners, '*Ensemble*'

TEACH YOURSELF BOOKS

BASIC FRENCH

Jean-Claude Arragon

TEACH YOURSELF BOOKS
Hodder and Stoughton

First published 1988
Third impression 1990

Copyright © 1988
Jean-Claude Arragon

No part of this publication may be reproduced or transmitted
in any form or by any means, electronically or mechanically,
including photocopying, recording or any information storage
or retrieval system, without either the prior permission in
writing from the publisher or a licence permitting restricted
copying, issued by the Copyright Licensing Agency, 33–34
Alfred Place, London WC1E 7DP

British Library Cataloguing in Publication Data

Arragon, Jean-Claude
  Basic French. —— (Teach yourself books).
  1. French language — For non-French
  speaking students
  I. Title
  448.2´4

ISBN 0 340 42077 4

Printed and bound in Great Britain
for Hodder and Stoughton Educational,
a division of Hodder and Stoughton Ltd,
Mill Road, Dunton Green, Sevenoaks, Kent
by Richard Clay Ltd, Bungay, Suffolk.
Typeset by Macmillan India Ltd, Bangalore 25

Contents

Introduction

Learning a foreign language can be a highly fruitful and stimulating activity, but it presupposes a certain mental attitude if good and rapid progress is to be made. The following comments are intended to help you achieve that attitude.

You should always remember that each foreign language has its own identity. It would therefore be unreasonable to expect French to follow exactly the patterns of your mother tongue.

Although the same letters are used to write down French and English, the actual sounds they represent may not always be similar! Listening regularly to authentic foreign language material (records, radio broadcasts, etc.), is an essential part of the learning process.

You should also recognise and accept that the grammar rules of French are different from those of English. For instance, to express age in English, it is the verb 'to be' which is required: 'he is twenty', whereas in French, it is the verb 'avoir' (to have) followed by the word 'ans' (years) which is used in that context: 'il a vingt ans'.

Idiomatic phrases, sayings etc., will often be significantly different in the two languages. To help you appreciate that fact, several such phrases are included in each chapter.

Every language is governed by a number of fairly logical rules. Looking for those rules is also an essential part of the learning process. You should therefore train yourself to search for important clues. To help you refine this technique, 'Work It Out' sections have been included in most chapters. Look at the sentences presented and, before turning to the explanations, try and discover the relevant clues, as a good detective would. Draw your own conclusions, make your own rules. These may need to be revised, refined or even discarded as your learning progresses, but this exercise will help you look at the language in the right way.

'Passive' absorption of words, phrases, grammar rules etc., is only a small part of language learning. Use the material contained in each chapter to anticipate real-life situations in shops, offices, etc. Prepare in your own mind what you would say using and combining the phrases you have learnt, or better still, making your own sentences based on the models you already possess. The exercises found in each chapter will help you clarify and reinforce the knowledge already acquired.

Finally, you should make a conscious effort to develop your own powers of 'linguistic lateral thinking'. If you do not have at your disposal the words you need, try to express your thoughts in a different, simpler way. The 'Have a Try' passages for translation at the end of each unit give you the chance to use what you have learned.

If you follow these guidelines, you will find that learning French is an exciting and rewarding activity in which personal investigation, discovery and experimentation play a very important part. This is, after all, the true Teach Yourself approach.

Radio stations
In order to hear 'genuine' French material, you are strongly advised to listen to one of the following stations as often as you can; do not be put off by the fact that, at the beginning, you may have difficulty in understanding most of what is said. Be patient and remember that practice makes perfect!

France-Inter: 1829 on Long Wave (165 kHz)
Europe 1: 1666 on Long Wave (180 kHz)
Radio Luxembourg: 1271 on Long Wave (236 kHz)

Pronunciation

To communicate efficiently in spoken French, you need to pronounce it in a way which native speakers will understand.

This section is only a brief guide; the best way to improve your pronunciation is to listen to real French and imitate the sounds you hear as faithfully as you can.

The basic elements of the language, vowels and consonants, are presented below, together with their nearest English equivalents. Please note that 'English' in this context means 'Standard British English'.

Vowels

Important: All French vowels are 'tense'. This means that, when they are pronounced, the tongue, lips and jaws stay in the same position from the beginning to the end of the sound. This makes for a clear, 'crisp', sustained quality. In addition, French vowels retain their value whatever their position in a word. This is not so in English where, in a word like 'pre-pa-ra-tion' for instance, there is a strong vowel (that of the syllable -ra-) and a reduced one (that of the syllable -pa-). In the equivalent French word 'pré-pa-ra-tion', all vowels have virtually the same strength.

There are two types of vowels in French:

1 Oral vowels (the air escapes through the mouth). They are:

a	like the **a** in 'cat'	papa	sa
	or sometimes like the **a** in bath	hâte	mâle

Beware: the French *a* is *never* pronounced as that of 'fate' or 'late'.

e	like the **i** of 'fir', 'sir'	le	je
é	like the **i** or **y** of 'city'	allé	été
è/ê	like the **e** in 'net', 'set'	près	bête
i	like the **ee** in 'fee'	cri	si

o	like the **o** in 'not', 'pot'	comme **fort**
	or like the vowel sound in	
	'court', 'port'	p**o**se r**ô**le

Beware: the French *o* is *never* pronounced as that of 'nose' or 'rose'.

| **u** | similar to the **i** but with lips pushed out and rounded | d**ur**   s**ur** |

Beware: this sound is *not* that found in 'full' or 'pull'.

Notes:
—**y** has the same value as **i** above;
—the combinations 'au' or 'eau' produce a vowel sound similar to that found in 'taught' or 'caught', but with the lips pushed out and rounded;
—the combination 'ou' produces a sound similar to that of the vowel in 'fool' or 'pool', but the lips are pushed out and rounded;
—the combination 'ai' is normally pronounced like the vowel sound of 'set' or 'bet' (i.e. like *è* or *ê* above);
—in most cases, the combination 'eu' is pronounced as the vowel sound in 'fir' or 'purr'.

2   *Nasalised vowels*

(*Note*:   there are no nasalised vowels in English.) These are articulated in the same way as the corresponding oral vowels but some of the outward going air escapes through the nose. The following trick may help you to pronounce them with a reasonable degree of accuracy: practise the agreement noise '*mm*!' (which you sometimes utter instead of 'yes' with your lips closed); learn to produce it whilst opening your mouth, then add that sound onto the appropriate vowel sound, as indicated below.

ain/ein/in
   like the **e** of 'net', *plus* the nasal escape   m**ain**   f**în**
an/en
   like the **a** of 'bath', *plus* the nasal escape   **an**   d**ent**
un
   like the **i** in 'fir', *plus* the nasal escape   br**un**   **un**
on
   like the **ou** of 'nought', *plus* the nasal escape   b**on**   m**on**

Consonants

(The consonants which are *not* listed below are pronounced in an identical or almost identical way in both languages.)

c	like th **c** of 'car', when followed by **a**, **o**, **u**, or when at the end of a word, *or*	cage	bec
	like the **c** of 'face', when followed by **e** or **i**	ici	race
	Note: if the **c** preceding **a**, **o**, **u** bears a cedilla (ˌ), it will be sounded as that of 'race'	ça	reçu

Beware: the combination c + h normally produces a sound similar to the *sh* of 'shave' but *never* like that of *ch* in 'chap'.

g	like the **g** of 'gap' if followed by **a**, **o**, **u**, or at the end of a word, *or*	garde	guide
	like the **s** in 'leisure' if followed by **e** or **i**	âge	rougi

Beware: this sound does *not* incorporate the (d) element found in the English 'page' or 'rage' (pa(d)ge, ra(d)ge).

h In theory, there are two values of 'h' in French: 'mute' (=silent) and 'aspirated'. In practice, both are silent. The distinction is kept, however, because a 'mute h' does not prevent a clash of vowels between two words, whereas an 'aspirated h' does: compare: l'hôtel (hotel = 'mute') and: le haut (summit = 'aspirated')

Note: in modern dictionaries, the 'aspirated h' is signalled in the phonetic transcription by an asterisk (*) or an apostrophe (')

j	like the sound of **g** in 'âge'	je	jour

Beware: this sound does *not* incorporate a 'd' element either.

l	all French **l** sounds, whatever their position in the word, are pronounced like the **l** in 'let' or 'lip' (= clear l)	la	bal

q alone, or followed by *u*, is normally pronounced as the *k* of 'kit' or the *c* of 'cat'. co**q** **qu**e

r this sound is produced at the back of the
mouth (and not, as in English, at the front
with the tip of the tongue!) pa**r** **r**ue

Note: to practise the 'r' sound, pretend to gargle whilst holding
down the tip of your tongue (with a pencil for instance).

s if alone between two vowels, it will normally
be pronounced like the **z** in 'razor', *but* dé**s**ert o**s**é
in all other cases, it will have the same
value as its English counterpart **s** **s**ac **s**ur

Note: to retain the sound **s** between two vowels, the letter **s** must
normally be doubled.

compare: dé**s**ert (*desert*) (= **z**)
and: de**ss**ert (*dessert*) (= **s**)

Silent letters
In French, certain letters are not pronounced when they appear at the
end of a word (but see the section on liaison below). This is the case
for:
—the letter **s**: le**s** maison**s** (*houses*)
(the two final **s** letters are silent).
—the letters **t**, **x** and **z**: peti**t** (*small*); vieu**x** (*old*);
ne**z** (*nose*).

The word-final combination '**er**' is normally pronounced as é (similar
to the last sound of 'pretty' in English). The group '**et**' at the end of a
word is normally pronounced as è/ê, similar to the vowel sound in
'net'.

Liaison (word linking)
In order to avoid a clash of vowels between two adjoining words, the
last silent letter of the first word may sometimes be pronounced. The
normal sound value will be preserved except for:

—**s** and **x** which assume le**s** enfants (*the children*) sounded
  the sound **z**. as: 'le**z**enfants'.

six amis (*six friends*) sounded as: 'sizamis'.

—**d** which sometimes assumes the value of **t**.

grand ami (*great friend*) sounded as: 'gran**t**ami'.

Accents

Accents are signs used over certain letters (a, i, o, u) to distinguish between two words:

a (has); **à** (at),
ou (or); o**ù** (where),

or over 'e' to change the sound of that letter (see 'vowels' above).

1 Nouns   How to say 'the'

Nouns

Nouns are words used to name creatures or things: the words 'garçon' (boy/waiter), 'fille' (girl), 'chien' (dog), 'table' (table), 'sac' (bag) are all nouns. In English, a noun is generally said to be *masculine* if it denotes a male human being, *feminine* if it refers to a female human being and *neuter* if it denotes anything else. So 'man' or 'boy' are masculine and can be referred to as 'he'; 'woman' or 'girl' are feminine and can be referred to as 'she'; 'table' or 'bag' are neuter and can be referred to as 'it'. It is not uncommon, however, for an animal to be referred to as 'he' or 'she' according to its sex (which seems fairly logical), and for a car or a ship to be referred to as 'she' (which seems totally illogical!).

In French, the system is quite different. First of all, there is no neuter. Therefore, nouns can only belong to one of the two categories or *genders*: masculine or feminine. The seemingly daunting task of finding out and remembering whether a French noun is masculine or feminine will be greatly simplified if you learn to look (and listen) for clues. You will find, for instance, that *endings* can be very useful in many cases to determine the gender of nouns. You will also find that certain categories of nouns share a common gender. Not surprisingly, nouns denoting beings of the male sex are generally masculine, and nouns referring to beings of the female sex are usually feminine. Nouns denoting trees are often masculine, whereas names of flowers, fruit and illnesses are often feminine. But beware! There are always exceptions to most rules, just to make things interesting!

How to say 'the'

Besides the above-mentioned clues which are carried by the noun itself, there are additional ones, given by other words in the sentence.

Such is the case with the French equivalent of the word 'the'. In English, 'the' does not carry any information about the gender (masculine, feminine, neuter) or the *number* (singular or plural) of the noun, and remains the same in all cases: 'the boy', 'the girl', 'the dog', 'the doors', 'the men'. This is not the case in French.

In the singular, if the noun is masculine, the French for 'the' will be 'le': 'le garçon' (the boy/waiter), 'le chien' (the dog). If the noun is feminine, the French for 'the' will be 'la': 'la fille' (the girl/daughter), 'la porte' (the door).

Note: This clue will not be available to you if the word which follows 'le' or 'la' begins with a vowel (a, e, i, o, u) or with a 'mute' (i.e. unpronounced) h; in such cases, 'le' and 'la' will be reduced to 'l'':

l'ami	*(male) friend*
l'amie	*(female) friend*
l'hôtel	*hotel (masculine)*
l'heure	*time/hour (feminine)*

The reason is that French hates a clash of vowels between two words and will avoid it by a variety of means whenever possible.

In the plural, i.e. to denote 'more than one', the French equivalent of 'the' is 'les' for both masculine and feminine.

Compare:

le garçon	— **les** garçons	the boy(s),
la fille	— **les** filles	the girl(s),
le chien	— **les** chiens	the dog(s),
la porte	— **les** portes	the door(s),
l'hôtel	— **les** hôtels	the hotel(s),
l'amie	— **les** amies	the friend(s).

So 'les' carries no clues telling you whether the noun is masculine or feminine. You will therefore have to look for such clues elsewhere.

Note: After examining the examples given above to illustrate the plural form of 'the' in French, it is possible to make the following observation: the six plural nouns used end in 's'. Could this mean that French nouns take an 's' in the plural as do most English ones? The answer is that the great majority of them do, but that there are, as in English, a few exceptions to that rule.

Remember: Training your mind to *look for clues* is an essential part of the language-learning process. The 'work it out' sections will help you to develop this skill. Active learning of this type is the key to speedy progress!

Work it out

Look carefully at the following list of French nouns and try to state a rule about their gender by looking at their endings. The last two words in the list have been added to help you realise that the rule has to be stated precisely!

1	la création (*creation*)	7	le ciment (*cement*)
2	la violence (*violence*)	8	le développement (*development*)
3	le moment (*moment/time*)	9	la clémence (*clemency*)
4	la prudence (*prudence*)	10	la situation (*situation*)
5	la perfection (*perfection*)	11	la dent (*tooth*)
6	le segment (*segment*)	12	le camion (*lorry*)

Conclusions
The following points should have emerged from this limited sample.

A Since 'création', 'perfection' and 'situation' are all preceded by 'la', but 'camion' by 'le', French nouns ending in 'tion' (but not just 'ion') appear to be feminine

B Since 'violence', 'prudence' and 'clémence' are all preceded by 'la', nouns ending in 'ence' appear to be feminine.

C Since 'moment', 'segment', 'ciment' and 'développement' are preceded by 'le' but 'dent' (tooth) by 'la', nouns ending in 'ment' (but not just 'ent') appear to be masculine.

The above rules are in fact very accurate. There are no exceptions to the first one; the only exception to the second one is 'le silence' (silence) and the only exception to the third one is 'la jument' (the mare).

Note:
1 Whenever you encounter a new French noun, you should always try to memorise it with its *definite article* 'le' or 'la' as applicable: do not just learn 'maison' (house) but 'la maison' (feminine), do not learn 'village' (village) but 'le village' (masculine) etc. In this way, you will avoid making a cascade of mistakes when building up sentences

and you will also give your mind some information which will enable it to work out useful rules about the gender of nouns.

2   In French, the articles 'le', 'la' and 'les' are far more frequently used than their English equivalent 'the'. The reason is that they give important information about the noun and should therefore not be omitted. In most cases, for instance, the plural form of a French noun sounds exactly the same as its singular one, the 's' of the plural being silent. That is why it is important to have the definite article to signal whether the noun is in the singular or the plural. In English the two forms sound distinctly different.

Exercise 1(i)
On the strength of the discoveries made in the above section, state which of the following nouns is masculine (m) or feminine (f), since, as we have said, 'l'' does not carry that information.

1 l'action (*action*) **2** l'audience (*audience*) **3** l'élément (*element*) **4** l'essence (*essence/petrol*) **5** l'équipement (*equipment*) **6** l'intention (*intention*) **7** l'armement (*armament*) **8** l'obstruction (*obstruction*) **9** l'apparence (*appearance*) **10** l'infection (*infection*).

Exercise 1(ii)
From what has been said in this chapter concerning the gender of certain categories of nouns (trees, fruit, illnesses), state which of the following nouns should be preceded by 'le' (=masculine) and which should take 'la' (=feminine).

1 rose (*rose*) **2** grippe (*flu*) **3** pin (*pine-tree*) **4** pomme (*apple*) **5** palmier (*palm-tree*) **6** tulipe (*tulip*) **7** pêche (*peach*) **8** rage (*rabies*) **9** chêne (*oak*) **10** fraise (*strawberry*).

Exercise 1(iii)
Put the following nouns and their article in the plural.

1 la tulipe **2** le pin **3** la fraise **4** l'élément **5** le palmier **6** l'action **7** le chêne **8** le moment

Ouf! C'est fini!
Phew! It's over!

2 Describing things and beings
How to say 'a' (or 'an')

Describing things and beings

If you want to give information about things or beings, you need words to *describe* them. Such words are called *adjectives:* small, tall, dear, black are all adjectives. In English, adjectives are nearly always placed before the noun they describe. The fact that the noun might refer to one or more beings of either sex or to one or more things has no effect on the shape of the English adjective.

Compare:
    the small boy(s)
    the small girl(s)
    the small cat(s)

In French, the situation is quite different. As already mentioned, French nouns fall into two distinct gender categories, masculine and feminine. This affects many other words in the sentence, not only *definite articles* (see Chapter 1), but also *adjectives, demonstratives, possessives*, etc., as we shall see in this and other chapters. That is why it is vitally important to know whether a given noun is masculine or feminine.

Note: To enable you to construct a variety of simple but very useful sentences, we shall at this stage introduce the following forms of the verb 'être' (to be) which is the most frequently used verb in the language:

    il/elle est (*he/she/it is*) and
    ils/elles sont (*they are*)

The verb will be presented in full in a later chapter.

Word list

Nouns

le chat	*cat*	la nuit	*night*
la dame	*lady/woman*	la robe	*dress*
la fleur	*flower*	le sac	*bag*
l'homme (masc.)	*man*	le vase	*vase*
la maison	*house*	la voiture	*car*

Adjectives

content	*pleased/glad*	noir	*black*
fatigué	*tired*	petit	*small*
fermé	*closed/locked*	sale	*dirty*
fort	*strong*	triste	*sad*
jeune	*young*	vert	*green*
joli	*pretty*	vieux	*old*
malade	*ill*		

Other words

et	*and*	elle	*she/it*
mais	*but*	ils	*they (masc.)*
il	*he/it*	elles	*they (fem.)*

Work it out

Look carefully at the following phrases and see what you can deduce about the way French adjectives behave, on the basis of the information available.

le chat noir   les chats noirs
   the black cat(s)

la robe noire   les robes noires
   the black dress(es)

le sac vert   les sacs verts
   the green bag(s)

la voiture verte   les voitures vertes
   the green car(s)

la jolie dame   les jolies dames
   the pretty lady (ladies)

le petit garçon   les petits garçons
   the little boy(s)

la petite maison   les petites maisons
   the small house(s)

Deductions

Bearing in mind that your remarks are based on a very limited sample, and may therefore need to be amended later, the following points should have emerged:

A Since 'noir', 'vert', 'joli' and 'petit' take an 'e' when used with a feminine noun, and an 's' in the plural, it appears that French adjectives form their feminine by adding an 'e' to the masculine, and their plural by adding an 's' in both cases.

B Some adjectives (here 'joli' and 'petit') appear before the noun, some (here 'noir' and 'vert') appear after the noun; adjectives of colour seem to appear after the noun.

Although the above deductions do not give you the whole picture about the behaviour and *agreement* of French adjectives, they provide sound basic information.

Elémentaire!
Elementary!

Note:

1   If an adjective ends in 'e' (without an accent on it) in the masculine singular, it will remain the same in the feminine singular. But if there is an accent on the final 'e' the normal rule will apply:

le vin roug**e**	*(the red wine)*
la robe roug**e**	*(the red dress)*
but:	
le sac fermé	*(the closed bag)*
la porte fermé**e**	*(the closed door)*.

In the plural, both will take an 's':

les robes roug**es**	*(the red dresses)*
les sacs fermé**s**	*(the closed bags)*

2   Adjectives ending in 'el', 'en', 'on' in the masculine singular: 'réel' (real), 'ancien' (ancient), 'bon' (good) . . . will double the last letter before taking the 'e' in the feminine:

la crise est rée**lle**	*(the crisis is real)*
la maison est ancie**nne**	*(the house is ancient)*
la pomme est bo**nne**	*(the apple is good)*

3   The adjectives 'beau' (beautiful), 'nouveau' (new) and 'vieux' (old), become in the feminine: 'belle', 'nouvelle' and 'vieille' respectively, and in the masculine plural: 'beaux', 'nouveaux' and 'vieux':

la be**lle** fleur	*(the beautiful flower)*
la nouve**lle** voiture	*(the new car)*
la viei**lle** dame	*(the old lady)*
Les nouveau**x** sacs sont beau**x**	*(the new bags are beautiful)*

Exercise 2(i)
Translate into English:

1 Le sac est noir. **2** La maison est petite. **3** La porte est fermée. **4** Les garçons sont contents. **5** Les fleurs sont jolies. **6** Les filles sont grandes. **7** Le chat noir est fatigué. **8** Le petit café est fermé. **9** La grande voiture rouge est vieille. **10** Les robes noires sont sales.

Exercise 2(ii)
Make the adjectives in brackets agree with the noun they describe:

1 La porte est (grand). **2** Les filles sont (petit). **3** La (vieux) dame est (content). **4** Les sacs (vert) sont (fermé). **5** La (joli) fleur est dans le (petit) vase (noir). **6** Les (nouveau) voitures sont (beau). **7** Les chats (noir) sont (fatigué). **8** La (jeune) dame est (malade). **9** Les (grand) garçons sont (fort). **10** Les robes (rouge) sont (joli) mais elles sont (grand).

How to say 'a' (or 'an')

French nouns, as we have already seen, fall into two gender categories: masculine or feminine. That is why there are two distinct words to translate the English *indefinite article* 'a' or 'an'.

For masculine nouns the word used will be 'un': 'un garçon' (*a boy*), 'un chien' (*a dog*), 'un sac' (*a bag*), 'un ami' (*a male friend*).

For feminine nouns, the word used will be 'une': 'une fille' (*a girl*), 'une amie' (*a female friend*), 'une porte' (*a door*), 'une table' (*a table*).

Note: In English the convention is that it is perfectly acceptable to use a noun on its own in the plural with the meaning of 'an unspecified number of', 'some', 'more than one': 'dogs' (= some dogs), 'boys' (= an unspecified number of boys), and so on.

In French this is not possible. The reason is that, in most cases, the plural form of a noun sounds exactly the same as the singular one (whereas in English it does not). Consequently, a word is needed to act as a signal for the plural. The word used in this case is 'des' for both genders: 'des filles' (girls), 'des amis' (friends), 'des sacs' (bags).

Exercise 2(iii)
In the following examples replace 'le, la, les' by 'un, une, des' or vice versa as applicable:

1 le segment   2 une porte   3 la dent   4 un camion   5 une rose
6 le pin   7 les actions   8 des pommes   9 les fraises   10 des amis

Have a try

Les petites filles sont tristes: le chat noir est malade. L'homme est jeune et il est fort. La dame est dans la maison. Elle est contente. La nuit est noire et le garçon est fatigué. La voiture verte est sale. Les roses et les tulipes sont dans le vase. Elles sont jolies. La porte est fermée. Les pommes vertes sont dans le sac.

Bon, ça suffit!
Well, that's enough!

3 How to describe and ask how (or where) things or beings are

How to describe how (or where) things or beings are

Thanks to the knowledge so far acquired, you are already capable of producing a large number of simple but very useful sentences describing things or beings. You should take advantage of the vocabulary and rules you now possess to create new sentences of your own. The best way to do so is to imagine a situation and work out phrases which would enable you to cope should that situation arise. As your vocabulary improves, you will be able to make such 'situations' more and more sophisticated and to prepare yourself for possible real-life conversations. That is the way to learn a language!

The next logical step is for you to be able to describe where things and beings are. To do so efficiently, you will need two additional 'ingredients'.

The first is the appropriate person of the verb 'être' (to be). We have already met two: 'est' (is) and 'sont' (are). The whole of the present tense of this verb is as follows:

je suis	*I am*
tu es	*you are (familiar singular)*
il est	*he/it is*
elle est	*she/it is*
nous sommes	*we are*
vous êtes	*you are (polite singular or normal plural)*
ils sont	*they are (masculine)*
elles sont	*they are (feminine)*

Beware: 'Tu' occurs very frequently in French, but is used specifically to address a close friend, a relative, or a person with whom you feel you have a lot in common, although you might not actually know him or her personally (students use it in that way). 'Tu' used to address anyone else is perceived as rude or condescending. It is therefore better at this stage for you to avoid using it unless invited to do so by the person you are talking to. 'Vous', on the other hand, is used in the same way as 'you' to address one single person or several people.

The second element required to clarify the position of things or beings is a special type of word, called a *preposition*, which will help you situate a given thing or being in relation to another: 'sur' (on), 'sous' (under), 'contre' (against) etc. Prepositions are *invariable*: they remain unaffected by the gender or number of the noun they relate to. The most frequently used ones are given in the Word list.

Word list

Nouns

un apéritif	*aperitif*	le client/la	*customer*
le bar	*bar*	cliente	*(male/female)*
la bouteille	*bottle*	la gare	*station*
la chaise	*chair*	le livre	*book*
la chambre	*bedroom*	le menu	*menu*
le chien	*dog*	le mur	*wall*
le cinéma	*cinema*	la sortie	*exit*
		le verre	*glass*

Adjectives*

bleu	*blue*	plein	*full*
gros (grosse)	*big/fat*	vide	*empty*
jaune	*yellow*		

Verbs

avoir	*to have*	ils/elles ont	*they have*
il/elle a	*he/she/it has*		

Other words

contre	*against*	mais	*but*
dans	*in*	où	*where*
derrière	*behind*	sous	*under*
devant	*in front of/outside*	sur	*on*
entre	*between*		

*The feminine or plural form of a particular adjective will only be given (in brackets) if it does not follow the normal agreement rule.

Work it out

Look carefully at the following sentences and try to find out the gender (masculine/feminine) and number (singular/plural) of the person(s) involved:

1	Vous êtes contentes	*You are pleased*
2	Je suis fatiguée	*I am tired*
3	Nous sommes grands	*We are tall*
4	Vous êtes vieux	*You are old*
5	Je suis malade	*I am ill*
6	Vous êtes bonne	*You are good*

Note: In the case of a mixed set of things or beings (masculine + feminine), the adjective takes the masculine plural form.

Conclusions

A Statement 1 is addressed to several females; if it were directed towards male (or male + female) persons, the adjective would be 'contents'; if it were addressed to one person (polite form) it would be 'content' (masc.) or 'contente' (fem.).

B Statement 2 indicates that the speaker is a woman: 'fatiguée' bears the 'e' of the feminine.

C Statement 3 refers to several people either all male or mixed (males + females), since 'grands' bears the 's' of the masculine plural.

D Statement 4 could refer either to one or to several male persons, since 'vieux' has the same form in the masculine (singular and plural), or to a mixed group composed of male(s) and female(s).

E Statement 5 could refer either to a male or to a female, since 'malade' does not alter in the feminine singular.

F Statement 6 can only refer to one female person. If it referred to several females the form of the adjective would be 'bonnes'; for one male it would be 'bon' and for several persons (male or male + female) it would be 'bons'.

Un jeu d'enfant!
Child's play!

Exercise 3(i)
Translate into English:

1 La vieille dame est derrière le bar. **2** La chaise est contre le mur. **3** Le menu est devant le restaurant. **4** La petite fille est derrière la grosse voiture rouge. **5** Les clients sont dans la

chambre verte. **6** Les apéritifs sont sur la table dans le café. **7** Les jolies fleurs jaunes sont dans le grand vase bleu. **8** Le chat noir est devant la porte. **9** Les bouteilles vides sont sous la table dans un sac. **10** La maison est entre le café et le cinéma.

Exercise 3(ii)
Translate into French:

1 The customer is in front of the bar. **2** The apple is on the table, behind the bottle. **3** The little girl and the old lady are in the bedroom. **4** We are in a small restaurant between the café and the cinema. **5** She has a beautiful little house behind the station.

How to ask where things and beings are

Since you can now competently *state* where a thing or being is located, it seems logical for you to learn how to *ask* about its location. In French, a simple way of asking such a question is to use the word 'où' (where) immediately followed by the correct person of the verb 'être' (to be) and the name of the thing(s) or being(s) you wish to enquire about:

Où est le chien?	*Where is the dog?*
Où sont les filles?	*Where are the girls?*

In English, once the thing or being has been identified in the question, there is no need to rename it (adjectives and all!) in the answer. You simply replace the noun by the appropriate '*pronoun*': I, you, he, she, they. For example, to the question: 'Where are the small green glasses?', you would only reply 'They are on the table' (and not 'The small green glasses are on the table'). The same applies in French. But you have to bear in mind the gender (masc./fem.) and number (sing./plur.) of the noun you are replacing:

Où sont les petits verres verts?	*Where are the small green glasses?*
Ils sont sur la table.	*They are on the table.*
Où est l'apéritif?	*Where is the aperitif?*
Il est dans le verre.	*It is in the glass.*

Exercise 3(iii)

Look at the drawing, then answer the following questions logically, using the words suggested in brackets:

1 Où sont les fleurs? (dans). **2** Où est le chat? (sous). **3** Où est le verre? (devant). **4** Où est la bouteille? (entre). **5** Où est le livre? (derrière). **6** Où sont la bouteille, le verre, le vase et les fleurs? (sur).

Have a try

Dear (*Chers*) friends,
We are in a little hotel between the station and the cinema. The rooms are small but they are pretty. The menus are good. The waiter is a friend. The hotel is almost empty. It has a garden with (some) trees and flowers. We are tired but the children are pleased. See you soon (*A bientôt*).
John and Mary.

Où est la sortie?
Where's the exit?

4 How to say 'I have, you have' etc.
How to ask a question
How to say 'there is' and 'there are'

How to say 'I have, you have . . .'

Now that you possess the necessary knowledge to state where things and beings are situated, it is important for you to be able to build sentences in which you can express the fact that someone possesses something. The verb which will enable you to do so is the verb 'avoir' (to have).

The present tense of this verb is as follows:

J'ai	*I have*
tu as	*you have (familiar singular)*
il a	*he/it has*
elle a	*she/it has*
nous avons	*we have*
vous avez	*you have (polite singular or normal plural)*
ils ont	*they (masc. plur.) have*
elles ont	*they (fem. plur.) have*
J'ai une bouteille dans la voiture.	*I have a bottle in the car.*
Nous avons un garçon et une fille.	*We have a boy and a girl.*
Ils ont un petit restaurant derrière la gare.	*They have a small restaurant behind the station.*

Note: The 'e' of 'je', which was present in 'je suis' (I am) is omitted in 'j'ai' to avoid a clash between 'je' and the first letter of 'ai' which is a vowel. This phenomenon will occur every time 'je' is followed by a word beginning with a vowel (a, e, i, o, u), or y, or a 'mute' h.

Word list

Nouns

l' agent (masc.)	*policeman*	le passeport	*passport*
l' auberge (fem.)	*inn*	le patron	*owner/manager*
le film	*film*	le potage	*soup*
l' hôtel (masc.)	*hotel*	le village	*village*
le magasin	*shop*		

Adjectives

chaud	*hot*	ouvert	*open*
cher (chère)	*dear/expensive*	pauvre	*poor*
froid	*cold*	rare	*rare, unusual*
furieux (furieuse)	*furious*	riche	*rich*

Other words

non	*no*	très	*very*
oui	*yes*	trop	*too, too much*

How to ask a question

There are, in French, three distinct ways of asking a question which you need to be able to recognize and use as required: (*a*) familiar, (*b*) standard, and (*c*) elevated. (The latter will be examined in another chapter (see pp. 28–9), since it is rarely used in spoken French and considered rather highbrow.)

(*a*)   The first is generally used in familiar or colloquial speech and it is the simplest one. All you need to do is use the same word-pattern as for a normal statement and merely raise the pitch of your voice at the end, as you would when asking a question in English:

Tu es malade.
You are ill.   } voice down: statement

Tu es malade?
Are you ill?   } voice up: question

(*b*)   The second way of asking a question, which we shall refer to as 'standard' in this and other chapters, is acceptable in spoken and written French. It is presented below.

Work it out

Examine the sentences overleaf, then describe the technique used for the formulation of questions:

Ils ont une fille. $\Big\}$ statement: down
They have a girl.

Est-ce qu'ils ont une fille? $\Big\}$ question: up
Do they have a girl?

Des clientes sont dans le
magasin.
down
*Some (female) customers
are in the shop.*

Est-ce que des clientes sont
dans le magasin?
up
*Are some (female) customers
in the shop?*

Deductions

Your investigation should have revealed the following points:

A In every case, the expression 'est-ce que' is used to change a statement into a question.

B The expression 'est-ce que' does not change, whatever the gender or number of the noun or the pronoun which follows. It is therefore simply a marker to indicate that a question is being asked and remains unaffected by what follows. The meaning of the phrase (lit.: is it that) is irrelevant.

C When a word beginning with a vowel or a 'mute' h follows immediately, 'est-ce que' becomes 'est-ce qu''.

Exercise 4 (i)

Formulate the questions which prompted the following answers, using 'est-ce que'. The key-words required in the questions are given in brackets:

1 Oui, elle est fatiguée. (la dame)   **2** Oui, nous avons un garçon. (vous)   **3** Non, ils sont tristes. (les clients — contents)   **4** Non, elle est ouverte. (la porte — fermée)   **5** Non, il est froid. (le potage — chaud)   **6** Oui, elles sont dans le vase. (les fleurs)

Exercise 4(ii)

Translate into English the following sentences:

1 Est-ce que les garcons sont tristes? Non, ils sont contents.   **2** Est-ce que le potage est bon? Oui, il est bon mais il est froid.　**3** Est-ce que vous avez un menu, garçon? Oui, il est sur la table devant la porte.　**4** Ils sont riches? Non, ils sont pauvres mais ils sont heureux.　**5** Est-ce que vous avez le sac? Non, il est dans la chambre derrière la porte.　**6** Est-ce que l'agent est devant la gare? Non, il est dans le petit café.　**7** Où est le passeport? Il est dans le sac bleu. Le sac est ouvert? Non, il est fermé.　**8** Est-ce que le patron est dans le restaurant? Non, il est dans la chambre. Il est malade? Non, il est fatigué.

Exercise 4(iii)
Translate into French:

1 She has a small black car in the garage.　**2** The old man has a daughter in the village.　**3** I have a green bag in the bedroom. **4** The house has a big garden.　**5** The girls have (some) red dresses.

How to say 'there is' and 'there are'

Some English learners seem to have difficulty in coping with this expression in French. It is in fact very simple.

Work it out

Examine the following sentences closely and formulate the rules which govern the use of 'there is' and 'there are' in French:

1　Il y a une fleur dans le vase.	*There is a flower in the vase.*
2　Il y a des pommes sur la table.	*There are (some) apples on the table.*
3　Il y a un agent derrière la maison?	*Is there a policeman behind the house?*
4　Est-ce qu'il y a des clients dans le restaurant?	*Are there customers in the restaurant?*

Deductions
On the strength of the examples provided, you should have noted the following points:

A There is only one expression in French to translate both 'there is' and 'there are'. That expression is 'il y a'. Note that it is the verb 'avoir' (to have) and not 'être' (to be) which is required.

B The expression is unaffected by the gender (masc./fem.) or the number (sing./plur.) of the noun which follows.

C The sentence containing this expression can be turned into a question by using one of the two methods (familiar or standard) presented earlier in the chapter.

Important: There are in French, as in English, different levels of language: slang, familiar, standard, elevated. It is better to use the standard level to begin with, since it is difficult, without a great deal of practice, to gauge accurately the impact of one's statements in the foreign language. So, beware of the use of 'tu' (you, familiar) and try to use the standard form for asking questions ('est-ce que. . .?'), unless otherwise instructed.

D'accord?
Agreed?

Exercise 4(iv)
Translate into French using the standard question form 'est-ce que', when applicable:

1 Are there some shops in the village? **2** Is there a garage behind the hotel? **3** There is a poor woman outside (= in front of) the door. **4** There are (some) customers in the café. **5** Is there a man in the car? No, but there is a young woman.

Have a try

—Bonjour *(Hello)*. Est-ce que l'hôtel est fermé?
—Non monsieur, il est ouvert *(open)*.
—Vous avez une chambre?
—Oui, bien sûr *(of course)*.
—Est-ce qu'elle est grande?
—Non, elle est petite mais elle est très jolie.
—Est-ce qu'il y a un restaurant dans l'hôtel?
—Non monsieur, mais il y a une petite auberge derrière la gare.
—Les menus sont chers?

—Oui, mais les repas sont très bons. Est-ce que vous avez des valises?
—Oui.
—Où sont-elles?
—Dans la voiture devant l'hôtel. . .
—Est-ce qu'il y a un bar dans l'hôtel?
—Oui, mais il est fermé.
—Dommage! *(pity!)*

Est-ce qu'il y a des problèmes?
Are there any problems?

5 How to say 'to go', 'to' or 'at'   How to state that something is going to happen

How to say 'to go'

We have so far encountered the present tense of the most frequently used verbs in the French language: 'être' (to be) and 'avoir' (to have). Another useful verb in French is 'aller' (to go). Its present tense is as follows:

Je vais	*I go*
tu vas	*you go (familiar singular)*
il va	*he/it goes*
elle va	*she/it goes*
nous allons	*we go*
vous allez	*you go (polite singular or normal plural)*
ils vont	*they go (masc. plur.)*
elles vont	*they go (fem. plur.)*

Note: In English, a verb can be used in the present in two distinct ways: (*a*) to express something which happens regularly, i.e. 'I go'; or (*b*) to express something which is happening at this very moment, i.e. 'I am going'.

In French, there is only one tense to cover both meanings; consequently 'Je vais' could mean 'I go' or 'I am going'. This is true for all verbs. The general meaning of the sentence will, of course, indicate which translation is appropriate. For the sake of convenience, it is the meaning (*a*) which will be given in the Word lists.

Word list

Nouns*

l'animal (masc.) (animaux)	*animal(s)*	l'atelier	*workshop*
l'arbre (masc.)	*tree*	l'autobus (masc.)	*bus*

les commissions (fem.)	*shopping*	la radio	*radio*
la course	*race/errand*	le repas	*meal*
l'école (fem.)	*school*	le taxi	*taxi*
l'église (fem.)	*church*	la télévision	*television*
l'enfant (masc. or fem.)	*child*	le/la touriste	*tourist*
le marché	*market*	le visiteur	*visitor*
le moment	*moment*		

*If the plural form of a noun is irregular, it will be given in brackets immediately after that noun.

Adjectives

sage	*well behaved*	surpris	*surprised*

Verbs

acheter	*to buy*	manger	*to eat*
arriver	*to arrive*	regarder	*to look at/watch*
écouter	*to listen (to)*	rester	*to stay/remain*
entrer	*to enter/go into*	visiter	*to visit*

Other words

avec	*with*	pour	*for/in order to*
ou	*or*	sans	*without*
merci	*thank you*		

How to say 'to' and 'at' (to indicate movement and location)

The words 'to' (indicating a movement) and 'at' (indicating position or location) can both be translated by 'à'. This word, however, has a strange effect on the articles 'le' and 'les' (the) when brought into contact with them.

Work it out

Look carefully at the following sentences and try to work out the way 'à' behaves when placed next to the articles 'le', 'la', 'les'. The gender and number of the nouns used have been put in brackets to assist you.

Il va à la maison (fem. sing.)	*He goes/is going to the house.*
Nous allons au cinéma (masc. sing.)	*We go/are going to the cinema.*
Les dames vont aux magasins (masc. plur.)	*The ladies go/are going to the shops.*

| Le garçon va aux tables (fem. plur.) | *The waiter goes/is going to the tables.* |
| Les clients sont à l'hôtel (masc. sing.) | *The customers are at the hotel.* |

Deductions

A Before masculine singular nouns (as in the case of 'le cinéma') 'à + le' combine into 'au'.

B Before a feminine singular noun (as in the case of 'la maison') 'à' and 'la' remain separate. (*Remember*: 'à la' will become 'à l'' if the next word begins with a vowel or a 'mute h'.)

C Before a plural noun of either gender (masc. (as with 'les magasins') or fem. (as with 'les tables')), 'à + les' becomes 'aux'. On the strength of the last example you could also venture the following guess:

D In the case of a masculine singular noun beginning with a 'mute h' (as in the case of 'l'hôtel'), or a vowel, 'à' and 'l'' remain separate. If they did not, there would be a vowel-clash between 'au' and the next word.

Beware, however: rule **D** will no longer apply if the clash disappears due to the insertion, between 'à' and the noun, of an adjective which does not begin with a vowel or 'mute' h.

Compare:

Il va **à l'**hôtel (clash with 'hôtel')	*He goes to the hotel*
Il va **au** grand hôtel (no clash because of 'grand')	*He goes to the big hotel*
Il va **à l'**énorme hôtel (clash with 'énorme')	*He goes to the enormous hotel*
Nous allons **à l'**école (clash with 'école')	*We go to school*
Nous allons **à la** vieille école (no clash because of 'vieille')	*We go to the old school*

Exercise 5(i)

Combine 'à' with the article 'le, la, les', as appropriate, in the sentences overleaf:

1 Les enfants sont . . . école. **2** La voiture est . . . garage.
3 Les clients sont . . . restaurant. **4** Est-ce que vous allez . . .
commissions? **5** Nous allons . . . magasins. **6** Le patron
est . . . hôtel. **7** Je vais . . . maison **8** Les touristes sont . . .
église.

Exercise 5(ii)
Translate into English:

1 Le garçon va au marché. Il a un grand sac. **2** La petite fille est au
lit. Elle est fatiguée. **3** Les touristes sont à la porte, mais elle est
fermée. **4** Nous allons aux commissions avec la voiture. **5** Vous
allez à l'hôtel? Impossible, il est plein. **6** Le patron va à l'atelier. Il
est furieux. **7** Est-ce que tu vas à l'école? Non, je suis
malade. **8** Les enfants sont au cinéma? Non, ils sont à la maison.

How to state that something is going to happen

We are now in a position to say where things and beings are, where
they go and what they have. But all these descriptions are confined to
the present. We shall now learn how to state that something is going
to happen. In English, this is done by using the required person of the
verb 'to go' in the present tense, followed by the infinitive of the verb
you wish to use:

> I am going to eat.
> The customers are going to arrive.

In the above sentences, 'to eat' and 'to arrive' are infinitives.
   In French, the principle is the same as in English:

> Je vais manger.
> Les clients vont arriver.

The required person of 'aller': 'je vais, ils vont. . .' is followed by the
infinitive: 'manger' (to eat) and 'arriver' (to arrive).

Important: In French (as sometimes in English) sentences using this
construction are ambiguous as they could mean either '. . . is about
to. . .' or '. . . is on his way to. . .'. Generally, the context will give a
clear idea of the sense.

Exercise 5(iii)

Answer the following questions affirmatively and in full, using the appropriate pronoun (or the one suggested when applicable):

1 Est-ce que vous allez rester à la maison? (nous)   **2** Est-ce que les enfants vont aller au restaurant?   **3** Tu vas visiter l'église?   **4** Est-ce que les dames vont entrer dans le magasin?   **5** Je vais aller à la gare? (tu)   **6** Est-ce que le taxi va arriver à l'hôtel?   **7** La petite fille va manger la pomme?   **8** Est-ce que nous allons acheter des fleurs? (vous)

Ça va?
Everything O.K.?

Have a try

I am about to go to the village. There is a market and I am going to buy some fruit. Are you going to visit the church and the castle, or stay at home (= at the house) to watch television or listen to the radio? The meal is on the table. There are some apples in the yellow bag behind the door. The bus is going to arrive in a moment. . . See you later (*A plus tard*)!

6 How to state that something has just happened   How to ask a question (formal)   How to say 'of' and 'from'   How to express possession

How to state that something has just happened

You are now in a position to express, albeit in a limited way, certain actions in two 'time-zones' (present and future). The next logical step is to examine a way of breaking into the third one (the past). One way of doing so is to form a tense to express that an action has just been taking place.

'He has just arrived' or 'we have just eaten' are two examples of this tense, which is sometimes referred to as the immediate past.

To form the French equivalent of it, you need the help of the verb 'venir' (to come), the present of which is as follows:

Je viens	*I come*
tu viens	*you come*
il vient	*he/it comes*
elle vient	*she/it comes*
nous venons	*we come*
vous venez	*you come*
ils viennent	*they come (masc.)*
elles viennent	*they come (fem.)*

This tense, which literally means that the performer is 'coming from doing' whatever action the main verb expresses, is constructed in the way outlined below: The suitable person of 'venir' in the present tense, preceded by the required noun or pronoun, may itself be accompanied by 'juste' (just) to emphasize the very recent nature of the action; this in turn is followed by 'de' (from), or 'd'' if the next word begins with a vowel or 'mute' h, and finally by the infinitive of the main verb.

The formula for this tense is therefore:

> present of venir + (juste) + de/d' + infinitive

Nous venons (juste) de manger le potage.	*We have just eaten the soup.*
Les enfants viennent (juste) d'arriver.	*The children have just arrived.*

Word list

Nouns

l'argent (masc.)	*money*	l'entrée (fem.)	*entrance*
la banque	*bank*	la mer	*sea*
le car	*coach*	la montre	*watch*
le château (châteaux)	*castle(s)*	le nez	*nose*
le chauffeur	*driver/chauffeur*	la route	*road/way*
le dessert	*dessert*	le soir	*evening*
le directeur	*manager/director*	la valise	*suitcase*

Adjectives

agréable	*pleasant*	facile	*easy*
charmant	*charming*	formidable	*wonderful/ formidable/ fantastic*
complet (complète)	*full/complete*		
difficile	*difficult*	neuf (neuve)	*new*
doux (douce)	*sweet/soft*	superbe	*superb*

Verbs

commander	*to order*	monter	*to go up/carry (something) up*
demander	*to ask (for)*		
discuter	*to discuss/to talk*	parler (à)	*to talk/speak (to)*
		téléphoner (à)	*to telephone*

Other words

allô!	*hallo! (telephone)*	maintenant	*now*
après	*after*	pendant	*during/for*
avant	*before*		

Exercise 6(i)

Translate the sentences on the following page into English:

1 Les touristes viennent d'arriver devant le château. Ils sont dans le car.   2 Nous venons de regarder un beau film à la télévision.   3 Le patron vient de téléphoner. Le taxi va arriver.   4 Est-ce-que vous venez de visiter l'église? Non, nous venons de regarder la mer.   5 Je viens de manger le dessert. Je vais commander un café.   6 Le jeune garçon vient d'acheter une montre. Elle est belle mais elle est très chère.

Exercise 6(ii)
Translate into French:

1 The coach has just arrived outside the station.   2 I have just ordered an aperitif at the bar.   3 She has just bought a new suitcase in the shop.   4 You have just spoken to the manager.   5 We have just eaten a cold meal.   6 A man has just entered (into) the bank with a big black bag.

How to ask a question in a formal way

The two most common ways of asking a question (familiar and standard) have already been presented. There is a third way which is generally used in formal written French or sometimes encountered in elevated forms of the spoken language. This form can be used instead of the standard one after such words as 'comment' (how), 'pourquoi' (why), 'où' (where), 'quand' (when) and 'qui' (who), but only if the subject is a pronoun on its own.

> Comment allez-vous?   *How are you? (lit. How do you go?)*
>
> Où sont-ils?   *Where are they?*

but:

> Où sont les enfants?   *Where are the children?*
> (and not: Où les enfants sont-ils?)

Work it out

Examine the following sentences and try to work out the way this type of question is formulated. To help you in your investigation, each question will be preceded by its corresponding familiar equivalent which, apart from the voice-pitch change, has exactly the same structure as a statement.

Il est fatigué?	
Est-il fatigué?	} *Is he tired?*
Ils sont malades?	
Sont-ils malades?	} *Are they ill?*
Elle a une fille?	
A-t-elle une fille?	} *Does she have a daughter?*
Les clients sont contents?	
Les clients sont-ils contents?	} *Are the customers pleased?*
La maison est jolie?	
La maison est-elle jolie?	} *Is the house pretty?*
Monsieur Dupont est charmant?	
Monsieur Dupont est-il charmant?	} *Is Mr. Dupont charming?*
J'ai des amis?	
Ai-je des amis?	} *Do I have (any) friends?*

Deductions

From the examination of the above sentences, the following points should have emerged:

A Asking a question in this way requires the inversion of the pronoun and the verb ('ils sont chez eux' becomes 'sont-ils chez eux').

B If the inversion is likely to give rise to a vowel-clash between the verb and 'il' or 'elle', a 't' will be inserted between the two words to avoid that clash.

C The verb and the pronoun are linked by a hyphen '-' in the written text.

D If a noun is used in the question to indicate the performer of the action, it will come first, followed by the verb, then by the appropriate pronoun: 'ils' in the case of 'clients' (masc. plur.), 'elle' in the case of 'la maison' (fem. sing.), 'il' in the case of 'Monsieur Dupont' (masc. sing.).

E In the case of 'j'ai' (I have), this way of asking a question will eliminate the vowel-clash. The 'e' of 'je' will therefore be restored ('j'ai' becomes 'ai-je').

Et voilà!
Here you are!
(lit.: and there!)

Exercise 6(iii)
Transform the following statements into formal questions, using the method outlined above:

1 Tu as une belle maison.   **2**   Il est content.   **3** Elle a une jolie montre.   **4** J'ai un bon livre dans la voiture.   **5** Les petites filles sont sur la route.   **6**   La jeune dame va téléphoner.   **7** L'hôtel a un restaurant.   **8** Les magasins sont vides.   **9** Le chauffeur est dans la banque.   **10** Le car va arriver.

How to say 'of' and 'from'

Having learnt the way of saying 'to' and 'at' to express movement and location, we shall now examine how to say 'of' and 'from'.

In French, the word which covers both those meanings is 'de'. When in contact with 'le' or 'les', it combines with them in the following way:

'de + le'	becomes	'du'
'de + les'	becomes	'des'
'de + la'	remain separate	

Je viens **du** village	*I come from the village*
Nous venons **des** com-missions	*We come from doing the shopping*
Le taxi vient d'arriver **de la** gare	*The taxi has just arrived from the station.*

Note: If the word immediately following 'du' or 'de la' begins with a vowel or 'mute' h, both expressions will be replaced by 'de l''.

How to express possession

In English, the idea of possession can be expressed in a variety of ways, some of which are presented below:

(*a*) When the 'owner' is a human being or an animal, possession is indicated by the possessive case:

> The customers' passports.
> The tourist's car.
> The dog's nose.

(*b*) When the 'possessor' is an object instead of a being, the relationship is expressed in the following way:

> The bedroom window. (The window of the bedroom.)
> The village church. (The church of the village.)

In French, possession is expressed with the help of **'du'**, **'de la'**, **'de l''**, **'des'** as appropriate:

> Les passeports **des** clients.
> La voiture **du** touriste.
> La fenêtre **de la** chambre.
> L'église **du** village.

Note: If, in the singular, the owner is referred to by name, 'du', 'de la' and 'de l'' will be replaced by **'de'** or **'d'**:

> La femme **de** Monsieur Dupont.   *Mr Dupont's wife.*
> La maison **d'**Anne.   *Anne's house.*

Exercise 6(iv)
Translate into French:

1 The bank manager has just gone into the restaurant. **2** The coach driver is going to close the door. **3** The lady's suitcase is empty. **4** The children's father is about to order the dessert. **5** The customers' meal is going to be cold. **6** The policeman's son has just spoken to the little boy.

Have a try

— Vous venez d'arriver?
— Oui, nous venons juste de descendre de la voiture!
— Est-ce que vous allez rester longtemps (*a long time*)?
— Non, juste une nuit. Est-ce qu'il y a des problèmes?
— Non, ça va! Vous avez un passeport?
— Oui, voilà.
— Merci! Vous avez des enfants?

—Oui, un garçon et une fille.
—Est-ce qu'ils sont grands?
—Non, ils sont très jeunes.
—Vous avez des animaux?
—Non.
—Bon, ça va . . . vous allez installer la caravane (put the caravan) derrière les arbres entre la tente (*tent*) bleue et la tente jaune. D'accord?
—D'accord!

7 Verbs, tenses, stems and endings
How to form the present tense of 'er' verbs
How to say 'here', 'there' and 'over there'

Verbs

Verbs, as we have already stated, are words which express actions: I go, he has, etc. These words can be modified in certain ways to situate the action in one of three time-zones: past, present, future and, within each time-zone, to express definite shades of meaning about the action: repetition; duration; isolated occurrence; certainty; doubt etc. These shades of meaning are given by particular forms of the verb called tenses.

Word list

Nouns

la carte	*card/map*	le lac	*lake*
le champ	*field*	la lampe	*lamp*
la chanson	*song*	la mère	*mother*
la cuisine	*kitchen/cooking*	le paysage	*scenery*
l'exposition (fem.)	*exhibition*	le père	*father*
		le porteur	*porter*
la fillette	*little girl*	le pourboire	*tip*
le garagiste	*mechanic/garage owner*		*(= money)*
		le train	*train*
le gardien	*keeper/warden*	la vache	*cow*
l'invitation (fem.)	*invitation*		

Adjectives

cassé	*broken*	élégant	*elegant*
délicieux (délicieuse)	*delicious*	timide	*shy*

Verbs

allumer	*to switch on*	jeter	*to throw*
appeler	*to call*	jouer	*to play*
avancer	*to advance/move forward*	marcher	*to walk/work (for a machine)*
chanter	*to sing*	réparer	*to repair*
charger	*to load*	travailler	*to work*
frapper	*to knock/strike (a blow)*		

Other words

aussi	*as well/also*	hélas!	*alas!*
bientôt	*soon*	pas du tout	*not at all*
déjà	*already*	trop tard	*too late*

Tenses

Simple and compound tenses

The ways in which tenses are constructed vary considerably from one language to another. The following two categories are found in English as well as in French:

1 simple (= one-word) tenses: I *go*, we *have*. . .
2 compound (= several-word) tenses: she *had gone*, I *have had*. . .

1 Simple tenses

In English, within a given tense of this type, the verb itself does not vary (except for the 3rd person singular of the present: he goes, she has. . .). As a result, the burden of distinguishing between its various persons falls upon the pronoun: I, you, he, she. . . In French on the other hand, that burden falls not only on the pronoun: je, tu, il, elle. . . but also on the verb itself. This is clearly visible when comparing the present of 'aller', which we have already encountered, with its English equivalent 'to go':

aller	to go
je vais	*I go*
tu vas	*you go*
il/elle va	*he/she/it goes*
nous allons	*we go*
vous allez	*you go*
ils/elles vont	*they go*

In English the form 'go' is used in all cases except for the 3rd person singular 'goes', whereas in French, the verb changes quite significantly for each person.

2 Compound tenses

In such tenses, a specific form of the verb is preceded by another verb called the auxiliary. It is the auxiliary which then has the task of providing the necessary information about the time-zone and other relevant shades of meaning. In English, the auxiliary used to construct compound tenses is 'to have': we have gone, she had been. . . In French, both 'avoir' (to have) and 'être' (to be) are used as auxiliaries. You cannot choose freely between them. Certain categories of verbs require 'avoir', others need 'être'. This will be clarified in a later chapter.

In addition to the verb forms mentioned above, there are some which do not carry any specific information about time-zones. They are:

(a) the infinitive, which merely states what the action is: to have, to be, to go, to see;
(b) the past participle, which expresses the completed aspect of the action: had, been, gone, seen;
(c) the present participle, which expresses the continuing aspect of the action: having, being, going, seeing.

Stems and endings

In English, the infinitive of a verb is easily recognised because it is preceded by the word 'to'. In French, the infinitive is signalled *not* by a word placed before it, but by a specific ending attached to a part of the verb called the stem or root. French infinitives are classified into a small number of categories according to their endings:

1 **'er' verbs:** 'ferm**er**' (to close), 'parl**er**' (to talk), 'travaill**er**' (to work). . .
2 **'ir' verbs:** 'fin**ir**' (to finish), 'sort**ir**' (to go out). . .
3 **'oir' verbs:** 'av**oir**' (to have), 'v**oir**' (to see). . .
4 **'re' verbs:** 'descend**re**' (to go down), 'êt**re**' (to be). . .

There are around 4,500 verbs in the 'er' category which is by far the largest; 'ir' verbs number approximately 400. The 'oir' and 're' verbs number about 100, many of which are irregular (they are counted together as a single category).

Note: A *regular* verb is a verb which, in a *given category and a given tense*, follows a predictable pattern of formation in terms of stem and ending, so that if you know the behaviour of one 'model' verb, you can anticipate the way *all* regular verbs of that category will function. An *irregular* verb is one which deviates from the regular pattern of tense formation either through its endings or — more often — through its stem.

How to form the present tense of 'er' verbs

The division of a verb form into stem and ending is of crucial importance in the construction of French tenses. For a given category of verb ('er', 'ir' or 're') and providing the verb behaves in a regular manner, a particular set of endings will be added to the appropriate stem. These endings will be the same for all regular verbs in that category.

Work it out

In the following sentences, 'er' verbs are used in the present tense. Look at the verb carefully and isolate the ending for each person. The infinitive has been given in brackets. The root for the present tense is normally the infinitive minus its 'er' ending.

1 Nous regardons le paysage. (regarder) *We are looking at the landscape.*

2 La fillette timide mange une pomme. (manger) *The shy little girl is eating an apple.*

3 Le garagiste répare la voiture. (réparer) *The mechanic is repairing the car.*

4 Les enfants chantent une chanson. (chanter) *The children are singing a song.*

5 Je frappe à la porte. (frapper) *I am knocking at the door.*

6	Est-ce que tu écoutes la radio? (écouter)	*Do you listen to the radio?*
7	Elles parlent au gardien. (parler)	*They are speaking to the keeper.*
8	Vous allumez la lumière. (allumer)	*You are switching the light on.*

Important: In most of the above examples, the French verbs have been translated by the 'ing' form which indicates that the action is in progress. They could equally have been translated by the present of habit since, in French, the present tense covers both meanings:

Nous regardons = We look *or* We are looking.
Elle mange = She eats *or* She is eating.

Close examination of the eight sentences given above reveals the following combinations (stem + ending):

1	nous	regard + **ons**		5	je	frapp + **e**
2	(elle)	mang + **e**		6	tu	écout + **es**
3	(il)	répar + **e**		7	elles	parl + **ent**
4	(ils)	chant + **ent**		8	vous	allum + **ez**

Conclusions

In the present tense (with the exception of 'aller'), the endings of 'er' verbs are as follows:

je	—**e**	nous	—**ons**
tu	—**es**	vous	—**ez**
il/elle	—**e**	ils/elles	—**ent**

Although 'er' verbs are very regular in their behaviour, some changes can occur in the stem. These changes are dictated not by grammar but by sound considerations.

1 'Er' verbs which have a stem ending in 'g', such as 'manger' (to eat), 'charger' (to load), 'engager' (to engage), will require the insertion of an 'e' between the stem and the 'ons' ending of the 'nous' form. If this were not done, the 'g', instead of being similar to the friction sound of 'leisure', would be pronounced in the same way as that of '**gap**'. (A similar problem will arise whenever the 'g' of the stem is followed by the vowels 'a' or 'u'.)

Compare:	Je charge	*I load*
and:	Nous chargeons	*We load*

2   In the case of verbs with a stem ending in 'c' such as 'avancer' (to advance), 'placer' (to place), 'lancer' (to throw), a cedilla ', ' will have to be placed under the 'c' before the 'ons' ending of the 'nous' form. If this were not done, the sound of 'c', instead of being similar to that of 's' in '**s**ay', would assume the value of 'k' in '**k**eep'. (A similar problem will arise whenever the 'c' of the stem is followed by the vowels 'a' or 'u'.)

Compare:	J'avance	*I advance*
and :	Nous avançons	*We advance*

3   Most verbs in 'eler' and 'eter' double their 'l' or 't' except in the 'nous' and 'vous' forms.

Compare:	J'appelle	*I call*
and:	Nous appelons	*We call*
	Vous appelez	*You call*
or:	Je jette	*I throw*
and:	Nous jetons	*We throw*
	Vous jetez	*You throw*

Exercise 7(i)

In the following sentences, replace the infinitive (in brackets) by the appropriate form of the present tense:

1 Vous (visiter) l'exposition avec les enfants?   **2** Je suis dans la cuisine! Je (préparer) le dîner!   **3** Les vaches sont dans le champ: elles (regarder) le train.   **4** Nous (appeler) un taxi pour le client.   **5** La petite fille (jeter) la bouteille vide dans le lac.   **6** Tu (casser) la fenêtre avec la chaise.   **7** Le monsieur (demander) la note au garçon.   **8** Les touristes (visiter) le vieux château.

Exercise 7(ii)

Translate the following sentences into English (using the 'ing' form to indicate that the action is in progress):

1 Nous achetons des livres dans le magasin.   **2** La petite fille joue dans le jardin.   **3** Les invités dansent sur la terrasse.   **4** Est-ce que tu écoutes le nouveau disque?   **5** Je refuse l'invitation des voisins.   **6** Tu allumes la lampe de la chambre.   **7** Le patron ferme le bar.   **8** Le garçon demande le pourboire.

How to say 'here', 'there' and 'over there'

The words 'here' and 'there' indicating location can be expressed in French by 'ici' and 'là' respectively. In modern informal speech, however, 'là' tends to be used almost systematically to translate both 'here' and 'there' regardless of distance, so long as no confusion is likely to arise:

Où sont les verres et la bouteille?	*Where are the glasses and the bottle?*
Ils sont **là**, sur la table!	*They are here/there on the table!*
Où est l'argent?	*Where is the money?*
Il est **là**, dans le sac.	*It is here/there in the bag.*

If, however, the general meaning of the sentence requires it (usually to emphasise a contrast) the opposition between 'ici' and 'là' will be re-established:

La gare est **ici** et le château est **là**.	*The station is here and the castle is there.*
Vous allez chercher **ici** et je vais regarder **là**.	*You are going to search here and I am going to look there.*

The expression 'over there' is translated in French by 'là-bas'.

Où est le village?	*Where is the village?*
Il est là-bas derrière les arbres.	*It is over there behind the trees.*
La voiture est là-bas devant la gare.	*The car is over there, in front of the station.*

In spoken English, the pronoun and the verb are often omitted in answers of the type given above; the same applies in French:

Compare:	Where is the green bag?	*There, behind the door.*
and:	Où est le sac vert?	*Là, derrière la porte.*

Exercise 7(iii)
Translate the sentences overleaf into French (use the standard question form when appropriate):

1 Where are the flowers? There, in the vase!   **2** The taxi is here and the bus is over there in front of the station.   **3** Where is the map? Here on the table, under the bag!   **4** Hallo! Is Robert there? Yes, he has just arrived.   **5** Are you there, Madam? Yes, I am in the kitchen.   **6** He is going to come here, and I am going to go over there.

Allons-y!
Let's go!
(lit.: Let's go there!)

Have a try

I have just arrived at the station with my (mon) father. We are waiting for the train from Paris. I look at my father's watch. The train is going to arrive soon. Here is the train, and here is Monsieur Dupont. He is tall and elegant; he is carrying a big black suitcase. He comes towards my father.

— Hello Robert!
— Hello John, everything alright?
— Yes, but I am very tired. Is there a porter in the station?
— No, but I am going to carry your case. . . The car is just in front of the station, we are going to go home. Marie has just prepared a delicious meal.
— Excellent! Where is the exit?
— Over there!

En route!
Off we go!
(lit.: in road!)

8 More about nouns and adjectives

More about nouns

Having acquired the basic information about the behaviour of French nouns and adjectives, we shall now refine this knowledge further.

We have seen that French nouns are divided into two gender categories, masculine and feminine, and that most of them form their plural by adding 's' to their singular form:

la porte	→	les portes
door		*doors*
le sac	→	les sacs
bag		*bags*

Don't forget: Since the singular and plural forms of French nouns sound exactly the same in most cases, it is imperative that they should be preceded by a word which will give advance warning of the gender/number: article, possessive or demonstrative adjective, etc. . .

Word list

Nouns

l'Anglais (masc.)	*Englishman*	l'histoire (fem.)	*story/history*
l'attitude (fem.)	*attitude*	l'inspecteur (masc.)	*inspector*
le ballon	*balloon/ball*	le matin	*morning*
le bulletin	*bulletin*	la météo	*weather forecast*
la chance	*luck/chance*	la moustache	*moustache*
la chanteuse	*singer (female)*	la moto(cyclette)	*motorbike*
la chaussure	*shoe*	le mouchoir	*handkerchief*
le costume	*costume/suit*	la musique	*music*
la facture	*bill (to pay)*	la police	*police*
le Français	*Frenchman*	la serveuse	*waitress*
les gens (masc. plur.)	*people*	le stylo (à bille)	*(ballpoint) pen*

Adjectives

adorable	*adorable*	italien (italienne)	*Italian*
affreux (affreuse)	*ugly/awful*	japonais	*Japanese*
considérable	*considerable*	perdu	*lost*
dernier (dernière)	*last*	pressé	*in a hurry/rushed*
espagnol	*Spanish*	rond	*round*
étonnant	*astonishing*	sec (sèche)	*harsh/dry*

Verbs

adorer	*to adore*	détester	*to hate/detest*

Other words

ensemble	*together*	même	*even/same*

More about the plural of nouns

1   Nouns ending in 's', 'x' or 'z' in the singular do not change in the plural:

> l'autobus (masc.) → les autobus
> *bus*   *buses*
> la voix   → les voix
> *voice*   *voices*
> le nez   → les nez
> *nose*   *noses*

2   A small number of nouns ending in 'ou' in the singular take an 'x' instead of an 's' in the plural. Such is the case for 'chou' (cabbage) and 'genou' (knee):

> Je suis sur les genoux.   *I am exhausted.* (lit.: . . . on my knees)

3   Nouns ending in 'au', 'eau', 'eu' in the singular will form their plural by adding an 'x':

> le bateau   → les bateaux
> *boat*   *boats*
> le chapeau   → les chapeaux
> *hat*   *hats*
> le feu   → les feux
> *fire/light*   *fires/lights*

But:

> le pneu   → les pneus
> *tyre*   *tyres*

4   Most singular nouns in 'al' change to 'aux' in the plural:

le cheval	→	les chevaux
horse		*horses*
le journal	→	les journaux
newspaper		*newspapers*

But:

le bal	→	les bals
dance		*dances*
le carnaval	→	les carnavals
carnival		*carnivals*

5   Surnames are not normally put in the plural in French:
Les Dupont sont ici!
The Duponts (= Dupont family) are here!

6   When addressing somebody politely in France you are likely to use the words 'Monsieur' (equivalent to Sir but less formal), 'Madame' (Madam) or 'Mademoiselle' (Miss). The plural of these are 'Messieurs', 'Mesdames' and 'Mesdemoiselles' respectively. You may, if you wish, add the name(s) of the person(s) concerned after these words:

Bonjour
Hello/good morning
{ Monsieur (Dupont)!
  Madame (Dubois)!
  Mademoiselle (Lebrun)!

If you are politely referring to people without talking to them directly, you should say:

le monsieur	→	les messieurs
gentleman		*gentlemen*
la dame	→	les dames
lady		*ladies*
la demoiselle	→	les demoiselles
young lady		*young ladies*

Important: In England, people tend to use Christian names much more readily than in France. As in the case of 'tu' (= you familiar), take your cue from the French.

7   *Beware*:   a small number of French nouns have an irregular plural:

un œil	→	des yeux
eye		*eyes*

le ciel	→	les cieux
sky/heaven		*skies*

More about the gender of nouns

At this stage, it is worth stating again that you can work out for yourself theories to help you determine the gender of French nouns. Those theories may not work every time, but they will help you to become aware of the logic of the language. We examined a few examples in Chapter 1: trees are generally masculine, fruits are often feminine, nouns ending in 'ence' are feminine except for 'le silence', etc.

We shall now add the following rules:

1 A large number of French nouns end in 'tion' and 'sion' in the singular; they are invariably feminine and they very often have the same meaning as their English counterparts, e.g.:

l'attention	*attention*
la confusion	*confusion*
la construction	*construction*

This 'rule' should increase your vocabulary dramatically!

2   A number of nouns referring to abstract ideas or qualities end in 'té' in the singular. They are virtually all feminine and many have a corresponding English form ending in 'ty', e.g.:

la beauté	*beauty*
la fidélité	*fidelity*

3 A number of nouns ending in 'age' in the singular also have equivalents or near-equivalents in English: most of them are masculine, e.g.:

le courage	*courage*
le passage	*passage*

But the following are feminine:

la cage	*cage*
l'image	*image/picture*
la nage	*swimming*

la page	*page(= paper)*
la plage	*beach*
la rage	*rage/rabies*

4   Generally, nouns ending in 'eur' or 'teur' are:

(*a*)   masculine if they refer to a person or a machine performing a specific task:

| Le conducteur monte sur le tracteur. | *The driver climbs onto the tractor.* |

(*b*)   feminine if they refer to an abstract notion or quality:

| La hauteur de la tour est considérable. | *The height of the tower is considerable.* |

5   Along with nouns which end in 'ence' in the singular, those in 'ense', 'ance' and 'anse' are also feminine:

| La violence est une mauvaise défense. | *Violence is a bad (form of) defence.* |
| Voilà la dernière chance. | *Here/there is the last chance.* |

6   Nouns ending in 'tude' or 'ture' (singular form) are also feminine. Many of the former have an equivalent (or near equivalent) in English:

| Il a une très bonne attitude. | *He has a very good attitude.* |
| Où est la facture? | *Where is the bill?* |

Additional comments on the gender of nouns
(*a*)   Sometimes a noun of a given gender (masculine or feminine) can refer to individuals of either sex:

| le témoin | *witness (male or female)* |
| la victime | *victim (male or female)* |

(*b*) Certain French nouns can be used either in the masculine or in the feminine according to the sex of the person they apply to:

le touriste	*tourist (male)*
la touriste	*tourist (female)*
un artiste	*artist (male)*
une artiste	*artist (female)*

(*c*) A small number of French nouns change their meaning if their gender is changed.

Compare:	le poste	*post/employment*
and:	la poste	*post-office*
or:	le radio	*radio operator*
and:	la radio	*radio/X-ray*

Be particularly vigilant about these!

Exercise 8(i)
In the following sentences put the nouns (given in brackets) in the plural:

1 Il y a des (pneu) dans le garage.   **2** Nous allons visiter les (château) de la Loire.   **3** Elle a les (œil) fermés.   **4** Où sont les (chapeau) des invités?   **5** Il y a des (cheval) sur la route.   **6** Les jeunes gens adorent les (bal).   **7** Nous avons des (oiseau) dans une cage.   **8** Ils vont allumer des (feu) sur la plage.

More about adjectives

Beware: In English, adjectives are nearly always placed before the noun they relate to. In French, a great many are placed after it, but some of the most frequently used ones occur before:

> Le vieux chat noir est   *The old black cat is*
>   sur la petite table ronde.   *on the small round table.*

If a verb form (past participle or present participle form) is used as an adjective, it will be placed after the noun:

> Un chien perdu.   [verb: perdre (*to lose*)] *A stray (lit.*
>   *lost) dog*
> Le voyageur fatigué.   [verb: fatiguer (*to tire*)] *The tired*
>   *traveller*

Adjectives of nationality are always placed after the noun and are not written with a capital except when used as nouns to refer to inhabitants of a given country:

> les vins francais   *French wines*
> des chaussures italiennes   *Italian shoes*

but:

    Il y a deux hommes dans le   *There are two men in the taxi: an*
    taxi: un Anglais et un   *Englishman and a Frenchman.*
    Français.

A small number of French adjectives change their meaning according
to their position. The most common are presented below.

Compare:	Une pauvre femme	*A poor (wretched) woman*
	Une femme pauvre	*A poor (penniless) woman*
	Une triste histoire	*A sad (unfortunate) story*
	Une histoire triste	*A sad (tear-jerking) story*
	Ma propre voiture	*My own car*
	Ma voiture propre	*My clean car*

Exercise 8(ii)
Translate into French:

1 The Spanish waitress is with the English customers. **2** There is an
interesting story in the newspapers this morning. **3** He is going to
buy the black hats in the small shop. **4** She is going to eat some
fresh cream. **5** The old man is an American tourist. **6** My own
car is very dirty.

Exercise 8(iii)
Translate into English:

1 L'inspecteur a une fausse moustache. **2** Le directeur a une voix
très sèche. **3** Il y a de la musique douce à la radio. **4** Votre
chemise est propre mais mon propre costume est sale. **5** La jeune
dame est une chanteuse italienne. **6** J'ai une histoire étonnante mais
vous êtes un homme pressé. **7** Ils ont une maison neuve dans la
vieille ville. **8** Nous allons acheter une petite moto japonaise.

Ça va?
Everything O.K.?
(lit.: that goes?)

Have a try

Le bulletin météo est excellent. La mer et le ciel sont bleus; nous allons

avoir un carnaval formidable! Les magasins sont fermés et les rues
sont déjà pleines *(full)* de gens: des Français, mais aussi des Anglais,
des Italiens, des Espagnols et même des Japonais! Il y a aussi des
agents et des inspecteurs de police, mais l'atmosphère *(atmosphere)*
est excellente. Les costumes sont très beaux. Les enfants sont heureux.
Ils ont des ballons rouges, bleus et verts et des chapeaux adorables.
Ah, il y a un petit garçon perdu . . . Non, voilà la mère. Et voilà la
reine *(queen)* du carnaval. Elle est belle et très élégante . . . Ce *(this)*
soir, les gens, riches et pauvres, vont danser, chanter et manger
ensemble et ils vont allumer des feux sur la plage . . . J'adore le
carnaval.

> Moi aussi!
> *Me too!*
> *(lit.: Me also!)*

9 How to say 'I have gone' or 'I went' etc. Past participles   'Avoir' or 'être'?

How to say 'I have gone' or 'I went' etc.

We are now, thanks to the immediate past, in a position to express an action which has just taken place:

> Il vient (juste) d'arriver dans le bureau.　　*He has just arrived in the office.*

Although this tense is very useful, it does not allow us to express an action, now completed, which occurred further back in the past. If we wish to do so, we need a tense called the perfect, which we shall now examine. The perfect, as previously mentioned, is a compound (= two-word) tense made up of the following elements:

> auxiliary + past participle of the main verb.

This tense exists in English and in French, but there are several important differences in its usage between the two languages. The two crucial points to remember are as follows:

1   The first is that, whereas in English the perfect is always formed with 'to have' (I have eaten, I have been . . .) both 'avoir' (to have) and 'être' (to be) are used in French. It is not a matter of free choice, however: although the great majority of verbs require 'avoir' as their auxiliary, some must be constructed with 'être'. This point will be clarified later on in this chapter.
2   The second crucial difference is that, whereas in English the perfect emphasises the fact that the action in *now* over, e.g. I have (now) eaten, he has (now) been, etc., its French equivalent, which can also have the same meaning, is used predominantly to indicate that an action, considered as a distinct, isolated event, took place in the past.

Consequently:

　　J'ai mangé.

could mean:

　　(*a*)　I have (now) eaten.

or:

　　(*b*)　I ate.

and:

　　Vous avez cassé la montre.

could be translated as:

　　(*a*)　You have broken the watch.

or:

　　(*b*)　You broke the watch.

Although for the sake of convenience only one of the possible translations of the French perfect will normally be given, don't forget that the two interpretations are usually possible!

Beware:　In French, the task of the perfect is merely to indicate that the action took place in the past, regardless of duration, repetition, etc. If you need to emphasize the fact that it lasted, was repeated or was in progress when another occurred, you must use a different tense called the imperfect which we shall study in due course.

Past participles

In Chapter 7 we noted that French verbs are divided into a small number of categories, based on the endings of their infinitives: 'er', 'ir', 'oir', 're' and that simple tenses are formed in the following way:

stem + ending

This mode of formation also applies in the case of the *past participle*, which is the verb-form expressing the completed aspect of an action: 'eaten', 'gone', 'rung' etc. Since the past participle is a crucial component of the perfect tense, the rules for its formation will now be given.

1　*Stem* + *'é'* for all 'er' verbs including 'aller':

travaill**er**	*(to work)*	travaillé	*(worked)*
cherch**er**	*(to search)*	cherché	*(searched)*
parl**er**	*(to talk)*	parlé	*(talked)*

2 *Stem + 'i'* for most 'ir' verbs:

part**ir**	*(to go)*	part**i**	*(gone)*
fin**ir**	*(to finish)*	fin**i**	*(finished)*

but:

ven**ir**	*(to come)*	ven**u**	*(come)*

3 *Reduced stem + 'u'* for most 'oir' verbs:

av**oir**	*(to have)*	**eu**	*(had)*
v**oir**	*(to see)*	**vu**	*(seen)*

Verbs in 'evoir' lose 'ev' in the past participle, e.g.:

re**cevoir**	*(to receive)*	re**çu**	*(received)*
aper**cevoir**	*(to perceive)*	aper**çu**	*(perceived)*

4 *Stem + 'u'* for most 're' verbs:

descend**re**	*(to go down)*	descend**u**	*(gone down)*
attend**re**	*(to wait)*	attend**u**	*(waited)*
vend**re**	*(to sell)*	vend**u**	*(sold)*

but there are exceptions, e.g.:

prend**re**	*(to take)*	pr**is**	*(taken)*
ê**tre**	*(to be)*	ét**é**	*(been)*

Nous avons trouvé la solution.	*We found the solution.*
Ils ont pris le train pour Paris.	*They took the train to (=for) Paris.*
Elle a eu des problèmes.	*She has had some problems.*

Note: These rules only apply with certainty to regular verbs in each category, i.e. those which behave in a predictable way in terms of stem and ending formation. Irregular past participles will, from now on, appear in word lists after the relevant infinitive, in the manner indicated below:

couvrir (couv**ert**)	*to cover (covered)*
mourir (**mort**)	*to die (dead)*

Avoir or être?

Most French verbs form their perfect with the help of the auxiliary 'avoir' (to have). This is always the case in English:

J'**ai** parlé.	*I spoke/have spoken.*
Nous **avons** écouté.	*We listened/have listened.*
Elles **ont** fini.	*They finished/have finished.*

There are, however, some verbs which require 'être' (to be) instead of 'avoir' (to have) as their auxiliary. They are sometimes classified as 'verbs indicating a change of position' or referred to as 'the famous 14'. In the list below, they are presented in pairs, normally with opposite meanings. Some have already been encountered in previous chapters.

aller	*to go*	naître	*to be born*
venir	*to come*	mourir	*to die*
arriver	*to arrive*	passer	*to pass*
partir	*to leave/go*	retourner	*to return*
descendre	*to go down*	rester	*to stay*
monter	*to go up*	tomber	*to fall*
entrer	*to enter*		
sortir	*to go out*		

Note: Verbs which are formed by adding a *prefix* (small particle placed at the beginning of the word and modifying the meaning) to one of the above 14, will *also use 'être'* in the perfect:

Je suis **re**parti.	*I left again.*
(**re** + partir)	
Il est **re**descendu.	*He went down again.*
(**re** + descendre)	
Il est **de**venu fou.	*He became mad.*
(**de** + venir)	

Remember: In French, the perfect can have two distinct shades of meaning:

Il est arrivé.
could mean:
He has (now) arrived.
or
He arrived.
and:
Nous avons mangé.
could mean:
We have (now) eaten.
or
We ate.

Word list

Nouns

l'addition (fem.)	*bill*	le sable	*sand*
le chemin	*way*	la salle à manger	*dining room*
le disque	*record*	la serviette	*towel/serviette/*
l'écriteau (masc.)	*sign/notice*		*napkin*
le garage	*garage*	le tableau	*painting*
le maillot de bain	*swimsuit*	la villa	*villa*
le plateau	*tray*	le voyageur (-euse)	*traveller (masc./*
le poulet	*chicken*		*fem.)*
le propriétaire	*owner/proprietor*		

Adjectives

dégoûtant	*disgusting/awful*	excellent	*excellent*

Verbs

lire	(lu)	*to read*	prendre	(pris)	*to take*
offrir	(offert)	*to offer*	rire	(ri)	*to laugh*
ouvrir	(ouvert)	*to open*	suivre	(suivi)	*to follow*
préférer		*to prefer*	voir	(vu)	*to see*

Other words

attention!	*caution/beware!*	enfin	*at last/finally*
défense de (+infin.)	*it is forbidden to*	hier	*yesterday*
	(official notices)	longtemps	*(a) long (time)*

Work it out

We saw earlier in this chapter that the perfect tense behaves in a different way in the two languages. There is another important difference which you will now be asked to investigate.

The past participle used in the formation of the perfect behaves in a different way depending on the auxiliary (être or avoir) used. Look at the examples given below and try to fathom out the difference. The appropriate gender and number information is given whenever necessary.

1 Elle a mangé une grosse pomme verte. — *She ate a big green apple.*

2 Nous (fem. plur.) sommes entrées dans le magasin. — *We went into the shop.*

3 Le directeur a fermé la banque. — *The manager closed the bank.*

4 Je (fem. sing.) suis arrivée devant le garage. — *I arrived in front of the garage.*

5	Est-ce que vous (fem. sing.) êtes partie de l'hôtel?	*Did you leave (=depart from) the hotel?*
6	Vous (masc. plur.) avez écouté le disque de Paul?	*Did you listen to Paul's record?*
7	Le monsieur et la dame ont parlé à l'agent.	*The gentleman and the lady spoke to the policeman.*
8	Les enfants sont restés à la maison.	*The children stayed at home.*

Conclusions

Your conclusions, based on the above examples, should be as follows:

A   In the above sentences, past participles used with 'avoir' remain invariable: they do not agree in gender or number with the subject (performer):

> Elle a mangé. (sentence 1)
> Vous avez écouté. (sentence 6)
> Ils ont parlé. (sentence 7)

B   By contrast, the past participles following 'être' agree in gender and number with the subject (performer):

> Nous sommes entrées. (sentence 2 — fem. pl.)
> Je suis arrivée. (sentence 4 — fem. sing.)
> Vous êtes partie. (sentence 5 — fem. sing.)
> Ils sont restés. (sentence 8 — masc. pl.)

In other words, the past participle of a verb used with être as an auxiliary agrees like an adjective with the subject (= performer) of the sentence.

Très curieux!
Very strange!

Exercise 9(i)

Translate into English, *without* making use of the English perfect tense!

1 La montre de Robert est tombée dans l'eau.   **2** Les voyageurs sont montés dans le train.   **3** La serveuse a apporté le plateau.   **4** Monsieur Dupont a demandé l'addition.   **5** Nous sommes partis de la maison pendant la nuit.   **6** Est-ce que vous avez fermé les valises?   **7** J'ai acheté des pêches au marché.   **8** Les amis ont commandé un apéritif. **9** Les enfants sont partis hier matin. **10** Nous avons passé une soirée formidable.

Exercise 9(ii)
Put the following sentences into the perfect:

1 Je regarde le film. **2** Nous mangeons au restaurant. **3** Ils ont un petit accident. **4** Le train arrive à la gare. **5** Les voyageurs descendent du car. **6** Les touristes admirent le tableau.

Exercise 9(iii)
Translate the following sentences into French (using the perfect tense):

1 The woman closed the door. **2** The customer talked to the manager. **3** She went down into the dining room and ordered the wine. **4** The cat got up onto the chair and ate the chicken. **5** The suitcase fell on the head of the traveller. **6** We arrived in front of the shop before the manager.

Have a try

When we arrived at the villa, we found the door locked. I telephoned the owner and we waited an hour in the car, in (= under) the sun. Finally, the owner arrived with the key. He opened the door and said, 'There you are! (Have a) good holiday!' Then he left. We put the cases in the bedrooms and I asked, 'Do you wish to eat or to go to the beach?' The children shouted, 'To the beach!' I put the towels and the swimsuits in a bag and we went towards the sea. We walked (for) a long time. Finally, we arrived on the beach. The children asked, 'Where are the people? The beach is empty. Ah! There is a sign over there!' We went towards the sign and we read: Beware: pollution. No swimming!

> Pas de chance!
> *Bad luck!*
> *(lit.: No luck!)*

10 How to say 'this', 'that', 'these' and 'those'
How to turn positive sentences into negative ones

How to say 'this', 'that', 'these' and 'those'

The words 'this', 'that', 'these' and 'those' placed before a noun are called *demonstrative adjectives* and are used to call attention to certain specific things or beings in preference to others. The corresponding French words: 'ce', 'cet', 'cette' and 'ces' behave differently from their English counterparts in two respects:

(*a*) In their above-mentioned form, they do not allow for the distinction which exists in English between 'this' and 'that' or between 'these' and 'those'.

(*b*) Since they can, if required, be used to replace the definite article ('le, la, les'), they too will carry information about the gender (masc./fem.) and the number (sing./plur.) of the noun they relate to.

Word list

Nouns

l'accident (masc.)	*accident*	la note	*bill*
l'ambulance (fem.)	*ambulance*	le panneau	*(road) sign*
		la pierre	*stone*
la cathédrale	*cathedral*	le pull-over	*jumper*
le champagne	*champagne*	la sculpture	*sculpture*
la collision	*collision*	le stop	*stop (sign)*
le docteur	*doctor*	le supermarché	*supermarket*
la glace	*ice-cream*	la viande	*meat*
le/la malade	*sick person/patient*		

Adjectives

abominable	*abominable*	dangereux (dangereuse)	*dangerous*
blessé	*wounded/ hurt*	énorme	*enormous*

fâché	*angry/cross/*	malade	*ill/sick*
	annoyed		*badly damaged*
horrible	*horrible/awful*		*(familiar)*
intelligent	*intelligent*		

Verbs

cacher	*to hide (something)*	payer	*to pay*
éviter	*to avoid*	penser	*to think*
freiner	*to brake*	refuser	*to refuse*

Other words

aujourd'hui	*today*	jamais	*never*
comment	*how*	loin (de)	*far (from)*
demain	*tomorrow*	près (de)	*near (to)*
depuis	*since/for*	que	*that/whom/which*
encore	*still/yet/again*	toujours	*always/still*

Work it out

Study the following sentences carefully to find out the way demonstrative adjectives behave in French. The gender and number of the relevant nouns have been included to help you in your investigation.

1 Cet animal (masc. sing.) est très dangereux.
This/that animal is very dangerous.

2 Est-ce que tu vas fermer cette porte (fem. sing.)?
Are you going to close this/that door?

3 Ce tableau (masc. sing.) est splendide.
This/that painting is splendid.

4 Ces livres (masc. plur.) sont excellents.
These/those books are excellent.

5 J'ai acheté ces énormes pommes (fem. plur.) au supermarché.
I bought these/those enormous apples at the supermarket.

6 Nous venons de visiter cette adorable ville (fem. sing.).
We have just visited this/that adorable town.

7 J'aime ce charmant hôtel (masc. sing.) et cette vieille église (fem. sing.).
I like this/that charming hotel and this/that old church.

8 Elle déteste cet horrible garçon (masc. sing.).
She hates this/that horrible boy.

Deductions

From the study of the above sentences, the following points should have emerged:

A   'Ce' is used before a masculine singular word (adjective or noun) which does not begin with a vowel (sentence No 3).

B   'Cet' occurs before a masculine singular word (adjective or noun) beginning with a vowel or 'mute' h (sentences Nos 1 and 8).

C   'Cette' appears before a feminine singular word (adjective or noun), regardless of the letter it begins with (sentences Nos 2, 6 and 7 = cette église).

D   'Ces' is used before masculine plural or feminine plural words (adjectives or nouns) regardless of the letter they begin with (sentences Nos 4 and 5).

Note: We have seen that the demonstrative adjectives as presented above do not indicate relative closeness or distance as do their English equivalents this/that and these/those. If it becomes important to make such a distinction, the words '-ci' (= here) and '-là' (= there) can be placed after the relevant nouns.

Ce costume-ci est superbe mais ce costume-là est horrible.	*This suit is superb but that suit is horrible.*
Je n'aime pas cette table-ci . . . Je préfère cette table-là.	*I do not like this table . . . I prefer that table.*

C'est clair?
Is that clear?

Exercise 10(i)

Translate the following sentences into French, using '-ci' and '-là', whenever appropriate, to remove ambiguity:

1 We love this house. **2** I detest that dress but I like this jumper. **3** That little girl is adorable. **4** He is going to eat that meat! **5** This painting is wonderful but that sculpture is abominable. **6** These children are very intelligent. **7** This enormous stone is about to fall on(to) the road. **8** Did you watch that film? **9** This room is too dear! **10** Those dogs are always in the garden.

How to turn positive sentences into negative ones

You are now able to construct a variety of sentences indicating where things or beings are, what they do, etc. We shall now examine the way in which those positive statements can be turned into negative ones. The French equivalent of 'not' needed for that purpose is 'ne . . . pas'.

Note: In familiar or colloquial speech, French people have a tendency to 'drop' the first part of the negative phrase and use only 'pas'. Although it is important for you to know that fact, you should refrain from doing the same thing at this stage.

Work it out

Study the following negative statements carefully, so as to draw the relevant conclusions concerning the behaviour of 'ne . . . pas'.

1	Je ne ferme pas la porte.	*I am not closing the door.*
2	Nous ne regardons pas la télévision.	*We are not watching television.*
3	Vous n'avez pas mangé la glace.	*You have not eaten the ice-cream.*
4	Elle n'est pas descendue ce matin.	*She did not come down this morning.*
5	Les touristes ne vont pas rester ici.	*The tourists are not going to stay here.*
6	Est-ce que le taxi n'est pas arrivé?	*Hasn't the taxi arrived?*
7	N'as-tu pas regardé le film?	*Haven't you watched the film?*
8	Les clients ne sont-ils pas contents	*Aren't the customers pleased?*

Conclusions

Your conclusions should be as follows:

A 'Ne' loses its 'e' whenever the next word begins with a vowel (or, presumably, a 'mute' h).
B In the case of a simple (= one word) tense like the present, 'ne' is placed before the verb and 'pas' after (examples 1 and 2).
C In the case of a compound (= two-word) tense like the perfect,

'ne' is placed before the auxiliary (avoir or être) and 'pas' immediately after (examples 3 and 4). The past participle will be placed after 'pas'.
D   In the case of the immediate future (present of aller + infinitive) 'ne' is placed before 'aller' and 'pas' immediately after. The infinitive will be placed after 'pas' (example 5).
Note: The same will apply in the case of the immediate past (venir de + infinitive).
E   In questions introduced by 'est-ce que', 'ne . . . pas' behaves exactly as in the corresponding statement (example 6). This would also be the case with 'informal' questions, in which a rise in voice-pitch is all that is required to turn a statement (example 1 to 5) into a query.
F   In questions where an inversion is used (formal or elevated style), the group *verb + pronoun* is treated as a whole; 'ne' is placed before the group and 'pas' immediately after (example 7).

Beware: If a noun is used in this type of question (as in example 7), it will be placed *before* the negative expression and the pattern will be:

> noun + ne + verb + pronoun + pas

> Le docteur ne vient-il pas?
> *Isn't the doctor coming?*

The above findings can be summarised thus:

1   In French the negative form 'ne . . . pas' is used in the following way: 'ne' is placed before the simple-tense verb or the auxiliary and 'pas' immediately after.
2   Any past participle or infinitive will be placed *after* the negative expression:

> ne + verb + pas (+ past participle/infinitive)

Exercise 10(i)
Using the information gathered in the previous section, put the following sentences into the negative:

1 Le vieux monsieur monte dans le taxi.   2 La serveuse est dans la salle à manger.   3 Nous allons visiter la cathédrale.   4 Est-ce que les magasins vont fermer demain?   5 Ils ont commandé le champagne.   6 Les voyageurs sont restés dans le car.   7 Le garçon a-t-il apporté l'apéritif?   8 Tu viens de téléphoner au docteur?

Exercise 10(ii)

Translate the following sentences into French (use the standard type of question whenever applicable):

1 We are not eating there!   2 Are the tourists not tired?   3 He is not going to stay in the shop.   4 The meals are not very good in this restaurant.   5 The visitors have not arrived.   6 I did not buy that black jumper.   7 The children are not in the house.   8 She is not going to go into that hotel.

C'est tout pour le moment!
That's all for the moment!

Have a try

—Il y a longtemps que vous êtes ici?
—Depuis ce matin.
—Est-ce que vous avez vu l'accident?
—Oui, et vous?
—Non, je viens juste d'arriver.
—Voilà comment l'accident est arrivé: au croisement, le jeune homme avec la moto est sorti de la petite route; il n'a pas vu le panneau du 'stop' et il a traversé la route nationale. Le conducteur de la voiture a freiné mais il n'a pas évité la collision. Le jeune homme est blessé et la moto et la voiture sont malades! J'ai téléphoné à l'ambulance et à la police. . . Ah voici l'ambulance; mais les agents ne sont pas encore là!
—Est-ce que vous allez attendre?
—Bien sûr, je suis le seul témoin!

Ah bon!
I see!
(*lit.: Ah good!*)

11 How to say 'my', 'your', etc.   How to express quantity (from one to one hundred) and rank

How to say 'my', 'your', etc.

Having learnt how to use 'du', 'de la', 'des' to express the idea of possession, you will now be able to understand the way the English *possessive adjectives* — my, your, his, her, etc. — are translated and behave in French.

French possessive adjectives function on the same principle as definite articles, which they can replace when required: in the singular, they have two separate forms, one for the masculine and one for the feminine to cope with the two-gender system. In the plural, however, there is only one set, which is common to both genders (masculine and feminine).

Here is the list of possessive adjectives in French:

Meaning	Masculine (singular)	Feminine (singular)	Plural (masc. and fem.)
my	mon	ma	mes
your (fam.)	ton	ta	tes
his/her/its	son	sa	ses
our	notre	notre	nos
your (polite sing. or normal plural)	votre	votre	vos
their	leur	leur	leurs

So far everything seems fairly simple and straightforward, but beware: the way in which French possessive adjectives function is significantly different from the way English ones do! This will be made clear in the section which follows the Word list.

Word list

Nouns

l'an (masc.)	*year*	le kilo(gramme)	*kilo(gram)*
la balle	*ball*	la limonade	*lemonade*
la bière	*beer*	les lunettes	*glasses (for*
le biscuit	*biscuit*	(fem. pl.)	*vision)*
le bureau	*office/desk*	l'oncle (masc.)	*uncle*
le cheval	*horse(s)*	le pain	*bread*
(chevaux)		le petit	*breakfast*
la clé (or clef)	*key*	déjeuner	
le cousin/la	*cousin (male/*	la seconde	*second*
cousine	*female)*	la semaine	*week*
le croissant	*croissant*	la sœur	*sister*
le fauteuil	*armchair*	la tante	*aunt*
le fromage	*cheese*	le vélo	*bicycle*
l'idée (fem.)	*idea*	le weekend	*weekend*

Adjectives

curieux	*curious/strange*	sûr	*sure/reliable/safe*
(curieuse)			
mauvais	*bad*		

Verbs

apporter	*to bring*	trouver	*to find*
casser	*to break*		

Other words

adieu	*goodbye*	s'il te plaît	*(if you) please*
alors	*then/in that*		*(familiar sing.)*
	case	s'il vous plaît	*(polite sing. or*
			normal plural)

Work it out

See if you can fathom out the way in which French possessive adjectives behave, by studying the following sentences. The gender of the relevant noun has been included to assist you.

1. Mon frère (masc. sing.) est content mais ma sœur (fem. sing.) est fâchée. — *My brother is pleased but my sister is cross.*

2. Est-ce que ta mère (fem. sing.) et ton père (masc. sing.) sont là? — *Are your mother and (your) father here?*

3 Marie est triste: sa tante (fem. sing.) et son oncle (masc. sing.) sont malades.	*Mary is sad: her aunt and (her) uncle are ill.*
4 Leurs passeports (masc. plur.) sont dans leur chambre (fem. sing.).	*Their passports (one each) are in their bedroom (one between them).*
5 Nos parents (masc. plur.) ont téléphoné hier soir.	*Our parents telephoned yesterday evening.*
6 Mon amie (fem. sing.) Louise est venue ce matin.	*My friend Louise came this morning.*
7 J'aime ce village et son église (fem. sing.).	*I like this village and its church.*
8 Ton idée (fem. sing.) n'est pas mauvaise.	*Your idea is not bad.*

Deductions

The following points should have come to light: In French, the possessive adjective does not agree with the owner as it does in English, but with the being or thing 'owned'; hence 'son' frère because 'frère' is masculine singular and 'sa' sœur because 'sœur' is feminine singular. This, of course, means that 'son frère' could be translated as 'his brother' or 'her brother', and 'sa sœur' as 'his sister' or 'her sister'.

This point having been clarified, how can the contradictions occurring in sentences 6, 7 and 8 be explained? 'amie' (fem. sing.) is preceded by 'mon', 'église' (also fem. sing.) is preceded by 'son' and 'idée' (again fem. sing.) is used with 'ton', all of which are masculine singular forms! The reason is simple: whenever a feminine singular noun begins with a vowel or 'mute' h, the masculine singular form of the possessive adjective will be used instead of the feminine singular one, to avoid ugly-sounding vowel-clashes (as in 'ma amie', 'ta idée', 'sa église').

Important: In sentences of types 2 and 3, it is normal to omit the second possessive adjective in English (hence the brackets). In French, however, that possessive cannot be left out because of its role as a gender and number marker.

Ingénieux!
(Ingenious!)

Exercise 11(i)
Translate into English:

1 J'ai appelé ma sœur au téléphone. **2** Tu vas casser mon vélo! **3** Robert est heureux; son frère et sa sœur sont arrivés hier. **4** Je viens de voir vos enfants sur la plage. **5** Elle a acheté son pull-over dans mon nouveau magasin. **6** Je déteste ton amie; ses idées sont ridicules.

Exercise 11(ii)
Translate into French using the standard question form when appropriate:

1 I am going to go (in)to my bedroom. **2** Have you seen his new house? **3** She is watching her daughter. **4** The waiter is bringing our wine. **5** Where are your bags, my friends? **6** I have put my jumper in his case. **7** My sister and her husband are over there! **8** The girl broke my beautiful vase with her ball.

How to express quantity (from one to one hundred)

Expressing quantity is a skill we constantly use. We shall now learn how to do so in French. Before introducing numbers, however, we should make a few simple but important remarks about their behaviour. In French, 'cardinal' numbers such as 'deux' (two), 'dix' (ten), etc., are normally invariable, i.e. they remain the same whatever the gender or number of the noun they refer to. The only exceptions which need to be mentioned at this stage are 'un' (one), which becomes 'une' before a feminine singular noun, and 'vingt' (twenty), which takes an 's' in the expression 'quatre-vingts' (eighty) if no number follows (see also chapter 24).

Compare	un jour	*one day*
and	une semaine	*one week*
or	quatre-vingts kilos	*eighty kilos*
and	quatre-vingt-cinq ans	*eighty five years*

In French, the numbers from one to nineteen are:

un(e)	*one*	onze	*eleven*
deux	*two*	douze	*twelve*
trois	*three*	treize	*thirteen*
quatre	*four*	quatorze	*fourteen*
cinq	*five*	quinze	*fifteen*
six	*six*	seize	*sixteen*
sept	*seven*	dix-sept	*seventeen*
huit	*eight*	dix-huit	*eighteen*
neuf	*nine*	dix-neuf	*nineteen*
dix	*ten*		

The 'decimal sets' (= tens) from twenty to one hundred are:

vingt	*twenty*	soixante-dix	*seventy*
trente	*thirty*	quatre-vingts	*eighty*
quarante	*forty*	quatre-vingt-dix	*ninety*
cinquante	*fifty*	cent	*one hundred*
soixante	*sixty*		

Numbers from 20 to 69

To express quantities between twenty and sixty-nine, all you need to do is select the 'decimal set' you want: 'vingt, trente, quarante. . .' and add to it the required number: 'un, deux, trois. . .':

    36 = trente-six
    47 = quarante-sept
    54 = cinquante-quatre
    68 = soixante-huit, etc. . .

Note, however, that in the case of the following numbers: 21, 31, 41, 51 and 61, the word 'et' (and) has to be inserted before 'un' (or 'une'):

    21 = vingt et un
    31 = trente et un
    61 = soixante et un, etc . . .

Numbers from 70 to 100

In France (unlike Belgium or Switzerland) there is no single word to express either 70, 80 or 90. Those numbers are therefore made up as follows:

    70 = soixante-dix   *(sixty + ten)*
    80 = quatre-vingts   *(four twenties)*
    90 = quatre-vingt-dix   *(four twenties + ten)*

So, to make counting less clumsy, numbers from one to nineteen are used between 61 and 79 and between 81 and 99:

72 = soixante-douze
79 = soixante-dix-neuf
93 = quatre-vingt-treize
98 = quatre-vingt-dix-huit

Note: For 71, 'et' must be inserted between 'soixante' and 'onze' ('soixante et onze'). This is not the case for 81 (= quatre-vingt-un) or 91 (= quatre-vingt-onze). The word for nought is 'zéro'. It is a noun and will therefore take an 's' in the plural:

Il a eu deux zéros en   *He has had two noughts in*
français.   *French.*

How to express rank

The (cardinal) numbers presented so far simply indicate quantity. There is another related set designed to indicate rank, sometimes referred to as the *ordinal numbers*: first, second, third, fourth and so on. In order to form ordinal numbers in French, you simply remove the final 'e' of the cardinal number (if applicable) and add the ending 'ième':

quatre   *(four)*   becomes quatrième
dix   *(ten)*   becomes dixième
douze   *(twelve)*   becomes douzième

Exceptions: 'Un' becomes 'premier' (or 'première' before a fem. sing. noun) when used on its own, but 'unième' in compound numbers; 'deux' can become 'second' (or 'seconde' before a fem. sing. noun) or 'deuxième' (only the latter can be used in compound numbers); 'neuf' becomes 'neuvième' (on its own or in compound numbers).

Note: Ordinal numbers can be put in the plural in French:

Ils sont arrivés troisièmes.   *They arrived third.*
Nous allons être les premiers. *We are going to be the first.*

Important remarks concerning the use of numbers:

1 When expressing age in French, the relevant number must be

preceded by 'avoir' (and not 'être') and followed by the word 'an(s)':

Elle a vingt-huit ans.   *She is twenty-eight (years of age).*

2   Dates are normally expressed in figures rather than in words:
le 6 juin 1944   *6 June 1944 ('D. Day')*
le 14 Juillet   *14 July ('Bastille Day')*

Days of the month are expressed by an ordinary (cardinal) number except for the first.

| *Compare:* | Le 1er (premier) avril | *1 April* |
| *and:* | le 2 (deux) ou le 3 (trois) mars | *2 or 3 March* |

Exercise 11(iii)
Translate the following sentences into English:

1 Elle va avoir vingt et un ans.   **2** Garçon, trois bières et deux limonades, s'il vous plaît!   **3** Ton père a eu cinquante-sept ans hier.   **4** Nous avons regardé douze films en une semaine.   **5** Ce cheval est arrivé neuvième dans la troisième course.   **6** Une seconde s'il te plaît.

Exercise 11(iv)
Translate into French:

1 I have just bought twelve beautiful apples in that little shop. **2** This old man is one hundred years old tomorrow. **3** There are seventy-five paintings in this castle.   **4** He has eaten eleven biscuits this morning.   **5** She has thirty seven records in her bedroom.   **6** I am going to order six croissants for breakfast.

Have a try

—Quick, the taxi is outside! We are going to be late at the airport!
—No, we've got time . . . Are the suitcases ready?
—Yes, they are downstairs . . . Do you have the passports?
—They are on the table in the kitchen, but I have lost the tickets . . . Where are they?
—Stay calm! They are in my handbag! Don't forget the envelope with the money!

— It's in my pocket ... That's strange! ... I have just put my watch here ... Where is it?

— Look, it's here. It has fallen under the bed!

— Quick, or we are going to miss the plane ... And then, goodbye to our weekend in Paris!

Pessimiste va!
You pessimist! (familiar)

12   Verb groups   The present of 2nd group verbs   3rd group verbs The present of 3rd group verbs

How to distinguish between verb groups

French verbs, as already pointed out, can be classified into a small number of categories according to the endings of their infinitives ('er', 'ir', 'oir' or 're'). The advantage of such a classification is that most verbs in a given category tend to behave in a regular and predictable way as regards tense formation. We have seen for instance that, with the exception of 'aller' (to go) and a few occasional modifications, the majority of 'er' verbs (also known as first group verbs) follow a fixed pattern for the formation of their present tense (see chapter 7).

In the case of 'ir' verbs, the situation is slightly more complex because they fall into two distinct categories. How can they be distinguished? The clue lies in the shape of their *present participle* (the equivalent of the English 'ing' form, which indicates that an action is in progress). The present participle ending of *all* French verbs is 'ant': 'cherchant' (looking for), 'finissant' (finishing), 'partant' (leaving). Certain 'ir' verbs, like 'finir' (to finish) or 'grandir' (to grow), add 'iss' between the stem and the 'ant' ending of the present participle. Such verbs are known as second group verbs.

Compare:

cherch + ant	(inf. = chercher —	1st group)
fin + iss + ant	(inf. = finir	— 2nd group)
part + ant	(inf. = partir	— 3rd group)
grand + iss + ant	(inf. = grandir	— 2nd group)

Any verb with a present participle ending in 'issant' is a second group verb and is totally regular. Learning one 'model', for instance 'finir', will give you all the clues you need to form all the tenses of any other second group verb.

In future Word lists, the present participle ending 'issant', characteristic of that group, will appear (in brackets) after the infinitive, as indicated below:

> choisir (issant) — to choose
> réussir (issant) — to succeed

The *past participle* of second group verbs, i.e. the form indicating the completed aspect of an action (equivalent to the 'ed' form of regular English verbs (fini = finished, réussi = succeeded), is constructed as follows:

$$\boxed{\text{stem} + \text{i}}$$

Il a fini le travail.	*He has finished the work.*
Vous avez réussi.	*You have succeeded.*
Les enfants ont grandi!	*The children have grown!*

Word list

Nouns

le bien	*good*	la précaution	*precaution*
le courrier	*mail*	la réparation	*repair*
le dîner	*dinner*	le réservoir	*tank*
la faim	*hunger*		*(= container)*
l'intérêt (masc.)	*interest*	la soif	*thirst*
la lettre	*letter*	le soin	*care*
maman	*mum(my)*	la solution	*solution*
le miracle	*miracle*	la stupidité	*stupidity*
l'ouvrier/	*worker*	la tête	*head*
l'ouvrière	*(masc./fem.)*	le travail	*work*
papa	*dad(dy)*	le voisin/la	*neighbour*
la porte	*door*	voisine	*(masc./fem.)*

Adjectives

beau (belle)	*beautiful*	paresseux	*lazy*
bon (bonne)	*good*	(paresseuse)	

Verbs

accomplir	*to accomplish/*	choisir (issant)	*to choose*
(issant)	*achieve*	croire (cru)	*to believe (believed)*
agir (issant)	*to act*	entendre	*to hear*
chercher	*to look for/search*	finir (issant)	*to finish*

grandir (issant)	*to grow (in size)*	remplir (issant)	*to fill up*
garantir (issant)	*to guarantee*	réussir (issant)	*to succeed*
investir (issant)	*to invest*	saisir (issant)	*to seize/catch*
pâlir (issant)	*to turn pale*	sortir	*to go out*
partir	*to go away/leave*	souffrir	*to suffer*
réfléchir (issant)	*to think/ponder*	(souffert)	*(suffered)*

Other words

à l'heure	*on time*	tant pis!	*too bad!*

How to form the present of second group verbs

Work it out

Examine the endings of the second group verbs used in the following sentences to obtain the necessary information concerning the construction of their present tense:

1 Nous finissons notre travail.   *We are finishing our work.*
2 Si vous réfléchissez, vous allez trouver une solution.   *If you think carefully (lit.: reflect), you are going to find a solution.*
3 Robert grandit très vite.   *Robert is growing up very quickly.*
4 Les ouvriers blanchissent les murs.   *The workers are whitewashing (lit.: whitening) the walls.*
5 Tu pâlis. Est-ce que tu es malade?   *You are turning pale. Are you ill?*
6 J'agis dans votre intérêt.   *I am acting in your interest.*

Deductions

You should have extracted the following information from the above sentences:

A The stem used for the present of second group verbs is the infinitive *minus* the 'ir' ending.

B The endings of the present tense of second group verbs are:

je	**-is** (sentence 6)
tu	**-is** (sentence 5)
il/elle	**-it** (sentence 3)

nous	**-issons** (sentence 1)
vous	**-issez** (sentence 2)
ils/elles	**-issent** (sentence 4)

Vous saisissez?
Do you get it? (familiar)
(lit.: do you grasp?)

Exercise 12(i)
In the following sentences, replace the infinitive of each second group verb (in brackets) by the suitable form of the present tense:

1 Je (réfléchir) à votre proposition. **2** Elle (investir) son argent avec soin. **3** Aujourd'hui, les docteurs (accomplir) des miracles. **4** Est-ce que vous (garantir) la réparation? **5** Tu (nourrir) les chats de la voisine? **6** Elles (réussir) à finir le travail à l'heure. **7** Le petit garçon (saisir) le beau ballon rouge. **8** Nous (remplir) le réservoir.

Exercise 12(ii)
Translate the above sentences into English.

Third group verbs

Logically enough, third group verbs are those which do not belong to the first group (infinitive in 'er') or the second group (infinitive in 'ir' and present participle in 'issant').

Although a number of third group verbs follow a fairly predictable pattern in the formation of their various tenses, some are irregular either because of their ending or, more commonly, because of modifications in the stem within a given tense. In addition, their past participle form is often unpredictable:

Infinitive	*Past Participle*
couvrir *(to cover)*	couvert *(covered)*
savoir *(to know)*	su *(known)*
courir *(to run)*	couru *(run)*
mourir *(to die)*	mort *(dead)*
souffrir *(to suffer)*	souffert *(suffered)*

Irregular past participle forms are included in the Word lists. The general rules concerning the formation of the present and past participles of 'regular' third group verbs are given below. This completes the information already presented in Chapter 9.

'ir' verbs

> present participle = stem (infinitive minus 'ir') + ant.
> past participle = stem (same as above) + i.

partir (*to leave* (= *go*))	partant (*leaving*)	parti (*left*)
sortir (*to go out*)	sortant (*going out*)	sorti (*gone out*)

Beware:

offrir (*to offer*)	offrant (*offering*)	offert (*not* offri) (*offered*)
ouvrir (*to open*)	ouvrant (*opening*)	ouvert (*not* ouvri) (open(ed))

'oir' verbs

> present participle = stem (infinitive minus 'oir') + ant.
> past participle = stem (often reduced) + u.

Note: Normally, a reduced stem is one in which some final letters are missing:

devoir (*to owe*)	devant (*owing*)	dû (*not* 'devu') (*owed*)
pouvoir (*to be able to*)	pouvant (*being able to*)	pu (*not* 'pouvu') (*been able to*)
pleuvoir (*to rain*)	pleuvant (*raining*)	plu (*not* 'pleuvu') (*rained*)

Beware:

avoir (*to have*)	ayant (*having*)	eu (*had*)
asseoir (*to sit*)	asseyant (*sitting*)	assis (*sat*)

're' verbs

> present participle = stem (infinitive minus 're') + ant.
> past participle = stem (as above) + u.

attendre (*to wait*)   attendant (*waiting*)   attendu (*waited*)
descendre (*to   descendant (*going   descendu (*gone
go down*)   down*)   down*)

Beware:

prendre (*to take*)   prenant (*taking*)   pris (*taken*)
vivre (*to live*)   vivant (*living*)   vécu (*lived*)

How to form the present of third group verbs

The 'regular' endings for the present tense of third group verbs are given below. They are to be added to the stem which is usually (but not always!) the infinitive minus its ending.

	'ir' verbs	*'oir' verbs*	*'re' verbs*
je	-s	-s	-s
tu	-s	-s	-s
il/elle	-t	-t	-d
nous	-ons	-ons	-ons
vous	-ez	-ez	-ez
ils/elles	-ent	-ent	-ent

Nous partons ce soir (partir)   *We are leaving this evening.*
Il perd la tête! (perdre)   *He is losing his head.*
Le taxi attend devant la   *The taxi is waiting outside*
porte (attendre).   *(lit.: in front of) the door.*
Elle reçoit beaucoup de   *She receives many letters.*
lettres (recevoir).

Beware: The following verbs: 'couvrir' (to cover), 'offrir' (to offer), 'ouvrir' (to open), 'souffrir' (to suffer) and their compounds (if any), have the same present tense endings as 'er' verbs:

Elle souffre beaucoup   *She suffers a great deal.*
(souffrir).
J'ouvre la fenêtre (ouvrir).   *I open the window.*

Important: A number of third group verbs have two (or three) distinct stems in the present:

'croire'   je crois, tu crois, il croit,
(*to believe*) nous croyons, vous croyez, ils croient.

'dire'   je dis, tu dis, il dit,
(*to say*)   nous disons, vous dites, ils disent.

'mourir'   je meurs, tu meurs, il meurt,
(*to die*)   nous mourons, vous mourez, ils meurent.

'prendre'   je prends, tu prends, il prend,
(*to take*)   nous prenons, vous prenez, ils prennent.

'recevoir'   je reçois, tu reçois, il reçoit,
(*to receive*) nous recevons, vous recevez, ils reçoivent.

Note: Verbs ending in 'cevoir', such as 'apercevoir' (to catch sight of), 'décevoir' (to disappoint) etc., follow the same pattern as recevoir (shown above). In addition, they change their 'c' to 'ç' before 'o' and 'u' to preserve the sound 's' of the stem (otherwise, the sound would be 'k' before those letters!).

> Vous prenez quelque chose?
> *Are you going to have a drink?*
> *(lit.: are you taking something?)*

Exercise 12(iii)
In the following sentences, replace the infinitive (in brackets) by the appropriate person of the present tense.

1 Tu (descendre) avec nous? Non (j'attendre) mon frère. **2** Elle (sortir) avec ses amis ce soir? Oui, mais elle (prendre) l'autobus. **3** Est-ce que le dîner est prêt? Nous (mourir) de faim. **4** Il (rire) de ma stupidité et il (ouvrir) la porte. **5** Est-ce que vous (recevoir) beaucoup de courrier? **6** Nous (croire) que nous (entendre) le train.

Exercise 12(iv)
Translate into English.

1 Je crois que je comprends son attitude. **2** Est-ce que tu prends la voiture pour aller au bureau? **3** Nous ne croyons pas à votre histoire.   **4** Nous allons trouver un café: les enfants meurent de soif.   **5** Est-ce que tu as ouvert ma lettre?   **6** Il a pris la précaution de téléphoner avant de partir.

Have a try

—Maman, où es-tu?
—Je suis dans la cuisine, je prépare le dîner.
—Est-ce qu'il est prêt?
—Il va être prêt dans un petit moment. Tu es pressé?
—Oui, je crois que je vais aller au cinéma avec Jean et Robert.
—Encore? Mais tu es déjà sorti hier soir! Et ton travail? Il est fini?
—Non, je vais le finir avant de sortir!
—Non, mon garçon! Ce soir, tu vas rester à la maison. Tu vas venir manger et après tu vas monter dans ta chambre travailler!
—Oh, maman! . . . C'est un film formidable, et c'est le dernier soir!
—J'ai dit non! Tu sors trop; et tu ne travailles pas à l'école! Ton père n'est pas content!
—Maman, s'il te plaît . . .
—Non! . . . je parle dans ton intérêt. Ton attitude n'est pas bonne. Tu es intelligent, mais tu es paresseux . . . Est-ce que le fils des voisins va au cinéma trois ou quatre fois dans la semaine? Non! Il reste à la maison et il travaille.
—Il est stupide!
—Pas du tout! Il est premier en français, en anglais, en histoire . . . Tu es toujours dernier!
—Tu es horrible!
—Tant pis! C'est pour ton bien!
—Je vais aller demander à papa pour le cinéma!

Comme tu voudras!
Please yourself!
(lit.: as you will want!)

13 How to say 'me', 'you', 'him', 'her' etc. A question of agreement

How to say 'me', 'you', 'him', 'her', etc.

You are now in a position to express the performance of an action by a subject in the present, the past and the future.

Il appelle.	*He is calling.*
J'ai regardé.	*I watched.*
Vous allez manger.	*You are going to eat.*

You can also state that a given thing or being is subjected to the action in question:

Il appelle le nouveau garçon.	*He is calling the new waiter.*
J'ai regardé le vieux film policier.	*I watched the old thriller.*
Vous allez manger cette belle pomme rouge.	*You are going to eat this beautiful red apple.*

Those statements are excellent in themselves. But let us suppose that they represent the answers to the following questions:

> Est-ce qu'il appelle le nouveau garçon?
> Est-ce que tu as regardé le vieux film policier?
> Est-ce que je vais manger cette belle pomme rouge?

They now sound clumsy and repetitive, since the being or thing subjected to the action—the new waiter, the old thriller and the beautiful red apple, which grammar books normally refer to as 'the direct object phrase'—has already been clearly stated once.

It is therefore logical to have a set of words to replace the direct object phrase, thereby avoiding those tiresome and inelegant repetitions. Such words are called *direct object pronouns*.

Important: Being able to spot the direct object phrase (if there is one!) in a sentence is crucial if you want to replace it by the suitable pronoun. In English, one simple — if not foolproof — method of doing so, is to ask the question whom? or what? after the verb.

> I eat the meat. I eat what? = the meat (direct object).
> He calls the young policeman. He calls whom? = the young policeman (direct object).

The same method can be applied in French. The answer to the questions 'qui?' (whom?) or 'quoi?' (what?) will reveal the direct object phrase (if any). Using the same two examples we would have:

> Je mange la viande. (Je mange quoi? = la viande).
> Il appelle le jeune agent. (Il appelle qui? = le jeune agent).

Beware: Certain English verbs like 'to telephone someone', 'to tell someone something', 'to remind someone of something', 'to give someone something', are *not* constructed with a direct object in French!

Here is the list of the French direct object pronouns. The corresponding subject pronouns are also included:

Subject pronouns		*Direct object pronouns*	
je	*I*	me	*me*
tu	*you (familiar)*	te	*you*
il	*he/it*	le	*him/it*
elle	*she/it*	la	*her/it*
nous	*we*	nous	*us*
vous	*you (polite sing. /normal plur.)*	vous	*you*
ils	*they (masc. pl.)*	les	*them*
elles	*they (fem. pl.)*	les	*them*

Word list

Nouns

le bifteck	*steak*	le douanier	*customs officer*
la boisson	*drink*		
le cadeau (cadeaux)	*gift(s)*	la femme	*wife/woman*
		le film policier	*thriller (film)*
la chose	*thing*	le fils	*son*

le gâteau	cake	la politique	politics
le mari	husband	(usually sing.)	
minuit	midnight	la salade	salad/lettuce
la minute	minute	le sherry	sherry
la mode	fashion	la situation	situation
la pêche	peach	la sorte	sort
le plat	dish	la tombée	nightfall
la poche	(paper)	de la nuit	
(en papier)	bag		

Adjectives

amical	friendly	merveilleux	wonderful
(amicaux)		(merveilleuse)	
décontracté	relaxed	mûr	ripe
économique	economic/economical		

Verbs

boire (bu)	to drink	renvoyer	to fire
	(drunk)		(=dismiss)
inspecter	to inspect		send back
inviter	to invite	servir	to serve
rejoindre	to (re)join	vérifier	to check
(rejoint)	((re)joined)		

Other words

| souvent | often/frequently | tard | late |

Work it out

After examining the following sentences carefully, draw the relevant conclusions concerning the behaviour of French direct object pronouns.

1	Tu aimes la salade?	*Do you like salad?*
	Oui, je l'adore.	*Yes, I adore it.*
2	Est-ce que vous avez regardé le film policier?	*Did you watch the thriller?*
	Oui, nous l'avons regardé	*Yes, we watched it.*
3	Allez-vous manger ces belles pommes rouges?	*Are you going to eat these beautiful red apples?*
	Oui, nous allons les manger.	*Yes, we are going to eat them.*
4	Est-ce que le douanier inspecte les bagages?	*Does the customs officer inspect the luggage?*
	Non, il ne les inspecte pas.	*No, he does not inspect it.*

5	Est-ce que tu as écouté mon disque?	*Have you listened to my record?*
	Oui, je viens juste de l'écouter.	*Yes, I have just listened to it.*
6	Je suis le directeur. Vous désirez me voir?	*I am the manager. Do you wish to see me?*
7	Attention Robert! L'agent te regarde!	*Look out, Robert! The policeman is looking at you!*
8	Je suis ici avec ta mère. Tu nous cherches?	*I am here with your mother. Are you looking for us?*
9	Paul, Marie! Papa vient de vous appeler!	*Paul, Mary! Daddy's just been calling you!*

Remarks

A The final vowel of the direct object pronouns 'le' and 'la' is replaced by an apostrophe (') whenever the next word begins with a vowel (or, presumably, a 'mute' h) (Nos 1 and 2).

Note: This also applies in the case of 'me' and 'te'.

B In No 1 (present tense), the pronoun 'l'' replacing 'la salade' is placed before the verb (adore).

C In reply No 2 (perfect), 'l'' replacing 'le film policier' occurs *before the auxiliary* (avons) and not before the past participle!

D In reply No 3 (immediate future), the pronoun 'les' replacing 'ces belles pommes rouges' (fem. pl.) is placed *immediately before the infinitive* 'manger' *and not* before 'allons'.

E In reply No 4 (present), 'les' replacing 'les bagages' (masc. pl.) occurs *after 'ne'* and *before the verb* (inspecte).

F In reply No 5 (immediate past), 'l'' replacing 'le disque' also occurs *immediately after 'de'* and *before the infinitive* (écouter).

G In sentences 6, 7, 8 and 9, the position of the object pronouns ('me', 'te', 'nous' and 'vous') conforms with that of 'le', 'la' or 'les' as examined in the preceding sentences.

Summary In the case of the tenses studied so far, the direct object (if any) occurs before the verb in the present, before the auxiliary in the perfect, and before the infinitive in the immediate past or the immediate future.

Pas vrai?
Isn't that so?
(lit.: not true?)

Note: The fact that a masculine singular noun phrase can be replaced (if required) by the direct object pronoun 'le', a feminine singular one by 'la' and a plural noun phrase of either gender by 'les' will simplify your task considerably, since those pronouns are identical to the corresponding definite article. (A noun phrase is a group composed of a noun with its appropriate article *or* possessive *or* demonstrative and relevant adjective(s) if any).

Exercise 13(i)

Bearing in mind the discoveries made in the 'Work it out' section, rephrase the following sentences using the appropriate pronoun to replace the direct object noun phrase:

1 J'ai mangé **le gros gâteau**.   **2** Tu vas fermer **la fenêtre de la chambre**.   **3** Nous venons de voir **le nouveau directeur**.   **4** Nous n'avons pas accepté **le cadeau du client**.   **5** Il achète **le beau costume bleu?**   **6** Elle voit **les chiens de Monsieur Dupont?**

Exercise 13(ii)
Translate into English:

1 Vous avez vu Robert? Oui, je l'ai vu hier matin.   **2** Tu vas visiter l'exposition? Non, je viens juste de la visiter.   **3** Est-ce que tu aimes la télévision? Oui, je la regarde souvent.   **4** Vous allez poser vos valises ici. Le douanier va les vérifier.   **5** Est-ce que le patron t'a écouté? Non, il m'a renvoyé!   **6** Le garçon va vous servir dans une minute.   **7** Est-ce que vous nous appelez? Non, nous ne vous appelons pas!   **8** Voici les plats; la serveuse les apporte.

Exercise 13(iii)
Translate the following sentences into French, using the "standard" question form wherever appropriate:

1 We bought a beautiful steak and your dog has eaten it!   **2** Here is the taxi driver; I am going to pay him.   **3** Do you have the bill? No, I don't have it.   **4** Are you going to invite them? No, they hate me.   **5** I'm listening to you, my boy. (familiar singular)   **6** She has just found him in the garage.

A question of agreement

We have now seen how to improve the elegance of our replies by using direct object pronouns to replace noun phrases which have occurred previously. We must now clarify the influence of those pronouns on the shape of the past participle when the verb is in the perfect.

You will remember that, when the perfect is constructed with 'être', the past participle agrees like an adjective:

Il est tombé. (masc. sing.)	*He fell.*
Elle est tombée. (fem. sing.)	*She fell.*
Ils sont tombés. (masc. plur.)	*They fell.*
Elles sont tombées. (fem. plur.)	*They fell.*

If, in constructions with 'avoir', the direct object phrase (i.e. the answer to the question 'qui?' (who(m)?) or 'quoi?' (what?) asked after the verb), is placed after the past participle, no change is required:

Il a mangé les pêches. (Il a mangé quoi? = les pêches)	*He ate the peaches.*

If, however, a direct object pronoun occurs *before* the past participle, as shown earlier in this chapter, you will have to check the gender and number of the noun phrase it replaces and make the past participle agree accordingly:

Il a mangé les pêches? Oui, il les a mangées.	*Did he eat the peaches? Yes, he ate them. ('les' replaces 'les pêches' (fem. plur.) and occurs* before *the past participle)*
Voici les ouvriers: le patron les a appelés.	*Here are the workers: the manager has called them ('les' refers to several workers = masc. plur.)*
Marie, est-ce que ta mère t'a vue?	*Mary, has your mother seen you?('t'' refers to one female and occurs* before *the past participle)*

Exercise 13(iv)

In the following sentences, make the past participle (in brackets) agree as required:

1 Ton frère? Je l'ai (vu) ce matin au marché.   **2** Votre voisine et son fils sont ici. Je les ai (appelé) il y a cinq minutes.   **3** Ta tante est furieuse: je ne l'ai pas (invité) au mariage.   **4** Les serveuses sont contentes: je les ai (remercié).   **5** Voilà les voleurs. Nous les avons (arrêté) ce matin.   **6** Je suis ta mère et tu ne m'as pas (écouté).

Terminé!
Finished!

Have a try

We have (some) charming neighbours. They work in a bank. The wife is beautiful, young and elegant. The husband is very friendly and he is an excellent cook. Last night, they invited us for dinner. We arrived at nightfall. The wife opened the door:

— I am sorry, my husband is in the kitchen, he is preparing the meal. He is going to join us in a minute. Are you going to have an aperitif?
— Yes please.
— We have whisky, sherry and beer.
— I am going to have a beer.
— And you, Anne?
— A small sherry, please. . .
— There you are. . . A beer for you, John, and a sherry for you, Anne. . . Ah, here is my husband! Have you finished in the kitchen, darling?
— Yes, everything is ready, but I am going to drink a small whisky.

After the aperitif, we went into the dining-room and we ate a marvellous meal. We spoke about children, politics, the economic situation, fashion and music in an excellent and very relaxed atmosphere. We came home very late!

Vous avez bien dormi?
Did you sleep well?

14 How to say 'this one', 'that one', 'these', 'those', 'a certain amount of', 'some' and 'any'

How to say 'this one', 'that one', 'these', 'those'

As we have seen in chapter 13, there are sets of words called pronouns which can, when required, replace whole noun phrases (article + adjective(s) + nouns(s) . . .), thus eliminating unwelcome and tiresome repetitions. Demonstrative pronouns such as 'this (one)', 'that (one)', 'these' or 'those' can be used to perform a similar function. They enable the speaker(s) to single out particular things or beings from a previously mentioned group.

As with the corresponding adjectives, French demonstrative pronouns can be followed by the words '-ci' (here) and '-là' (there). In principle, pronouns followed by '-ci' refer to things or beings relatively closer to the speaker whereas those followed by '-là' indicate things or beings relatively more distant (both in spatial or emotional terms). In practice, however, '-là' tends to be used in preference to '-ci' unless the idea of a clear opposition needs to be preserved.

Word list

Nouns

le boulanger/la boulangère	the baker (male/female)	le fruit	(piece of) fruit
le bagage (usually plural)	the luggage	la monnaie	change (coins)
le chocolat	chocolate	la poire	pear
l'eau (fem.)	water	le style	style
l'énergie (fem.)	energy	le théâtre	theatre
l'expérience (fem.)	experience	la tomate	tomato
le frère	brother		

Adjectives

curieux (curieuse)	*strange/ curious*	minéral	*mineral*
désolé	*sorry*		

Verbs

énerver	*to irritate*	réserver	*to reserve/book*
essayer	*to try*		

Other words

absolument	*absolutely*	en retard	*late (not on time)*
bon marché (always masc. sing.)	*cheap*	non alors!	*most definitely not!*
en avance	*early (not on time)*		

Work it out

Close examination of the following sentences should enable you to draw the necessary conclusions concerning the form and use of demonstrative pronouns. The gender of the relevant nouns is included for your guidance:

1   Nous avons des tables (fem.) libres. Préférez-vous celle-ci ou celle-là?

   We have several tables free. Do you prefer this one or that one?

2   La cliente a deux gros sacs (masc.). Tu vas porter celui-là et je vais prendre celui-ci.

   The (lady) customer has two big bags. You are going to carry that one and I'm going to take this one.

3   Est-ce que vous désirez acheter des fleurs (fem.)? Oui, je vais prendre celles-ci; celles-là ne sont pas très jolies.

   Do you wish to buy some flowers? Yes, I am going to take these; those are not very pretty.

4   Nos voisins (masc.) sont charmants! Ceux-ci? Non, ceux-là.

   Our neighbours are charming! These? No, those.

5   Ma voiture (fem.) est en panne. Nous allons prendre celle-là!

   My car has broken down. We are going to take this/that one!

Conclusions
Your conclusions should be as follows:

A   The demonstrative pronouns used to replace a masculine singular noun phrase are: 'celui-ci' or 'celui-là' (sentence 2).
B   The demonstrative pronouns required to replace a feminine singular noun phrase are 'celle-ci' or 'celle-là' (sentence 1).
C   To replace a feminine plural noun phrase, the pronouns needed are 'celles-ci' or 'celles-là' (sentence 3).
D   The demonstratives required to replace a masculine plural noun-phrase are 'ceux-ci' or 'ceux-là' (sentence 4).
E   As previously mentioned, if the need to express a clear opposition does not arise, '-là' will be used in preference to '-ci' (sentence 5).

Note: 'Celui-là', 'celle-là', 'ceux-là', 'celles-là', can be used as appropriate to express moral disapproval, contempt (feigned or real), or dislike:

> Mon frère n'est pas encore arrivé? Il est toujours en retard celui-là!
>
> *Hasn't my brother arrived yet? Him! (lit.: that one) He is always late!*

Beware: Sometimes the English pronoun 'it', although meaning 'this' or 'that', cannot be translated by one of the above French demonstratives because it refers *not* to something clearly recognizable as masculine or feminine, but rather to an idea, an opinion, etc. . . In such cases the French pronouns required will be 'ceci', 'cela' or 'c'' and the related adjective or past participle will be in the masculine singular.

> La voiture est ici. Cela est curieux.
>
> *The car is here. It (= this/ that) is strange.*

(It is not the car which is strange but the fact that it is here.)

> La lettre est arrivée. C'est intéressant.
>
> *The letter has arrived. It (= this /that) is interesting.*

(It is not the letter which is interesting but the fact that it has arrived.)

Exercise 14(i)
Translate into English:

1 Est-ce que vous aimez ces robes-ci? Non, je préfère celles-là.   **2** Nous avons deux menus aujourd'hui: celui-là est cher mais celui-ci est bon marché.   **3** Je vais réserver quatre fauteuils. Ceux-ci? Non, ceux-là.   **4** Ce restaurant est plein; nous allons aller dans celui-là!   **5** Le théâtre n'est pas dans cette rue, il est dans celle-là!   **6** Denise et Christine ont mangé mon chocolat! Ah, celles-là. . . !

Exercise 14(ii)
Fill in the gaps with the appropriate form of the demonstrative pronoun, using the opposition '-ci'/'-là' (in that order), if required:

1 Vous allez manger une poire? Oui, je vais prendre . . .   **2** Cet hôtel-ci est complet. Nous allons essayer . . .   **3** Je désire acheter des mouchoirs . . . . ? Non, . . .   **4** Nous venons de visiter ces deux églises . . . est superbe, mais . . . n'est pas très belle.   **5** Vous n'aimez pas ma sœur? Ah non alors, je la déteste . . . !   **6** As-tu écouté mes deux nouveaux disques? J'ai écouté . . ., mais pas . . .

How to say 'a certain amount of/some' and 'any'

In English the words 'some' and 'any' can be used with a noun in the singular to mean 'a certain amount of' and with a plural one to express 'a certain number of'. Generally, 'some' is reserved for positive statements, whereas 'any' is used with negative statements or questions.

Compare	I have some money.
and	We have some friends.
or	Do you have any money?
and	We do not have any friends.

In French, there is no such distinction between positive or negative statements and questions; the words used to translate 'some' and 'any' are the same as those we studied to express 'of the/from the', i.e. 'du, de la, de l' and des'.

| Je désire du fromage et des fruits. | *I want (= wish for) some cheese and (some) fruit.* |
| Est-ce que vous avez de l'argent? | *Do you have any money?* |

Important: In negative constructions (i.e. with 'ne . . . pas'), 'du', 'de l'', 'de la' or 'des' meaning 'some' or 'any' all reduce to 'de' (or 'd'' before a vowel or 'mute' h).

Compare	J'ai de l'argent.	*I have some money.*
and	Je n'ai pas d'argent.	*I do not have any money.*
or	Elle a du travail.	*She has (some) work.*
and	Elle n'a pas de travail.	*She does not have any work.*

Beware

1 If, however, the meaning of 'du', 'de l'', 'de la' or 'des' is 'of the' or 'from the'; the above-mentioned reduction rule will *not* apply:

Elle ne vient pas du cinéma.   *She is not coming from the cinema.*

Ce n'est pas la femme du boulanger.   *That is not the baker's wife.*

2 With phrases expressing quantity like 'beaucoup' (much/many), 'peu' (little/few), 'une foule' (a crowd/lot), 'bon nombre' (a good many), 'une poignée' (a handful) etc, 'du', 'de la', 'de l'' and 'des' will reduce to 'de' (or 'd'' when appropriate).

Compare	Nous avons de l'argent.	*We have some money.*
and	Nous avons beaucoup d'argent.	*We have much money.*
or	J'ai des billets.	*I have some notes.*
and	J'ai une poignée de billets.	*I have a handful of notes.*

Exercise 14(iii)
Translate into English:

1 Vous avez de la chance: je viens juste d'acheter de l'essence. 2 Est-ce que vos parents ont des bagages? 3 Nous avons acheté du chocolat et de l'eau minérale au super-marché. 4 Tu as de l'énergie mais tu n'as pas de classe. 5 Est-ce que vous avez beaucoup de travail cette semaine? 6 Elle n'a pas d'enfants mais elle a une foule d'amis.

Exercise 14(iv)
Translate the sentences overleaf into French (use the standard question form where appropriate):

1 Did you have any luck at the races?   **2** I am sorry, I do not have any change.   **3** She has some courage but she does not have any experience.   **4** We have just ordered some cheese and some fruit.   **5** We are going to have some organisation in this office!   **6** Waiter, can you bring some coffee and some croissants, please? Sorry, sir, we do not have any croissants, but I am going to bring you some coffee in a minute.

Enfin!
At last!

Have a try

— Good morning!
— Good morning. Do you have any lettuces please?
— Yes of course! They have just arrived and they are absolutely superb. Do you want this one or that one?
— That one please.
— Just a second. I am going to put it in a paper bag.
— Thank you . . . I am going to take a kilo of pears.
— These?
— No, they are not very ripe! I prefer those.
— There you are! One kilo of pears.
— Thank you.
— Is that all?
— No, I think I have forgotten something . . . Oh yes, a kilo of tomatoes!
— Ripe?
— No, not too much.
— Is that alright?
— Yes, perfect. How much?
— Fifteen francs twenty-five.
— There you are. Goodbye . . .

Et votre monnaie?
What about your change?

15 How to say 'never', 'nobody', 'no more', 'nothing'   How to say 'to go to' or 'to be in' a town or country and 'to — or from —' somebody's house or shop

How to say 'never', 'nobody', 'no more', 'nothing'

The method for turning a positive statement into a negative one by using 'ne . . . pas' (not) has already been investigated. There are a number of expressions in French which behave in a similar way to 'ne . . . pas'. They are 'ne . . . jamais' (never), 'ne . . . personne' (nobody/no one), 'ne . . . plus' (no more/no longer), 'ne rien' (nothing):

Vous n'écoutez jamais.	*You never listen.*
Vous n'écoutez personne.	*You listen to nobody.*
Vous n'écoutez plus.	*You no longer listen.*
Vous n'écoutez rien.	*You listen to nothing.*

In general, these expressions behave in the same way as 'ne . . . pas': 'ne' goes before the simple tense verb or the auxiliary and the second part of the negation is placed after the verb or the auxiliary but before the past participle or the infinitive, except in the case of 'personne'.

Compare	Il n'a rien dit et il ne va rien dire.	*He said nothing and he is going to say nothing.*
and	Il n'a vu personne et il ne va voir personne.	*He has seen no one and he is going to see no one.*

Word list

Nouns

l'Allemagne (fem.)	*Germany*	la bienvenue	*welcome*
l'Angleterre (fem.)	*England*	la boutique	*shop/boutique*

la Bretagne	*Brittany*	l'Italie (fem)	*Italy*
la cafétéria	*cafeteria*	le lit	*bed*
la charcuterie	*pork butcher's*	Londres	*London*
le charcutier/la	*pork butcher*	la main	*hand*
charcutière	*(male/female)*	le mal	*evil/ache*
le cigare	*cigar*	le Maroc	*Morocco*
la cigarette	*cigarette*	les Pays-Bas	*Netherlands*
le congé (normally	*holiday(s)*	le pont	*bridge*
plural)		le retour	*return*
l'Espagne (fem.)	*Spain*	le sac à main	*handbag*
les Etats-Unis	*United States*	le salon	*lounge*
(masc. plur.)		la traversée	*crossing*
la ferme	*farm*		*(=journey)*
le ferry	*ferry*	la voie	*track/way*
le frein (à main)	*(hand) brake*	le voyage	*journey*
l'intérieur	*inside/interior*		

Adjectives

| bête | *silly/stupid* | hors-taxes | *duty free* |
| épuisé | *exhausted* | interdit | *forbidden* |

Verbs

dire (dit)	*to say (said)*	passer	*to spend/pass*
falloir (3rd pers.	*to be*	stationner	*to park*
sing. only)	*necessary*	toucher (à)	*to touch*
laver	*to wash*	vivre (vécu)	*to live (lived)*
organiser	*to organise*		

Other words

à bord	*on board/*	par avion	*by air/plane*
	aboard	personne	*nobody*
à la main	*by hand*	prière de	*please . . . (offi-*
à peu près	*approximately*	(+infinitive)	*cial notices)*
de retour	*back (again)*	quelque chose	*something*
en retard	*late*	quelqu'un	*somebody*
environ	*approximately*	rien	*nothing*

Exercise 15(i)

Translate the following sentences into English:

1 Est-ce que vous n'avez rien trouvé sous le lit? **2** Nous n'avons rencontré personne dans la rue. **3** Ils ne vont rien dire à leurs parents. **4** Je n'ai plus d'argent pour payer l'hôtel. **5** Je suis désolé mais Monsieur Dubois n'habite plus ici. **6** Ta secrétaire n'est jamais en retard. **7** Ne pas toucher S.V.P. (s'il vous plaît). **8** Prière de ne rien donner aux animaux.

Exercise 15(ii)
Answer the following questions fully, using the negative form suggested in brackets:

1 Tu as vu quelqu'un? Non . . . (personne)   **2** Les enfants ont mangé quelque chose? Non . . . (rien)   **3** Elle travaille toujours? Non . . . (plus)   **4** Ils viennent souvent le voir? Non . . . (jamais)   **5** Le téléphone sonne. Tu vas répondre? Non . . . (pas)

> Ça ne fait rien!
> *It doesn't matter!*
> *(lit.: that does nothing!)*

How to express movement to — or position in — a town or country

We already know that the expression required to translate 'to the' is 'au', 'à la', 'à l' ' or 'aux' depending on the gender and number of the noun concerned.

Est-ce que tu rentres à l'hôtel	*Are you going back to the hotel?*
Non, je vais au cinéma.	*No, I am going to the cinema.*

If, however, you wish to express movement to — or position in — a town, the only element you require is the preposition 'à':

Ils vont à Paris ce week-end.	*They are going to Paris this week-end.*
André habite à Lyon.	*André lives (lit.: dwells) in Lyons.*

The only exception to this rule is when the name of the town begins with a definite article, e.g. Le Touquet, La Baule, Les Andelys (North West of Paris). In such cases, 'à' combines with 'le' or 'les' in the usual way:

Je suis (*or* je vais) au Touquet.	*I am in (or I am going to) Le Touquet.*
Il est (*or* il va) à La Baule.	*He is in (or he is going to) La Baule.*
Ils sont (*or* ils vont) aux Andelys.	*They are in (or they are going to) Les Andelys.*

If you wish to express 'movement to' or 'position in' a country, two possibilities arise:

(*a*) If the country is feminine (most countries ending in 'e' are in this category), the word required is '**en**' (in) (or '**aux**' if the country is feminine plural):

Vous allez passer vos vacances **en** Espagne?	*Are you going to spend your holidays in Spain?*
Non, nous restons **en** Angleterre!	No, we are staying in England!
Il est parti **aux** Seychelles.	*He has gone to the Seychelles.*

(*b*) If the name of the country is masculine (countries ending in a letter other than 'e' are), the words required will be:

'**au**' (to/in) for masculine singular names, and '**aux**' (to/in) for those which are masculine plural.

Compare	Nous sommes allés **au** Portugal. (masc. sing.)	*We went to Portugal.*
and	Ils travaillent **aux** Etats-Unis. (masc. plur.)	*They work in the United States.*

Note: In general, the rule which applies to feminine countries also applies in the case of French regions of the same gender:

Je vais passer quelques semaines en Bretagne.	*I am going to spend a few weeks in Brittany*

If the name of the region is masculine singular, or feminine plural, the expression 'dans le', or 'dans les' will be used as appropriate:

Ils ont fait un voyage dans le Jura (masc. sing.) et dans les Alpes (fem. plur.).	*They travelled in the Jura and in the Alps.*
J'ai acheté une petite ferme dans les Pyrénées. (fem. plur.)	*I bought a small farm in the Pyrenees.*

The majority of English counties are masculine in French. They follow the rule laid out for regions:

Il habite dans le Yorkshire ou dans le Lancashire.	*He lives (lit.: dwells) in Yorkshire or Lancashire.*

How to express 'to come from' a country or region

In this case the rules are as follows:

1 With feminine nouns, the words 'd'', 'de' or 'des' are used as appropriate:

Ils reviennent d'Italie.   *They are coming back from Italy.*

Cette carte postale vient de Provence.   *This postcard comes from Provence.*

Ma sœur arrive des Seychelles ce soir.   *My sister arrives from the Seychelles this evening.*

2 With masculine nouns the word used is 'du' (or 'des' in the case of a masculine plural noun):

Ils sont de retour du Maroc.   *They are back from Morocco.*

Voici une lettre des Etats-Unis.   *Here's a letter from the United States.*

How to say 'to — or from —' someone's house or shop

The word required in this case is 'chez' ('to', or 'at' the house or shop of . . .).

Je viens de chez le boucher où j'ai acheté un bifteck.   *I have just come back from the butcher's where I bought a steak.*

Hier soir nous avons mangé chez Michel.   *Last night we ate at Michael's.*

Beware: 'Chez' can *only* be used with the name of a person, or that of his/her trade and *not* with the name of the shop itself:

RIGHT: Il est chez le charcutier.   *He is at the (pork) butcher's.*
  (name of the man)

WRONG: Il est chez la charcuterie.
  (name of the shop)

Exercise 15(iii)
In the following examples, fill in the blanks to indicate 'movement to or from' or 'position in' the relevant country, town or region:

1 Pour les vacances nous allons voyager . . . Espagne et . . . Portugal. (*to*).   **2** Ils ont passé quinze jours . . . Allemagne et . . . Pays-Bas. (*in*).   **3** Nous allons aller vivre . . . Canada ou . . . Australie!   (*in*).   **4** J'arrive juste . . . Paris et je vais . . . Marseille. (*from, to*).   **5** Mon cousin a une petite villa . . . Normandie. (*in*).   **6** Ah, vous êtes revenus . . . Italie? Oui, nous sommes arrivés . . . Venise par avion ce matin. (*from, from*).   **7** Il vient . . . Guatémala où il a passé six ans. (*from*).   **8** Je suis épuisée: nous sommes rentrés . . . Bretagne cette nuit à trois heures. Mais nous sommes contents d'être de retour chez nous . . . Paris. (*from, in*).

Exercise 15(iv)
Translate into English:

1 Les Dubois ont une maison à Caen, en Normandie.   **2** Nous allons aller en vacances en Grèce et en Italie cet été.   **3** Mes parents arrivent des Pays-Bas ce soir, par avion.   **4** Je vais aller passer une semaine en Provence.   **5** Est-ce que vous venez d'Espagne? Oui, de Madrid.   **6** Le patron a organisé une exposition au Japon.   **7** Vous partez en France pour les congés? Non, nous restons ici. Nous n'avons plus d'argent!

Quel dommage!
What a shame!

Have a try

"Mesdames, Messieurs,
Bienvenue à bord de ce ferry. Vous pouvez maintenant mettre le frein à main, descendre de votre véhicule et fermer les portes à clé. Ne laissez pas d'objets de valeur, sacs à main, portefeuilles, appareils-photos etc., à l'intérieur. Vous allez suivre les flèches jaunes pour monter sur le pont des passagers où vous allez trouver des fauteuils confortables, une excellente cafétéria et un restaurant. Il y a aussi un salon de télévision pour les enfants. Le film commence dans trente minutes. Sur le pont des passagers il y a une boutique hors-taxes où

vous allez trouver des boissons, des cigarettes, des cigares et des cadeaux à des prix intéressants. Le voyage va durer deux heures environ.

Il est interdit de retourner sur le pont des voitures avant la fin de la traversée. Merci."

Vous avez le mal de mer?
Are you sea-sick?
(lit.: Do you have the sea-sickness?)

16 Formulating requests; giving advice and orders   How to say 'before, after, for, against . . .'   How to say 'the weather is . . .'

Formulating requests; giving advice and orders

One simple way of giving 'impersonal' advice or orders (i.e. other than in face-to-face situations) in French, is to use the infinitive. This method is frequently found in cooking recipes, instructions for the use, care and maintenance of products, etc.:

Ouvrir avec soin.	*Open with care.*
Conserver au réfrigérateur.	*Keep refrigerated. (lit. : Conserve in the refrigerator.)*

'Negative orders' can also be constructed on the same basis:

Ne pas avaler.	*Do not swallow.*

If, however, you wish to direct your request towards one or more specific individuals, you require a tense called the imperative. It is a simple (= one-word) tense and is constructed according to the following pattern:

> stem + endings

Its two main features are as follows:

1   It has only three persons: 2nd singular ('tu' form), 1st plural ('nous' form), 2nd plural ('vous' form — polite singular or normal plural).
2   The verb form is used on its own, without the subject pronoun ('tu', 'nous' or 'vous'). This increases the sense of urgency of the statement.

Information concerning the way this tense is constructed is given after the Word list.

Word list

Nouns

la casserole	*pan/casserole*	le porte-monnaie	*purse*
le crédit	*credit*	la prudence	*caution/prudence*
le diable	*devil*	le réfrigérateur	*refrigerator*
le feu rouge	*traffic light*	le reste	*rest/remainder*
le nuage	*cloud*	la rue	*street*
l'orage (masc.)	*storm*		

Adjectives

chéri	*darling/dearest*	sourd	*deaf*
froissé	*creased/crumpled*	stupide	*foolish/stupid*
lourd	*heavy*		

Verbs

aider	*to help*	répondre	*to reply*
avaler	*to swallow*	rêver	*to (day)dream*
conserver	*to keep/conserve*	rincer	*to rinse*
crier	*to shout/scream*	sécher	*to dry*
cuire (cuit)	*to cook (cooked)*	tenir (tenu)	*to hold (held)*
grogner	*to grumble*	tomber	*to fall*
placer	*to place/put*	tordre	*to wring/twist*
poser	*to put (down)/ set/pose*	traverser	*to cross/go through*
refermer	*to reseal/close again*		

Other words

d'accord!	*alright/OK/agreed!*	eh bien!	*well then!*
à plat	*flat*	qu'est-ce que. . .?	*what. . .?*
dehors	*outside*	zut!	*bother!/blast!*

The rules governing the determination of the stem and endings applicable to each verb category are as follows.

Imperative of 'er' (1st group) verbs

With the exception of 'aller' (to go), all 'er' verbs have the endings shown overleaf. The stem corresponds to the infinitive form minus the 'er' ending:

> 2nd person sing.:   -e
> 1st person plur.:   -ons
> 2nd person plur.:   -ez

Regarde la carte. (regard + e)   *Look at the map. (familiar form)*

Mangeons notre repas.   *Let's eat our meal.*
  (mang + e + ons)

Avançons avec prudence.   *Let's proceed with caution.*
  (avanç + ons)   *(lit.: Let's advance with prudence)*

Ecoutez, le train arrive.   *Listen, the train is coming.*
  (écout + ez)   *(lit.: arriving)*

Don't forget: When the stem of the imperative ends in 'g' or 'c', as in manger or avancer, the verb form has to be altered in the following way:

(*a*)   an 'e' must be inserted between the 'g' and the 'ons' ending of the first person plural.

(*b*)   a cedilla ',' must be placed under the 'c' before the 'ons' ending of the first person plural (see chapter 7, p. 38)

Note: The imperative of 'aller' (to go) is:

va   *go (familiar)*
allons   *let's go*
allez   *go (polite sing./normal plural)*

Allez au lit!   *Go to bed!*
Allons prendre un verre   *Let's go and have a drink (lit.: take*
  au bar.   *a glass) at the bar.*
Va au diable! (familiar)   *Go to the devil/the blazes!*

Imperative of 'ir', 'oir' and 're' (2nd and 3rd group) verbs

In the case of the group 2 and 3 verbs, the endings of the imperative are, almost without exception, those of the corresponding persons of the present tense:

Réfléchissez avant de   *Think (lit.: reflect) before*
  répondre.   *answering.*

Attendons une minute.	*Let's wait a minute.*
Descends de là!	*Get down (lit.: . . . from there)!*
Prenez le train!	*Take the train!*

Beware: The imperative of 'avoir' (to have) and 'être' (to be) are as follows:

Avoir	*Etre*
Aie *(have – fam.)*	Sois *(be – fam.)*
Ayons *(let's have)*	Soyons *(let's be)*
Ayez *(have)*	Soyez *(be)*

Soyez prudents.
Be careful/take care.
(lit.: be prudent.)

If the negative expressions 'ne . . . pas' (not), 'ne . . . jamais' (never), 'ne . . . personne' (no-one), 'ne . . . rien' (nothing) are used with an imperative, 'ne' will be placed before it and the rest of the negative expression ('pas', 'jamais'. . .) will appear after:

| Ne posez pas de questions stupides. | *Don't ask stupid questions.* |
| N'invitons personne. | *Let's invite nobody.* |

Beware: If a direct object pronoun ('me', 'te', 'le', 'la', 'nous', 'vous', 'les') is used, the following rules will apply:

1 In the imperative positive (= do . . . !), they will be placed after the verb and 'me' (or 'm' ') will become 'moi':

Voilà les disques; écoutons-les.	*Here are the records, let's listen to them.*
Cette photo est excellente, regardez-la.	*This photo is excellent, look at it.*
Aide-moi!	*Help (me)!*

2 In the negative form (don't . . . !), the pronouns will resume their normal position before the verb and 'moi' will revert to 'me':

| Ne les écoutons pas. | *Let's not listen to them.* |

Ne la regardez pas.   *Don't look at her/it.*
Ne m'aide pas.   *Don't help me. (fam.)*

Tiens, tiens!
Well, well/Fancy that!
(lit.: Hold, hold!)

Exercise 16(i)
In the following sentences, replace the infinitive by the appropriate
form of the imperative. The person required is also indicated in the
brackets.

1 (Avoir — 2nd pers. plur.) du courage, la situation est
grave. **2** (Etre — 2nd pers. sing.) prudent, il y a beaucoup de
circulation sur les routes ce week-end. **3** (Réfléchir — 1st pers.
plur.) calmement. Le problème est difficile. **4** (Attendre — 2nd
pers. plur.)! Ne (partir — 2nd pers. plur.) pas tout de
suite! **5** (Sortir — 2nd pers. sing.) et ne (revenir — 2nd. pers. sing.)
jamais! **6** (Prendre — 2nd pers. plur.) ce médicament deux fois par
jour, matin et soir, avant les repas. **7** Ne (perdre — 1st pers. plur.)
pas la tête, (être — 1st pers. plur.) logiques. **8** (Finir — 2nd pers.
sing.) ton travail avant de sortir et ne (rentrer — 2nd pers. sing.) pas
trop tard ce soir.

Restez calme!
Keep your cool/stay calm!

Exercise 16(ii)
Translate into English:

1 Arrêtez la voiture là-bas, sous les arbres. **2** Vite, téléphonez au
docteur. **3** Ecoutez cette chanson, elle est formidable! **4** Ne
venez pas ce soir, nous sortons avec des amis. **5** Descendons, le taxi
est arrivé. **6** Placer dans une casserole et cuire à feu
doux. **7** Cherchez la clé et fermez la porte. **8** Si la télévision ne
marche pas bien, arrêtez-la!

Exercise 16(iii)
Translate into French. Use the familiar form ('tu') in the sentence
marked (fam.).

1 Paul, don't eat that peach, keep it for your sister. (fam.) **2** Let's go (and) ask for a room. **3** Don't shout, your father is not deaf! **4** Listen to the weather forecast: there are storms in Brittany. **5** Do not listen to that boy; he is silly. **6** Rinse with care and dry flat. Do not wring. (label) **7** Not to be washed by hand. (label)

How to say 'before, after, for, against . . . '

In past chapters we have encountered a number of words called prepositions: 'derrière' (behind), 'devant' (in front of), 'contre' (against), 'entre' (between), 'sous' (under), 'sur' (on). . . Prepositions enable us to express a variety of relations such as purpose, location, direction, opposition, etc., within a sentence:

Je suis contre cette idée.	*I am against this/that idea.* *(opposition)*
Le café est sur la table.	*The coffee is on the table.* *(location)*
Il vient pour discuter avec nous.	*He comes to talk with us.* *(purpose)*

More prepositions

Here is a further list of prepositions which will be useful to you at this stage:

à	*at, towards (+ ideas of purpose and ownership)*	avec	*with*
		chez	*at the house/ shop of*
à côté de	*near, next to, beside*	en	*in, into*
après	*after*	le long de	*along/alongside*
au-dessous de	*below*	malgré	*in spite of*
au-dessus de	*above*	pour	*for/in order to*
autour de	*around*	sans	*without*
avant	*before (time)*		

Important: Whereas all the above prepositions can be followed by a noun phrase, only a small number of them—'à', 'de', 'pour' and 'sans'—can be accompanied by a verb. If this is the case, the verb *must* be in the infinitive:

La nuit commence à tomber.	*Night is beginning to fall.*
Il est allé au lit sans manger.	*He went to bed without eating.*
Nous venons de téléphoner.	*We have just telephoned.*
	(lit.: We come from
	telephoning)

Frappez avant d'entrer
. *Knock before entering.*

How to say 'the weather is fine, hot, cold . . .'

The expression required to make statements about the weather in French is: 'il fait . . .' (it is . . .).

A list of the most common phrases used to refer to the weather is presented in the table below:

Il fait . . .	*The weather (= it) is . . .*
beau	fine
bon	pleasant (warm)
chaud	hot
frais	cool
froid	cold
humide	damp
mauvais	bad
orage	stormy
du brouillard	foggy
(du) soleil	sunny
du vent	windy

Beware: All the above expressions can be used *only* when referring to the weather.

Note: It snows = il neige
                It rains = il pleut

Il pleut des cordes!
It's raining cats and dogs!
(lit.: it's raining ropes!)

Have a try

—Pierre, où es-tu?

—Je suis là, chérie, j'arrive!

—Bon! Porte ces sacs s'il te plaît. Ils sont très lourds.

—Oui, chérie . . .

—Traversons la rue . . . Non, attends, le feu est rouge! . . . Ah, il est vert maintenant! Allons-y! Eh bien, qu'est-ce que tu attends? Tu rêves encore! Tu ne m'écoutes jamais!

—Désolé chérie.

—Ça ne fait rien . . . J'ai l'habitude! . . . Je vais aller dans ce magasin. Il ya des robes splendides! Attends-moi là.

—D'accord!

—. . . Pierre! viens ici. Regarde! J'ai trouvé une robe adorable. . . Et bon marché! Tu l'aimes?

—Oui, elle est jolie!

—Eh bien, je vais l'acheter. . . Zut! J'ai oublié mon porte-monnaie à la maison, dans mon vieux sac à main. Tu as de l'argent?

—Oui, je crois . . . Attends, je vais payer avec ma carte de crédit.

—Bonne idée! . . . Voilà . . . Porte la robe avec le reste . . . Non, pas dans le grand sac, elle va être toute froissée!

—Ecoute, ne crie pas, je ne suis pas sourd!

—Je ne suis pas sûre!

Tu es toujours dans les nuages!
You've always got your head in the clouds!
(lit.: You're always in the clouds!)

17 How to say 'to me', 'to you'   How to use the right pronoun with 'before', 'after', 'for'   Another way of expressing possession

How to say 'to me', 'to you'

As we have already seen, pronouns are words which can be used in place of previously formulated noun phrases to make statements simpler and less repetitive. For instance, a direct object noun phrase (representing the answer to the questions 'qui?' (who(m) ?) or 'quoi?' (what?) formulated after the verb), can be replaced by one of the following pronouns: me, te, le, la, nous, vous, les.

To the question:

> Est-ce que tu as montré le passeport de ta femme aux deux douaniers?
>
> *Did you show your wife's passport to the two customs officers?*

you could therefore reply:

> Oui, je l'ai montré aux deux douaniers.
>
> *Yes, I showed it to the two customs officers.*

with 'l'' replacing the phrase 'le passeport de ta femme'.

But what of the phrase 'aux deux douaniers', which represents the answer to the question 'à qui?' (to whom?), and is called an indirect object phrase?

It, too, can be replaced by a pronoun, but from a different set called indirect object pronouns. Indirect object pronouns are given in the table opposite, together with the corresponding subject and direct object ones.

Subject pronouns		Direct object pronouns		Indirect object pronouns	
je	*I*	me	*me*	me	*to me*
tu	*yóu (fam.)*	te	*you*	te	*to you*
il	*he/it*	le	*him*	lui	*to him*
elle	*she/it*	la	*her*	lui	*to her*
nous	*we*	nous	*us*	nous	*to us*
vous	*you*	vous	*you*	vous	*to you*
ils	*they (masc.)*	les	*them*	leur	*to them*
elles	*they (fem.)*	les	*them*	leur	*to them*

Note: In the last two sets, several pronouns look alike. Remember, however, that their roles are different.

(a) *direct object pronouns* replace the noun phrase representing the answer to 'qui?' (who(m)?) or 'quoi ?' (what?) *formulated after the verb*.

(b) *indirect object pronouns* replace the noun phrase representing the answer to 'à qui?' (to whom?) or 'à quoi?' (to what?) also *formulated after the verb*.

Important: If any one of the indirect object pronouns is used with a given verb, it can only be accompanied by either 'le', 'la', 'l'' or 'les'. No other combination is allowed.

Word list

Nouns

l'alcool (masc.)	*alcohol*	la malle	*(car)boot*
le balcon	*balcony*	le mois	*month*
le bouchon	*cork*	le scandale	*scandal*
le bruit	*noise*	le tire-bouchon	*corkscrew*
le coffre	*(car)boot*	les vacances (fem. plur.)	*holidays*
le document	*document*		
le livre de cuisine	*cookery book*	le vin	*wine*

Adjectives

propre *tidy/clean/own*

Verbs

amener	*to bring (person)*	garder	*to keep*
bouger	*to move/stir*	laisser	*to leave (behind)*
commencer	*to begin*	prêter	*to lend*
compter (sur)	*to count (on)*	raconter	*to tell (a story)*
déclarer	*to declare/say*	revenir	*to come back/return*
demander à quelqu'un	*to ask somebody*	servir	*to serve*
		voyager	*to travel*
donner	*to give*		
emmener	*to take away (person)*		

Other words

juste	*just*	tout le temps	*all the time*

Work it out

In the sentences below, both direct and indirect pronouns will be used in a variety of constructions. Try to sort out the rules governing their position in relation to each other and also to the verb:

1 Est-ce que tu as gardé le tire-bouchon des voisins? Non, je le leur ai rendu la semaine dernière.

Have you kept the neighbours' corkscrew? No I gave it back to them last week.

2 Je vais prêter ma voiture à Jean. Tu vas la lui prêter? Tu es fou!

I am going to lend my car to John. You are going to lend it to him? You are mad!

3 Garçon, nous n'avons pas la carte des vins. Je ne vous l'ai pas donnée? Je suis désolé!

Waiter, we don't have the wine list. Haven't I given it to you? I am sorry!

4 Je laisse les passeports dans le sac? Non, tu me les donnes!

Do I leave the passports in the bag? No, you give them to me!

5 Avez-vous la note? Oui, le patron nous l'a apportée.

Do you have the bill? Yes, the manager has brought it to us.

6 Les enfants adorent ce livre, donne-le leur!

The children adore this book, give it to them!

7 Je vais raconter cette histoire à votre mari. Non, ne la lui racontez pas maintenant, il y a trop de bruit.

I am going to tell this story to your husband. No, don't tell him it now, there's too much noise.

Remarks

A In the first answer (perfect tense), the direct object 'le' (= le tire-bouchon) is placed before the indirect object 'leur' (to them) and they both precede the auxiliary (ai).

B In the second answer (immediate future), the direct object 'la' (= la voiture) precedes the indirect object 'lui' (to him) and both occur before the infinitive (prêter).

C In answer 3 (perfect), the direct object 'l'' (= la carte des vins) comes after the indirect object 'vous' (to you). Both are placed before the auxiliary (ai). Note the position of the negative 'ne' (before both pronouns).

D In answer 4 (present), the direct object 'les' (= les passeports) is placed after the indirect object 'me' (to me) and both are positioned before the verb (donnes).

E In answer 5 (perfect), the direct object pronoun 'l'' (= la note) follows the indirect object one 'nous' (to us). The auxiliary comes after both.

F In sentence 7 (imperative positive), the direct object 'le' (= ce livre) comes first, followed by the indirect object 'leur' (to them). This time, however, both are placed after the verb.

G In sentence 7 (imperative negative), the order of the two pronouns is the same as in the previous sentence: 'la' (= l'histoire) precedes 'lui' (to him) but in this case they are placed before the verb.

Summary:

1 When direct object and indirect object pronouns are both present in a sentence, the indirect pronouns 'me', 'te', 'nous' and 'vous' will *precede* the direct object pronouns 'le', 'la', 'les'.

2 The indirect pronouns 'lui' and 'leur' will *follow* the direct object pronouns 'le', 'la' and 'les'.

3 In the case of simple (= one word) and compound (= two word) tenses (e.g. perfect), the pronouns are placed *before* the verb or the auxiliary. This, however, does not apply exactly in the case of the imperative positive, where the relative order of the two pronouns outlined above still applies but both follow the verb.

Remember: In the negative imperative (i.e. with 'ne . . . pas', 'ne . . . jamais') the pronouns return to their normal place *before* the verb.

Important: In the imperative positive the pronoun 'me' is replaced by 'moi' but in the negative the normal form is restored:

| *Compare* | Donnez-moi la clé. | *Give me the key.* |
| *and* | Ne me donnez pas la clé. | *Don't give me the key.* |

C'est clair?
Is it clear?

Exercise 17(i)
Translate into English:

1 Est-ce que tu as envoyé la lettre à Michel? Oui je la lui ai envoyée ce matin.   **2** Les Dupont ne nous ont pas laissé la clé. Je la leur ai demandée trois fois.   **3** Ma balle! Tu vas me la donner ou j'appelle mon père!   **4** Oui, nous avons votre échelle; une seconde, nous allons vous la rendre.   **5** Nous désirons le petit déjeuner. Est-ce que vous allez nous le monter?   **6** Voici les livres de Jean! Bon, vous allez me les donner et je vais les lui envoyer.   **7** Tu as ma valise? Non, je ne l'ai pas, tu ne me l'as pas prêtée!

Exercise 17(ii)
Translate into French using the information you gathered in the *work it out* section:

1 Is my suitcase in the bedroom? No, madam; I brought it down to you.   **2** If this story is very sad, do not tell it to me.   **3** The meal is ready. I am going to bring it to you.   **4** Here is the bill, give it to her.   **5** This is a secret; do not repeat it to them!   **6** Has my paper arrived? Bring it to me on the balcony.   **7** We have the results; you sent them to us last month.   **8** I wish to talk to the director! I am sorry, you cannot talk to him. He is not here.

How to use the right pronouns with 'before', 'after', 'for'

In French, as in English, a preposition—'à' (to/at), 'sur' (on) etc.—can be followed by a pronoun:

Il est derrière nous.   *He is behind us.*
Je reste avec vous.   *I am staying with you.*

In French, however, most of the pronouns used in that position are different from the direct and indirect ones which we have already examined. They are listed below as prepositional pronouns against the corresponding subject ones:

Subject pronouns		Prepositional pronouns	
je	*I*	moi	*me/myself*
tu	*you*	toi	*you/yourself (fam.)*
il	*he/it*	lui	*him/himself* *it/itself*
elle	*she/it*	elle	*her/herself* *it/itself*
nous	*we*	nous	*us/ourselves*
vous	*you (polite singular or normal plural)*	vous	*you/yourself/ yourselves*
ils	*they (masc.)*	eux	*them/themselves*
elles	*they (fem.)*	elles	*them/themselves*

Ils travaillent pour moi. *They are working for me.*
Nous voyageons avec eux. *We are travelling with them.*
Après toi, mon garçon. *After you, my boy.*

Important: In addition to the above-mentioned use, those pronouns can also serve to emphasize subject pronouns (I, you, he, she, etc.) by either replacing or accompanying them:

Qui a cassé le verre? Moi! *Who broke the glass? I did.*
 (and not 'je'!)
Lui, il reste ici; toi, tu vas He *is staying here*; you *are*
 aller au magasin!   *going to go to the shop.*

Note: One subject pronoun which has not so far been mentioned is 'on' (one/somebody). In both standard and elevated French it is the equivalent of 'one' and is used (like 'il' or 'elle') with verbs in the third person singular:

On frappe à la porte. *Somebody is knocking at* *the door.*
On vient!   *Someone is coming!*

In this case, the corresponding prepositional form is 'soi' (oneself):

　　On travaille pour soi.　　　*One works for oneself.*

In familiar French, 'on' is very frequently used for 'nous':

　　On reste ici. (= Nous　　　*We are staying here.*
　　　restons ici.)
　　On mange? (= Nous　　　*Are we eating (soon)?*
　　　mangeons?)

In this case, the corresponding prepositional form is of course 'nous':

　　On va emmener le chien　　*We are going to take the dog*
　　　avec nous.　　　　　　　*with us.*

Another way of expressing possession

The prepositional pronouns 'moi', 'toi', 'lui', etc. . . can be used with
the preposition 'à' to express ownership:

　　Est-ce que ce livre est à toi?　*Does this book belong to you?*
　　Non, il est à lui.　　　　　　*No, it belongs to him. (It is*
　　　　　　　　　　　　　　　　his.)

Exercise 17(iii)
Complete each sentence using the prepositional pronoun
corresponding to the subject one:

1 Ils restent ici pour les vacances. Ils sont heureux chez . . .　**2** Est-
ce que vous avez amené vos enfants avec . . .?　**3** Ne bouge pas: il y a
un gros chien derrière . . .　**4** Je vais au marché. Tu viens avec
. . .?　**5** Le patron garde les pourboires pour . . . C'est un
scandale!　**6** Marie n'est pas prête. Nous allons commencer sans
. . .　**7** Nous sommes furieux: il est arrivé après . . . et il vient d'être
servi.　**8** Tu vas gagner la course, je compte sur . . .

Have a try

—Good evening sir, madam . . . Your passports please. . . Thank
　you. Are you returning from your holidays?
—Yes.
—Which countries did you visit?
—We stayed in France all the time.
—You did not go to Spain?

— No.
— Have you read this document?
— Yes.
— Do you have anything to declare?
— No, just the normal quantities of cigarettes, wine and spirits.
— Did you buy any presents?
— Yes, two or three records, a cookery book, a dozen glasses . . .
— Where are those things?
— In a suitcase in the boot of the car.
— Get out of (= down from) the car please, and open the boot . . .
   Thank you!
— I am sorry, the boot is not very tidy (= clean) . . .
— Open this suitcase please!
— That one?
— No, not that one, this one.
— Alright . . . There you are.
— Well, well! You have several bottles of Spanish alcohol in this case,
   sir . . . I am sorry, but you are going to come with me; and ask your
   wife to come as well . . .

Par ici, s'il vous plaît!
This way please!
(lit.: by here please!)

18 How to say 'here is/here are, there is/there are'   How to say 'every, all, everyone, everything'   How to translate 'of, from, about, to it, or to them'

How to say 'here is/here are, there is/there are'

In the course of previous chapters we have encountered the expressions 'ici' or '-ci' (here) and 'là' (there) in a variety of constructions:

La bouteille est ici et les verres sont là.	*The bottle is here and the glasses are there.*

or

Vous désirez cette chambre-ci ou celle-là?	*Do you want this room or that one?*

We have also stated that although 'ici' or '-ci' is supposed to indicate the closeness of things or beings and 'là' their distance in relation to the speaker, 'là' tends to be used much more frequently than 'ici' (or '-ci'), except when an opposition needs to be clearly stated. The same remarks apply to 'voici' (here is/are) and 'voilà' (there is/are), which come from the fusion of a particular person of the verb 'voir' (to see) and the above-mentioned words 'ici' and 'là';

     'voici' (*here is/are*) = voyez ici (*see here*)
and   'voilà' (*there is/are*) = voyez là (*see there*)

This explains why both expressions can be used in sentences without a verb:

Voici le train.	*Here is the train.*
Voilà mon frère.	*There is my brother.*

'Voici' and 'voilà' can be used to express movement towards the speaker as well as position. Consequently, 'voici le train' and 'voilà

•mon frère' could also mean 'here comes the train' and 'here (lit.: there) comes my brother' respectively.

The difference in sense between 'voilà' and 'il y a', which also means there is/are, can be represented visually in the following way:

| Voilà un autobus. | **There** *is a bus.* |
| Il y a un autobus. | *There* **is** *a bus.* |

The first sentence indicates the position (or movement towards the speaker) of the bus, whereas the second merely states its existence.

Note: 'Voici' and 'voilà' are frequently used in exclamative sentences of the following type:

Voici ma cousine!	*Here comes my cousin!*
Voici le camion du boulanger!	*Here comes the baker's van!*
Et voilà!	*There you are! (signalling that an action has been completed)*
Vous désirez un apéritif?	*Do you want an aperitif?*
. . . Voilà Monsieur!	*. . . Here you are, sir!*

'Voici' and 'voilà' preceded by a direct object pronoun ('me, te, le, la, nous, vous, les') can be used as pronouns to translate here/there I am, here/there you are, etc . . .

| Est-ce que vous avez votre billet? Oui, le voici. | *Do you have your ticket? Yes, here it is.* |
| Vous venez avec moi? Oui, nous voilà. | *Are you coming with me? Yes, here we come.* |

Word list

Nouns

l'appareil-photo (masc.)	*camera*	la cravate	*tie*
		le détail	*detail*
l'appartement (masc.)	*apartment*	le facteur	*postman*
		le melon	*melon*
le billet	*ticket/note*	l'orage (masc.)	*storm*
le cabinet de travail	*study*	l'ouvrier/ l'ouvrière	*worker (masc./fem.)*
le camion	*lorry*	la photo (gra- phie)	*photo(graph)*
le colis	*parcel*		

la pièce	*room/coin/play*	le rendez-vous	*appointment*
la région	*region/area*	la visite	*visit*
le règne	*reign*		

Adjectives

| libre | *free/available* | prêt | *ready* |
| nécessaire | *necessary* | royal (royaux) | *royal* |

Verbs

accepter	*to accept*	pardonner	*to forgive*
changer	*to change*	redescendre	*to go down again*
fouiller	*to search*	regretter	*to regret*
inciter	*to urge/incite*	reparler	*to talk again*
oublier	*to forget*	vendre	*to sell*

Other words

| par | *through/by* | trop tard | *too late* |
| plusieurs | *several* | | |

Exercise 18(i)
Translate into English:

1 Voici les ruines du château, et voilà l'église, là-bas, derrière les arbres. 2 Ah, te voilà enfin! Le directeur désire te voir tout de suite. 3 Voilà l'orage. Nous allons rester ici un moment. 4 Garçon, l'addition s'il vous plaît! Voilà Madame! 5 Est-ce que tu as trouvé ma montre? Oui, la voici. 6 Les visiteurs vont arriver dans une minute. Ah, les voilà!

Exercise 18(ii)
Translate into French, using 'voici' or 'voilà' as appropriate:

1 We are waiting for the bus . . . Here it comes at last! 2 One kilo of apples and a melon . . . There you are, sir. 3 Have you bought the bread? Yes, here it is. 4 Here comes the postman . . . He is carrying a parcel. 5 Here is the camera. Good, we are going to take some photographs. 6 You wish to talk to me? Here I am.

How to say 'every, all, everyone, everything'

Because of the two gender system which operates in French, the equivalent of 'every' or 'all' will have four distinct forms:

masc. sing.:	tout
fem. sing.:	toute
masc. plur.:	tous
fem. plur.:	toutes

The appropriate form will be selected according to the gender and number of the noun phrase it relates to:

Toute la ville parle de cet événement.
The whole town (lit.: all the town) is talking about this event.

Tout le travail est fini.
All the work is finished.

Nous avons tous les papiers nécessaires.
We have all the necessary papers.

Je regrette, toutes les places sont prises.
I am sorry (lit.: I regret), all the places are taken.

'Tout' (masc. sing.) can also be used on its own as a pronoun, to express a global quantity (= everything). Note that the verb which follows is in the third person singular:

Tout est prêt.
Everything is ready.

Note: The opposite of 'tout' (everything) is 'rien' (nothing). It is used with the negative particle 'ne', but 'pas' must be omitted.

Rien n'est prêt (and not : rien n'est pas prêt).
Nothing is ready.

'Tous' and 'toutes' can also be used as pronouns to replace masculine or feminine noun phrases.

J'ai parlé aux ouvriers. Tous sont d'accord.
I have spoken to the workers. All of them agree.

Nous avons invité plusieurs amies; toutes ont accepté.
We invited several (girl) friends; all of them accepted.

Tout va bien!
Everything is fine!
(lit.: all goes well!)

Exercise 18(iii)
Put the appropriate form (tout, toute, tous, toutes) before the noun

phrase (given in square brackets) in each of the following sentences:

1 Nous avons visité [la région] pendant nos vacances.   **2** Ici [les hôtels] sont très chers mais ils sont excellents.   **3** Nous avons fouillé [les chambres] et nous n'avons rien trouvé.   **4** Il passe [son temps] à lire des livres stupides.   **5** Ils sont restés [une semaine] au lit.

Exercise 18(iv)
Translate into French:

1 She is not very pleased: her baby cried all night.   **2** The whole family arrives in an hour.   **3** The storm has broken all the trees.   **4** Everything is finished between us.   **5** Nothing is ready for the picnic.   **6** We have seen the photographs of the wedding. They are all superb.   **7** I forgive everything but I forget nothing!   **8** We have met his friends. They are all charming.

How to translate 'about it, from it, of it, to it/them'

If you wish to translate into French such expressions as 'about it', 'from it', 'of it', 'to it (or them)', you need the two pronouns 'en' and 'y'. They will enable you, as other pronouns do, to avoid the repetition of previously mentioned noun phrases and therefore improve the quality of your language.

Work it out

In the following sentences, examine the way repetition of the noun phrase has been avoided and draw the necessary conclusions concerning the use of 'en' and 'y'.

1	Est-ce que vous êtes allé à la banque?	*Have you been (lit. gone) to the bank?*
	Non, j'y vais maintenant.	*No, I am going (to it) now.*
2	Tu viens du marché?	*(Have) you come from the market?*
	Oui, j'en viens.	*Yes, I (have) come from there (lit. from it).*

3 Est-ce qu'ils ont parlé des vacances?	*Did they talk about the holiday?*
Oui, ils en ont parlé en détail.	*Yes, they talked about it in detail.*
4 Avez-vous pensé à ma proposition?	*Have you thought about my proposal?*
Oui, oui, j'y ai pensé!	*Yes, I have (thought about it)!*
5 Vous vendez des cravates?	*Do you sell ties?*
Non, désolé, je n'en vends pas.	*No, sorry, I don't sell any (of them).*
6 Vous allez aux courses?	*Are you going to the races?*
Non, nous n'y allons pas, malheureusement.	*No, we're not going (to them), unfortunately.*
7 Etes-vous allés au supermarché?	*Did you go to the supermarket?*
Nous venons d'y aller, mais nous allons y retourner.	*We have just been (to it), but we're going to go back (to it).*
8 Vous ne parlez pas de cette affaire!	*You don't talk about this matter!*
Trop tard! Nous venons d'en parler et nous allons en reparler.	*Too late! We have just talked about it, and will talk about it again.*

Conclusions

A   The pronoun 'y' is used to translate 'to it' (or them), or 'about it' (or them) (sentences 1, 4, 6 and 7).

B   The pronoun 'en' is used to express 'of it' (or them) or 'from it' (or them) (sentences 2, 3, 5 and 8).

C   'y' replaces noun phrases which are preceded by the preposition 'à' (at, to . . .).

D   'en' replaces noun phrases which are preceded by the preposition 'de' (about, from, of).

E   Normally, 'en' and 'y' are placed immediately before a simple tense verb or before the auxiliary in a compound (= two-word) tense verb.

F   In negative sentences with 'ne . . . pas', 'ne . . . jamais', etc., 'en' and 'y' are placed between 'ne' (or 'n'') and the verb or auxiliary (sentences 6 and 8).

Beware: 'y' cannot be used before the future of 'aller':

Est-ce que vous irez au   *Will you go to the theatre*
    théâtre demain soir?   *tomorrow evening?*
Oui, nous irons. (and not: *Yes, we will (go).*
    nous y irons).

On en reparlera!
We'll talk about it again/the matter isn't closed!

Exercise 18(v)

Answer the following questions, using 'en' or 'y', as appropriate, to replace the noun phrase:

1 Est-ce que tu vas à la plage? Oui, . . .   **2** Les voisins ont parlé du film? Oui, . . .   **3** Est-ce qu'il vient du village? Non, . . .   **4** Votre fils va à la boulangerie? Non, . . .   **5** La dame descend-elle du train? Oui, . . .   **6** Tu vas acheter des huîtres? Non, . . .

Exercise 18(vi)

Translate into French, using the standard form of question when applicable:

1 This problem is not important! We do not think about it!   **2** Are your parents going to the hotel? Yes, they are (going to it).   **3** They are not in the house. I (have just) come from it.   **4** Is your husband going to the match this week-end? No he is not (going to it), he has too much work (to do).   **5** The situation is bad. I have spoken to the director about it.   **6** The exhibition is open. Have you been to it? No, I am going to go (to it) this afternoon.

Allons-y.
Let's go.
(lit.: let's go there)

Have a try

—Bonjour!
—Bonjour!
—Vous attendez l'autobus?
—Oui . . .
—Moi aussi. Nous allons l'attendre ensemble . . . Il est en retard ce matin!

—Est-ce qu'il est souvent en retard?

—Rarement! Une ou deux minutes quelquefois . . . Je le prends tous les jours de la semaine . . . Le chauffeur est un ami à moi.

—Vraiment?

—Oui, oui!. . . Les voyages posent toujours un problème quand on n'a pas de voiture. Vous en avez une?

—Oui, mais elle est au garage pour une réparation. Et vous?

—Non! Je ne suis pas assez riche . . . Alors, il arrive cet autobus?

—Il y a beaucoup de circulation. Soyez patient!

—Soyez patient, soyez patient! J'ai un rendez-vous important dans vingt minutes!. . . C'est un scandale!. . . Je vais écrire une lettre à . . . Ah, le voilà, enfin!

—Oui, mais il est plein! Il n'y a pas une place libre!

—C'est terrible!. . . Et le prochain est dans une heure. Je vais être en retard . . . Venez avec moi! Nous allons prendre un taxi!

Vous venez, oui ou non? (fam.)
Are you coming or aren't you?
(lit.: Are you coming, yes or no?)

**How to form words like 'slowly, rapidly',
etc. and where to place them in the
sentence   How to say 'I am cold,
hot, hungry' etc.**

How to form words like 'slowly, rapidly', etc. and where to place them in the sentence

When we need to give details about the characteristics of a thing or being, we use one or more adjectives:

> *The tall brown-haired young man is over there.*
> Le grand jeune homme brun est là-bas.

Similarly, if we wish to refine the meaning of an adjective, a past participle or a verb, we require special words called adverbs. In the sentences:

> *The dog is rather old and extremely tired. He does not go very fast; let us walk slowly.*
> Le chien est plutôt vieux et extrêmement fatigué. Il ne va pas très vite; marchons lentement.

the words 'plutôt' (rather), 'extrêmement' (extremely), 'très' (very), 'vite' (quickly) and 'lentement' (slowly) are adverbs.

Note: Adverbs can also be used to refine the meaning of other adverbs. This is the case in the last sentence where 'très' (very) modifies the sense of 'vite' (quickly).

Word list

Nouns

l'auto-stop	*hitch-hiking*	l'habitude	*habit*
l'employé/e	*employee*	la lumière	*light*
(masc./fem.)		la machine	*machine*

| le mal à la tête | *headache* | le repos | *rest/time off* |
| | | la société | *society* |

Adjectives

absolu	*absolute*	immédiat	*immediate*
exact	*exact/ precise*	malheureux (malheureuse)	*unfortunate*
extraordinaire	*extraordinary*	récent	*recent*
extrême	*extreme*	terrible	*terrible/dreadful*
fréquent	*frequent*		

Verbs

| conduire (conduit) | *to drive/ lead* | transporter | *to carry (in a vehicle)* |
| déchirer | *to tear (up)* | traverser | *to go through/ to cross* |

Other words

à droite	*on the right*	quelques	*some/a few*
assez	*enough*	soudain	*suddenly*
à temps	*in (the nick of) time*	vite	*quickly*
presque	*almost/nearly*	un peu	*a little*
quelquefois	*sometimes*	une fois	*once*

How to turn certain adjectives into adverbs

In English, a large number of adjectives can be turned into adverbs by adding the ending 'ly':

> extreme → extremely
> slow → slowly

In French, a similar technique is used. Normally, the ending 'ment' is added to the feminine singular form of the appropriate adjective, as shown in the list below:

Adjectives		*Adverbs*
masc. sing	*fem. sing*	
curieux	curieuse	curieusement
curious		*curiously*
doux	douce	doucement
soft		*softly*
lent	lente	lentement
slow		*slowly*

There are, however, some modifications to this rule:

1   Adjectives which end in a vowel in the masculine singular, add the ending 'ment' onto the masculine form, instead of the feminine:

modéré	modérée	modérément
moderate		*moderately*
vrai	vraie	vraiment
true		*truly*

2   With the exception of 'lent' (slow), masculine singular adjectives ending in 'ent' and 'ant' change 'ent' into 'emment' and 'ant' into 'amment':

décent	décente	décemment
decent		*decently*
fréquent	fréquente	fréquemment
frequent		*frequently*
méchant	méchante	méchamment
unkind/vicious/ naughty		*unkindly (etc.)*
puissant	puissante	puissamment
powerful		*powerfully*

Beware: It is not possible to form adverbs in the way described above with *all* adjectives. It is, however, possible to incorporate the feminine form of the adjective into the expression:

    d'une manière/facon. . .   *in a . . . manner/way*

to obtain a similar meaning.

Il m'a reçu d'une facon charmante.	*He welcomed me in a charming way (= charmingly).*
Ils ont répondu d'une manière arrogante.	*They replied in an arrogant way (= arrogantly).*

Note: A small number of adjectives can be used as adverbs. Whenever this is the case, they will remain invariable whatever the gender and number of the noun concerned.

Compare	Elle est forte. (adj.)	*She is strong.*
and	Elle parle fort. (adv.)	*She speaks loudly.*

or   Les temps sont durs. (adj.) *Times are hard.*

and   Les employées travaillent   *The employees work hard.*
              dur. (adv.)

Where to place adverbs in the sentence

Work it out

In the sentences given below, adverbs of time and manner are used. Try to formulate the rules concerning their position. To help you, those adverbs have been printed in bold type.

1   Il vient **quelquefois** me voir.   *He sometimes comes to see me.*

2   Nous avons **rarement** mangé au restaurant mais nous sommes **fréquemment** allés au théâtre.   *We rarely ate at the restaurant but we frequently went to the theatre.*

3   Votre dernière lettre est arrivée **très** vite.   *Your last letter arrived very quickly.*

4   Cette maison est **trop** grande pour nous quatre.   *This house is too big for the four of us (lit.: for us four).*

5   Venez **immédiatement** mais ne restez pas **longtemps.**   *Come immediately but don't stay long.*

6   Vous allez payer la note **tout de suite** et sortir **rapidement.**   *You are going to pay the bill at once and get out/leave quickly.*

7   Je garde **toujours** cette photo des enfants.   *I always keep this photo of the children.*

Conclusions

A   In sentence 1, the adverb 'quelquefois' is placed after the simple tense verb (vient = present). This is also the case in sentence 7 (garde).

B   The adverbs 'rarement' and 'fréquemment' (in sentence 2) are placed between the auxiliary (avoir/être) and the past participle (mangé/allés).

C   (Sentence 3) The adverb 'très' is placed before the adverb 'vite' which it modifies.

D   (Sentence 4) The adverb 'trop' is placed before the adjective 'grande' which it modifies.

E   In sentence 5 the adverbs 'immédiatement' and 'longtemps' are placed after the verbs in the imperative positive (venez) and negative (ne restez pas). Note the position of 'pas'!

F   Sentence 6 outlines the position of adverbs modifying an infinitive. Both 'tout de suite' and 'rapidement' are placed after that form of the verb (payer/sortir).

Summary: In French, adverbs are placed after the verb they modify if it is in a simple (one-word) tense. This also applies in the case of the infinitive. In a compound tense, the adverb is placed between the auxiliary (avoir or être) and the past participle of the main verb.

Adverbs modifying adjectives and other adverbs are placed before them.

Beware: There are some exceptions to the above 'rules', particularly in the case of certain adverbs expressing notions of time: 'soudain' (suddenly), 'souvent' (often), 'quelquefois' (sometimes), etc. . . .

Compare:	Soudain, il a fermé la porte.	}	*Suddenly he closed the*
and:	Il a soudain fermé la porte.		*door.*
or:	Quelquefois, il vient me voir.	}	*He sometimes comes to*
and:	Il vient quelquefois me voir.		*see me.*

Exercise 19(i)
Transform the adjectives in square brackets into the corresponding adverbs, using the appropriate endings as indicated earlier in the chapter.

1 Je vous demande [simple] d'accepter mes excuses.   **2** J'espère que vous allez passer [agréable] la soirée avec eux.   **3** Nous allons réfléchir [calme] à ce problème.   **4** Avançons [prudent]. Il n'y a pas de lumière.   **5** Jean est [absolu] furieux. Son pantalon est déchiré.   **6** Ils ont [récent] eu la visite de mon oncle.   **7** Il est [extraordinaire] dynamique pour son âge.   **8** Elle frappe [furieux] à la porte.   **9** Notre société est [terrible] violente.

Exercise 19(ii)
Translate the above sentences into English, once the adjectives have been replaced by the appropriate adverbs.

How to say 'to be cold, hot, hungry' etc.

In English, there are a number of expressions indicating states of mind or body which are constructed with the verb 'to be' usually followed by an adjective: 'I am cold, she is hot' etc. . .

In French, the corresponding expressions are often constructed with 'avoir' followed by a noun. The most frequent are given below, together with their English equivalent.

Avoir . . .	*To be* . . .
besoin de	*in need of*
de la chance	*lucky*
envie de	*longing for*
faim	*hungry*
froid	*cold*
l'habitude de	*used to*
honte	*ashamed*
mal	*in pain*
peur	*afraid/frightened*
raison	*right*
soif	*thirsty*
tort	*wrong*

Tu trembles. Tu as froid? . . *You are shaking. Are you*
Non, j'ai peur.   *cold? No, I'm afraid.*
Est-ce que vous avez mal? *Are you hurt? No, but I am a*
Non, mais j'ai un peu honte. *little ashamed.*
Les enfants ont soif et nous *The children are thirsty and*
avons faim!   *we are hungry.*

Beware: Be sure to distinguish between 'j'ai chaud' or 'j'ai froid' and 'je suis chaud(e)' or 'je suis froid(e)'. The first two statements refer to the temperature of your body, the last two to your amorous capabilities!

Exercise 19(iii)
Translate into French:

1 I am going (back) in. I am beginning to be cold. **2** He is afraid to be late for dinner. **3** We are in need of a rest. Let's go on holiday. **4** She is not ashamed of her opinions. **5** Your husband is right, don't listen to the neighbours. **6** I hope (that) the children are not ill. **7** He is lucky. He always wins! **8** We are not used to driving on the right.

Have a try (use the 'vous', not the 'tu' form)

— Hello, young man! Are you going far?

— To Bordeaux! Can you take me with you?

— You are lucky. I'm going to Spain, but I'm going to cross Bordeaux. Give me your bag and climb in quickly . . . The traffic is dreadful today!

— Yes . . . Thank you very much!

— Where do you come from?

— From Paris. I left this morning very early . . . What are you carrying in your lorry?

— Some machines for the Spanish market.

— Do you cross the frontier regularly?

— Approximately once a week . . . Are you a student?

— Yes, I am going home for the holidays.

— Do you live in Bordeaux?

— Not exactly; my parents have a house near the town.

— Do you hitch-hike (= do some hitch-hiking) frequently?

— No, not very often; about once a month . . . I am not rich enough to have my own car.

— Poor student! I am sorry for you! . . . Listen, it is nearly midday. I am going to eat at a routier restaurant in a few minutes. Are you hungry?

— I'm not sure, I have a headache.

— That's because you are hungry! Come on, I invite you!

— Are you sure?

— No problem! I have some money. I'm not a student!

— Thank you very much!

J'ai une faim de loup!
I'm ravenous
(lit.: I have a wolf's hunger)

20 How to say that something 'used to happen, was happening'

As previously stated, French tenses are divided into two categories:

(*a*) simple tenses, constructed with a stem and endings; and
(*b*) compound tenses, made up of an auxiliary ('avoir' or 'être'), followed by the past participle of the main verb.

The tense which we are going to examine now is, like the present, a simple (one-word) one. It is called the imperfect and is used whenever the speaker or writer wishes to emphasize that a past action (*a*) lasted for some time; or (*b*) used to happen regularly; or (*c*) was in progress when another isolated action (expressed by a perfect) occurred; or (*d*) used to happen every time another action (also expressed by an imperfect) took place.

Important: If the aim is merely to record the occurrence of the action as an isolated event and not to insist on its duration, repetition etc., the perfect *must* be used:

Il a passé quinze jours à Paris, puis il est allé en Espagne où il est resté un mois.	*He spent a fortnight (lit.: fifteen days) in Paris, then he went to Spain where he stayed one month.*

A list of examples will be presented in the Work it out section following the Word list.

Word list

Nouns

l'après-midi (masc.)	*afternoon*	l'été (masc.)	*summer*
le besoin	*need*	l'excuse (fem.)	*excuse*
le bord	*edge/side*	la forêt	*forest*
le casino	*casino*	l'hiver (masc.)	*winter*
		l'invité (masc.)	*guest*

le luxe	*luxury*	le pique-nique	*picnic*
minuit	*midnight*	la promenade	*trip/walk*
le mois	*month*	la vie	*life*
le parapluie	*umbrella*		
le pied	*foot*		

Adjectives

grand	*tall/high/big*	simple	*simple*
incroyable	*incredible*	vrai	*true*
mouillé	*wet*		

Verbs

exister	*to exist*	nettoyer	*to clean*
faire (fait)	*to do/make*	pleuvoir (plu)	*to rain*
fumer	*to smoke*	rencontrer	*to meet*
inventer	*to invent*	rester	*to stay/remain*

Other words

chaque	*each/every*	pourquoi	*why*
comme	*as/like*	quand	*when*
diable!	*goodness gracious!*	tout	*everything*
fort	*hard (adv.)*	vite	*fast/quickly*
parce que	*because*		

Work it out

The sentences given below contain examples of verbs used in the imperfect. Examine them to find out (i) what the endings of that tense are; and (ii) how the stem is selected.

1 Quand j'étais jeune, j'allais souvent au cinéma.
When I was young I often used to go to the cinema.

2 Tu achetais des cigarettes quand je suis entré.
You were buying cigarettes when I came in.

3 Quand elle tombait malade, le docteur venait la voir.
Whenever she fell ill, the doctor used to come and see her.

4 Chaque soir, nous discutions avec le patron et vous lui donniez des détails sur la vie en Angleterre.
Every evening, we used to talk (= discuss) with the manager and you gave him details about life in England.

5 En vacances, ils mangeaient souvent au restaurant.
(When) on holiday, they often used to eat at the restaurant.

6 Quand il commençait à pleuvoir, elles ouvraient leurs parapluies.
Whenever it began to rain, they opened their umbrellas.

After studying the above sentences you should be in possession of the following information:

A Sentence 1:
(i) ending of the first person singular (je) = **ais**
(ii) stems: **ét** for 'être' (to be) and **all** for 'aller' (to go)
B Sentence 2:
(i) ending of the second person singular (tu) = **ais**
(ii) stem: **achet** for 'acheter' (to buy)
C Sentence 3:
(i) ending of the third person singular (il/elle) = **ait**
(ii) stem: **tomb** for 'tomber' (to fall) and **ven** for venir (to come)
D Sentence 4:
(i) ending of the first person plural (nous) = **ions**
  and of the second person plural (vous) = **iez**
(ii) stem: **discut** for 'discuter' (to talk/discuss)
  and **donn** for 'donner' (to give)
E Sentence 5:
(i) ending of the third person plural (ils) = **aient**
(ii) stem: **mang + e** for 'manger' (to eat)
Note: The 'e' is inserted between the 'g' of the stem and the 'a' of the endings when applicable, to preserve the value of 'g' as found in leisure.
F Sentence 6:
(i) ending of the third person singular (il) = **ait**, as in sentence 3.
(ii) stem: **commenç** for 'commencer' (to begin)
Note: The cedilla ',' is placed under the 'c' before the 'a' of the ending, to preserve the sound 's' as in race.
G Sentence 6:
(i) ending of the third person plural (elles) = **aient** as in sentence 5
(ii) stem: **ouvr** for 'ouvrir' (to open)

Summary: The stem used to form the imperfect is very often the infinitive minus the ending ('er, ir/oir, re'), but there are exceptions to this rule. A more reliable way to find the stem of the imperfect is to take the first person plural (nous) of the present and remove the 'ons' ending. It works well, so long as you know the present of the verb!

Neither of the above methods is totally foolproof; first group (= 'er') verbs and second group (= 'ir/issant') verbs, however, do not create any major problems. But beware of third group ones!

The endings of the imperfect are as follows:

je	-ais
tu	-ais
il/elle	-ait
nous	-ions
vous	-iez
ils/elles	-aient

Important:

(*a*) For a given verb, the stem used for the imperfect does not alter throughout the whole tense;

(*b*) the endings of the imperfect are the same for *all* verbs whatever their infinitive ('er', 'ir/oir', 're');

(*c*) for certain verbs the accent of the stem changes ('être' → 'ét').

Exercise 20(i)

In the following sentences, replace the infinitive, given in square brackets, by the appropriate person of the imperfect:

1 Quand nous [être] enfants nous [aller] souvent au bord de la mer. **2** Le soir je [manger] le repas puis je [regarder] la télévision. **3** Si les clients [arriver] trop tard, le garçon [refuser] de les servir. **4** Vous [écouter] des disques quand nous sommes arrivés. **5** Chaque matin le directeur [travailler] dans son bureau; l'après-midi il [aller] discuter avec les ouvriers. **6** A minuit, les invités [sortir] du casino et [rentrer] à l'hôtel. **7** Si je lui [offrir] un pourboire il [refuser] toujours.

Exercise 20(ii)
Translate into English:

1 Après le dîner, il fumait un cigare sur la terrasse. **2** Quand ses parents allaient le voir, il les emmenait au concert ou au théâtre. **3** Elle lavait le pull-over quand nous sommes rentrés à la maison. **4** Chaque semaine, son père lui donnait cent francs. **5** S'il arrivait en retard, il inventait toujours une excuse incroyable. **6** Quand il pleuvait trop fort, il ne sortait pas. **7** Pendant qu'il nettoyait la voiture, elle a préparé le déjeuner.

Exercise 20(iii)
Translate into French:

1 Each time I met him, he used to speak to me.   2 We were going to the market when we found the wallet.   3 When our father came here, he used to bring us presents.   4 He was tall and he walked quickly.   5 Every morning the waitress brought my breakfast into my room.   6 When she was tired, she used to cry and call (for) her mother.

Have a try

—Aujourd'hui la vie est très compliquée. Quand j'étais petit, les choses étaient simples.

—C'est vrai?

—Bien sûr! Nous n'avions pas de télévision . . .

—Pourquoi?

—Parce qu'elle n'existait pas! Le cinéma était rare et la voiture était un luxe: peu de gens en avaient une.

—Tu prenais l'autobus pour aller à l'école?

—Diable non! Nous allions à l'école à pied: quatre kilomètres le matin et quatre le soir. Nous partions très tôt et nous rentrions tard.

—Et quand il pleuvait!

—Eh bien, nous arrivions mouillés!

—C'était terrible!

—Pas du tout! Nous avions l'habitude d'être dehors hiver comme été . . . Maintenant, pour faire cent mètres, les gens ont besoin de leur voiture.

—Et le dimanche, vous restiez à la maison?

—Non, nous allions souvent faire une promenade dans la forêt, et un pique-nique, si le temps était beau . . . Aujourd'hui vous avez tout et vous êtes malheureux!

C'est la vie!
That's life.

21 How to compare things, beings and actions How to say 'more and more' (or 'less and less') and 'the more . . . the more' (or 'the less . . . the less') How to express 'the most, the least, the . . .-est'

How to compare things, beings and actions

Sometimes, instead of having to make straightforward statements about a given thing, being or action as in:

> The man is old.
> Your house is big.
> She works fast.

We have to say things like:

> This man is older than my father.
> Your house is as big as a castle.
> She works faster than you.

Such statements are called comparisons. There are, in French as in English, several degrees of comparison. They are presented in the 'Work it out' section which follows the Word list.

Word list

Nouns

l'admiration (fem.)	*admiration*	le collègue	*colleague*
l'agneau (masc.)	*lamb*	l'époque (fem.)	*era*
le bœuf	*ox*	le fou	*madman*
le boulot	*work (familiar)*	la folle	*madwoman*
le cochon	*pig/slovenly person*	le guide	*guide*
		le leader	*leader (political)*
		le musicien	*musician*

| le/la partenaire | *partner (male/ female)* | le programme | *programme* |
| | | la saison | *season* |

Adjectives

âgé	*old*	généreux (généreuse)	*generous*
agile	*agile/ nimble*	rapide	*quick/fast*
amusant	*amusing*	sincère	*sincere*
compliqué	*complicated*	suffisant	*sufficient*
confortable	*comfortable*	travailleur (travailleuse)	*hard-working*
fiable	*reliable*		
fort	*strong*		

Verbs

avoir faim	*to be hungry*	obliger	*to oblige/force*
devenir (devenu)	*to become*	récompenser	*to reward*
escalader	*to climb*	saboter	*to botch up/ sabotage*
gagner	*to win/earn/ gain*	terminer	*to finish*

Other words

| fort | *loudly* | d'habitude | *usually* |

Work it out

In the examples given below, examine the way in which comparisons ('as... as', 'more... than', 'less... than', 'not so... as', etc...) are expressed in French when adjectives (adj.) and adverbs (adv.) are involved:

1 Elle est aussi grande (adj.) que son frère.
She is as tall as her brother.

2 Nous allons au cinéma aussi souvent (adv.) que nos amis.
We go to the cinema as often as our friends.

3 L'autobus est moins rapide (adj.) que le train.
The bus is less quick than the train.

4 Nous marchons moins vite (adv.) que le guide.
We walk less quickly than the guide.

5 La cuisine est plus petite (adj.) que la salle à manger.
The kitchen is smaller than the dining-room.

6 Le film va commencer plus tôt (adv.) que d'habitude.
The film is going to begin earlier than usual.

7 Mon costume n'est pas aussi sale (adj.) que ta robe.
My suit is not as dirty as your dress.

8 Il ne chante pas aussi bien (adv.) que Michel.	*He does not sing as well as Michael.*

Conclusions

A   Adjectives and adverbs require the same structures when used in *comparative* sentences.

B   The comparative phrase 'as . . . as' is translated in French by 'aussi . . . que' (sentences 1 and 2).

C   The expression 'less . . . than' is translated by 'moins . . . que' (sentences 3 and 4).

D   'More . . . than' is expressed by 'plus . . . que' (sentences 5 and 6).

E   'Moins . . . que' can also be expressed as: 'ne . . . pas aussi . . . que' ('not so . . . as' or 'not as . . . as')—(sentences 7 and 8).

Notes:

1   As seen in **E** above, similar meanings can often be achieved by using totally different comparative expressions.

Compare:	Les trains sont plus confortables que les autobus.	*Trains are more comfortable than buses.*
and:	Les autobus sont moins confortables que les trains.	*Buses are less comfortable than trains.*
or:	Elle est plus travailleuse que son frère.	*She is more hard-working than her brother.*
and:	Son frère n'est pas aussi travailleur qu'elle.	*Her brother is not as hard-working as she is.*

2   The comparative 'aussi . . . que' ('as . . . as') can also be expressed by the word 'comme' (as/like).

Compare:	Il est aussi doux qu'un agneau.	*He is (as) mild as a lamb.*
and:	Il est doux comme un agneau.	

Beware: The adjective 'bon' (good) and the adverb 'bien' (well) do not form their comparative in the way outlined in sentences 5 and 6 above: the comparative of 'bon' is 'meilleur' (better) and that of 'bien' is 'mieux' (better).

Mon café est bon, mais celui-ci est meilleur.

My coffee is good, but this one is better.

Ce musicien joue bien, mais sa partenaire joue mieux.

This musician plays well, but his (female) partner plays better.

Comparatives and pronouns

If a pronoun such as I, you, he, etc . . . is used after a comparative phrase, it must be translated in French by one of the following, as appropriate: 'moi', 'toi', 'lui', 'elle', 'nous', 'vous', 'eux', 'elles' (prepositional set).

Il est plus âgé que moi.

He is older than I am.

Tu es aussi bête qu'eux.

You are as silly as they are.

How to say 'more and more (or less and less)' and 'the more . . . the more (or the less . . . the less)'

'More and more' is simply translated in French by 'de plus en plus' for adjectives and adverbs alike:

Notre travail est de plus en plus difficile.

Our work is (becoming) more and more difficult.

Le taxi va de plus en plus vite.

The taxi is going faster and faster.

'Less and less' is rendered by 'de moins en moins':

Les programmes sont de moins en moins intéressants.

Programmes are (becoming) less and less interesting.

Beware: Do *not* translate 'more and more' literally by 'plus et plus'; that is not French!

'The more . . . the more' and 'the less . . . the less' are translated by 'plus . . . plus' and 'moins . . . moins' respectively:

Plus je regarde ce tableau, plus je le déteste.

The more I look at this painting, the more I detest it.

Moins il travaille, moins il gagne.	*The less he works, the less he earns.*
Plus j'écoute cette chanson, moins je l'aime!	*The more I listen to this song, the less I like it!*

Beware: Do not translate 'the more . . . the more' by 'le plus . . . le plus' or 'the less . . . the less' by 'le moins . . . le moins'. That is not French either!

Exercise 21(i)
Translate into English:

1 Paris est plus grand que Marseille.   **2** En France, l'eau minérale est presque aussi chère que le vin de table.   **3** Madame Dubois va attendre une minute; elle est moins pressée que moi.   **4** Avec sa voiture de sport il roule comme un fou.   **5** Je ne suis pas aussi riche que vous mais je vais souvent au restaurant.   **6** L'orage est de plus en plus violent et nous n'avons pas de parapluie.   **7** Nous sortons de moins en moins le soir, nous préférons rester à la maison.   **8** Plus vous criez fort, moins les enfants vous écoutent.

Exercise 21(ii)
Translate into French (use 'comme' for 'as . . . as' whenever applicable):

1 That beach is quieter than this one.   **2** The more I eat, the hungrier I am.   **3** The peaches are bigger than the apricots but they are not as good.   **4** He is less preoccupied than I am because he is more optimistic.   **5** He is as strong as an ox and he is becoming taller and taller.   **6** Paul is smaller than his brother but he runs faster.   **7** You are not as happy as (you were) this morning.   **8** These machines are (becoming) more and more complicated and less and less reliable.

How to express 'the most, the least, the . . .-est'

The English expressions 'the most . . .', 'the . . .-est', 'the least . . .', which express 'the highest degree', are called *superlatives* and can be used with adjectives and adverbs alike. They are translated into French in the ways outlined opposite:

Adjectives

With adjectives, 'le, la, les plus' (the most) or 'le, la, les moins' (the least) is used as required by the gender and the number of the noun they relate to:

C'est le plus beau jour de ma vie.   *It is the best (lit.: the most beautiful) day of my life.*

Nous avions la plus grande admiration pour lui.   *We used to have the greatest admiration for him.*

Votre problème est le moins compliqué.   *Your problem is the least complicated.*

Beware: We have previously seen that some adjectives are placed before the noun and some after. The corresponding superlatives will follow the same rules as far as position is concerned.

Compare: L'homme fort.   *The strong man.*

and: L'homme le plus fort du monde.   *The strongest man in the world.*

or: Le programme intéressant.   *The interesting programme.*

and: Le programme le plus intéressant de la semaine.   *The most interesting programme of the week.*

or: Le petit détail.   *The small detail.*

and: Le plus petit détail.   *The smallest detail.*

Note: The adjective 'bon' (good) which has an irregular comparative ('meilleur'), also has an irregular superlative 'le meilleur' which will agree in gender and number with the noun it relates to:

Nous allons réserver la meilleure table.   *We are going to reserve the best table.*

Adverbs

With adverbs, 'le plus' (the most, the . . . est) or 'le moins' (the least) are the only form required.

C'est votre téléphone qui sonne le plus souvent.   *It is your phone which rings the most frequently.*

Les gens qui crient le plus fort n'ont pas toujours raison.   *People who shout the loudest are not always right.*

Note: The adverb 'bien' (well) which has an irregular comparative—'mieux' (better)—also has an irregular superlative: 'le mieux' (the best).

> C'est le soir que je travaille le   *It is in the evening that I*
> mieux.   *work (the) best.*

Exercise 21(iii)
Translate into English:

1 Les critiques pensent que ce film est le meilleur de la saison. **2** Nous avons escaladé la plus haute montagne. **3** François était l'enfant le plus sage de la classe. **4** Nous n'avons pas eu le plus petit problème pendant le voyage. **5** Voici la partie la moins intéressante de notre visite. **6** Le directeur va récompenser la secrétaire qui travaille le mieux. **7** Hier la livre est tombée à son niveau le plus bas. **8** Je suis sûr que cette solution est la plus acceptable.

Exercise 21(iv)
Modify the following statements so that the superlative form of the given adjective is used, bearing in mind position constraints:

1 La partie difficile du voyage est terminée. **2** Voici le grand leader politique de notre époque. **3** Je vais vous raconter l'histoire amusante. **4** Il cherche toujours les bons restaurants. **5** Acceptez mes vœux sincères pour Noël. **6** C'est le week-end qui passe vite. **7** Nous allons prendre le menu cher: nous avons faim. **8** Le travail dangereux est bien payé!

> Le plus dur est fait!
> *We are over the worst!*
> *(lit.: The hardest is done!)*

Have a try

—Entrez Dupont.

—Vous désirez me parler, Monsieur le Directeur?

—Oui, une seconde; je termine cette lettre . . . Voilà . . . Dupont, je vous ai demandé de venir parce que je ne suis pas content de vous!

—Pourquoi, Monsieur le Directeur?

—Ecoutez Dupont... Je ne suis pas plus bête que vous. Votre attitude au travail devient de plus en plus mauvaise.

—Mais, Monsieur le Directeur...

—Pas de 'mais': Vous arrivez en retard tous les matins, vous partez avant les autres ouvriers et vous êtes absent de plus en plus souvent. Et votre travail est déplorable. Ne protestez pas, vous travaillez comme un cochon Dupont!

—Mais, Monsieur le Directeur, j'ai des problèmes à la maison...

—Je suis désolé pour vous, mais ce n'est pas une raison suffisante pour saboter le boulot. Vous n'êtes plus fiable: hier, j'ai été obligé de demander à votre collègue Lemercier de vérifier tout votre travail. C'est votre dernière chance! La prochaine fois c'est la porte!

Plus de cadeaux!
No more favours!
(lit.: no more gifts!)

22 How to say that something will/shall happen, or would happen (if . . .)
How to say 'I should, you would, he could', etc.

How to say that something will/shall happen, or would happen (if . . .)

If you wish to express an action which is to take place very soon, the immediate future is an ideal tense:

Nous allons rentrer à la maison.	*We are going to return home.* *(lit.: to the house).*

If, however, you want to state that the action in question will take place less immediately, you need another tense called the future.

In English the future is a compound tense in which 'shall' and 'will' are used as auxiliaries: I shall go, he will return, etc. . .

In French, on the other hand, it is a simple (= one-word) tense formed in the usual way:

> stem + endings

As far as the endings are concerned, there is no difficulty for the following reasons:

(*a*)   They are those found in the present of 'avoir' (to have).
Have a look at the table at the top of the next page.
(*b*)   They are the same for *all* French verbs, whether 'er', 'ir', or 're'.

If the endings do not represent a problem, the stem does, in certain cases. The general rules are:

1   Almost all 'er' verbs use the whole of their infinitive for the stem of the future tense:

	Future endings	*Present of 'avoir'*
je	-ai	j'ai
tu	-as	tu as
il/elle	-a	il/elle a
nous	-ons	nous avons
vous	-ez	vous avez
ils/elles	-ont	ils/elles ont

J'entrerai dans le magasin et   *I shall go into the shop and (I*
   j'achèterai le livre.   *shall) buy the book.*

Only simple modifications are likely to occur: acheter→ achèterai.
Beware: The stem of 'aller' (to go) is 'ir' and that of 'envoyer' (to
send) is 'enverr':

Nous irons à la poste et   *We shall go to the post office and*
   nous enverrons le colis.   *(we shall) send the parcel.*

2   All second group verbs like 'finir' (to finish), which make their
present participle in '-issant' (see chapter 12), will use the *whole* of
their infinitive as the stem of their future tense:

Vous réfléchirez et ensuite   *You will think and then you will*
   vous agirez.   *act.*

3   For most third group verbs ending in '-ir', the infinitive will also
be used as the stem.

Ils sortiront du bureau à sept   *They will leave (= go out of)*
   heures et ils partiront   *the office at 7 o'clock and*
   en vacances aussitôt.   *they will go on holiday right*
                                away.

Beware: the stem of 'venir' (to come) is 'viendr', that of 'tenir' (to
hold) is 'tiendr'. The stems of 'courir' (to run) and 'mourir' (to die) are
'courr' and 'mourr' respectively.

Quand les enfants viendront à   *When the children come to the*
   la ferme, ils courront dans   *farm they will run in the*
   les champs.   *fields.*

(*Note*: in the above sentence the future, not the present, is used after
'quand' (when)!)

4   In the case of most 're' verbs, the stem will be the infinitive minus the final 'e':

> Je descendrai au village et je   *I will go down to the village*
>   prendrai l'autobus.   *and catch the bus.*

Beware: for 'être' (to be) and 'faire' (to do/make) the stems of the future are 'ser' and 'fer' respectively.

5   In the case of 'oir' verbs, the stem will have to be learnt individually. Here are some of the most usual:

avoir	*(to have)*	→ 'aur'
devoir	*(to have to)*	→ 'devr'
pouvoir	*(to be able to)*	→ 'pourr'
savoir	*(to know)*	→ 'saur'
voir	*(to see)*	→ 'verr'
vouloir	*(to want)*	→ 'voudr'

In addition, the two verbs which follow are only used in the 3rd person singular:

falloir	*(to be necessary)*	→ il faudra
pleuvoir	*(to rain)*	→ il pleuvra

Word list

Nouns

l'année (fem.)	*year*	le jardinier	*gardener*
le bouquet	*bunch/bouquet*	le litre	*litre*
le caviar	*caviar*	la salle de bains	*bathroom*
le départ	*departure*	le sandwich	*sandwich*
le domestique	*servant*	le/la secrétaire	*secretary*
l'épicier/	*grocer (masc./*		*(masc./fem.)*
l'épicière	*fem.)*	la terre	*ground/earth*
le jardin	*garden*	le timbre	*stamp*

Adjectives

ambitieux	*ambitious*	prochain	*next*
(ambitieuse)			

Verbs

revoir (revu)	*to see again (seen again)*

Other words

aussitôt	*immediately*	partout	*everywhere*
ensuite	*then/afterwards*		

Exercise 22(i)
In the following sentences, replace the infinitive (in brackets) by the appropriate person of the future tense, using the information given earlier in the chapter.

1 Allô Marie! Nous (arriver) ce soir à neuf heures! 2 Vous (finir) votre travail demain matin avant de sortir. 3 L'année prochaine, nous (aller) en vacances en France. 4 Tu (acheter) un litre de vin et un kilo de tomates chez l'épicier. 5 Ses amis (être) contents de le revoir. 6 Je ne vous (voir) pas avant mon départ. 7 Mon père ne (pouvoir) jamais payer la réparation! 8 Elle (venir) nous chercher à la gare.

Exercise 22(ii)
Having put the above sentences in the future tense, translate them into English.

How to say 'I should, you would, he could, etc. . .'

We sometimes need a tense to express the fact that an action would take place in the future if certain conditions were met. This tense is called the conditional. In English it is formed with an auxiliary (normally 'should' or 'would') and an infinitive without 'to':

(If I were rich) I would buy a big house.

In French it is a simple tense formed in the usual way:

> stem + endings

Having learnt the future and the imperfect, you will find this tense extremely simple to construct because:

(*a*) it uses exactly the same stem as the future, and
(*b*) it uses the endings of the imperfect:

je	-ais	nous	-ions
tu	-ais	vous	-iez
il/elle	-ait	ils/elles	-aient

Nous aimerions aller à la plage.	*We would like to go to the beach.*
Est-ce que vous voudriez avancer, s'il vous plaît?	*Would you like to move forward please.*
Je désirerais un timbre.	*I would like a stamp.*

The conditional tense is often used in French to soften a request or a command.

Compare:	Je veux la voiture.	*I want the car.*
and:	Je voudrais la voiture.	*I would like the car.*
or:	Est-ce que vous avez le journal?	*Do you have the paper?*
and:	Est-ce que vous auriez le journal?	*Would you (by any chance) have the paper?*

It is also used to indicate a moral obligation:

Il devrait téléphoner.	*He should (= ought to) telephone.*
Vouz pourriez demander où est la gare.	*You could ask (if you do/did not mind) where the station is.*

In journalistic style, it is used to express an unconfirmed event which is supposed to take place soon:

Le président viendrait en Angleterre en octobre.	*The president will probably come to England in October.*

Ce n'est pas sorcier!
It isn't overcomplicated!
(lit.: it is not wizard!)

Exercise 22(ii)

In the following sentences, replace the infinitive by the suitable person of the conditional:

1 Si j'avais le temps, je (prendre) des vacances. **2** Nous (désirer) une chambre avec salle de bains. **3** Est-ce que vous (pouvoir) venir ici, s'il vous plaît? **4** Je (vouloir) commander un bouquet de fleurs. **5** Tu (aimer) voir le film policier ce soir? **6** Vous (devoir) parler aux employés. Ils sont furieux!

Have a try

— Tu rêves?

— Oui, je pense à ce que je ferai quand je serai riche. . .

— Ah oui? Qu'est-ce que tu feras?

— Eh bien, je voyagerai. J'irai partout: au Japon, en Chine, au Pérou . . . Je rencontrerai toutes sortes de gens intéressants . . . Et toi?

— Oh moi, je déteste les voyages. Quand je suis sur un bateau j'ai le mal de mer; en avion, j'ai le mal de l'air; je suis même malade en voiture . . . Mais je serais heureuse d'avoir une grande maison . . .

— Où? A Paris?

— Non! Sur la Côte d'Azur, au bord de la mer, avec un grand jardin.

— Mais tu détestes travailler dans le jardin!

— Oui, mais j'aurais un jardinier professionnel, un cuisinier et une douzaine de domestiques pour faire tout le travail!

— Et tu mangerais du caviar et tu boirais du champagne du matin au soir, je suppose!

— Pourquoi pas?

— Tu ne penses pas que tu es un peu ambitieuse pour une secrétaire?

— Et toi, alors?. . . Ecoute, tu continueras ton rêve une autre fois; allons chercher nos sandwichs.

> Avec des 'si'. . . (on mettrait Paris dans une bouteille)
> *If pigs could fly . . .*
> *(lit.: with 'ifs'. . . (one could put Paris in a bottle))*

23 How to say 'mine, yours, his,' etc. How to say 'I wash (myself), you shave (yourself)' etc.

How to say 'mine, yours, his,' etc.

Possessive adjectives, which were examined in chapter 11, enable us to clarify 'ownership' of a thing or being.

> Mon frère est arrivé ce matin *My brother arrived this morning*
> avec sa femme. *with his wife.*

They are placed before the appropriate noun phrase ('frère' and 'femme' in the above sentence).

Possessive pronouns, on the other hand, will not only express possession but also replace the previously mentioned noun phrase, thereby eliminating clumsy repetitions of the following type:

> Si vous avez perdu votre *If you have lost your pen, I am*
> stylo, je vais vous prêter *going to lend you my pen.*
> mon stylo.

Since the identity of the 'possessed' item has already been established in the first part of the utterance, all you need to say in English is: '. . . I am going to lend you mine'.

The French equivalents of mine, yours, his, etc. . . are given after the Word list.

Word list

Nouns

l'allumette	*match (stick)*	le croisement	*crossroads/*
l'associé (masc.)	*associate/*		*crossing*
	colleague	le couteau à	*breadknife*
la campagne	*country(side)*	pain	
la carte postale	*postcard*	le défaut	*fault/defect*
le/la concierge	*concierge/caretaker*	l'escalier	*staircase/stairs*
	(masc./fem.)		

la fois	*the time* *(= occasion)*	la matinée	*morning* *(time-span)*
la frite	*chip*	le numéro (de téléphone)	*(phone) number*
la glace	*mirror/ice*	le rasoir	*razor*
les lunettes (de soleil) (fem. plur.)	*(sun)glasses*	le rocher	*rock*
		le stylo	*pen*

Adjectives

grave	*grave/serious*	tendre	*tender*
infect	*foul (food)*		

Verbs

s'adresser à	*to contact/to talk to (someone)*	s'excuser	*to apologize*
se cacher	*to hide (oneself)*	se faire mal	*to hurt oneself*
se coucher	*to lie down/to go to bed*	se lever	*to get up*
se couper	*to cut oneself*	se perdre	*to lose one's way/get lost*
se décider	*to make up one's mind/decide*	se préparer	*to prepare oneself*
se demander	*to ask oneself/ wonder*	se souvenir	*to remember*

Other words

directement	*directly*	si	*if*
en panne	*out of order/ broken down*	tout de suite	*at once/ immediately*

Gender and number of possessive pronouns

Since French nouns fall into two distinct gender categories and can be singular or plural, four sets of possessive pronouns are required. Note that each pronoun begins with a definitive article indicating the appropriate gender and number of the noun it replaces. See table at the top of the next page.

Vous avez mon numéro de téléphone mais je n'ai pas le vôtre.	*You have my telephone number but I don't have yours.*
Est-ce que tu as ta clé? J'ai perdu la mienne.	*Do you have your key? I have lost mine.*
Nous avons nos défauts; ils ont les leurs.	*We have our faults; they have theirs.*

Masculine		Feminine		Meaning
Sing.	*Plur.*	*Sing.*	*Plur.*	
le mien	les miens	la mienne	les miennes	*mine*
le tien	les tiens	la tienne	les tiennes	*yours (fam.)*
le sien	les siens	la sienne	les siennes	*his/hers/its*
le nôtre	les nôtres	la nôtre	les nôtres	*ours*
le vôtre	les vôtres	la vôtre	les vôtres	*yours*
le leur	les leurs	la leur	les leurs	*theirs*

Remember: possessive pronouns, like possessive adjectives, agree in gender and number *not* with the *possessor* as in English, but with the being or thing *possessed*.

> J'ai fait mes valises, il va   *I have packed (lit.: done) my*
>   faire les siennes.   *suitcases, he is going to*
>   *pack his.*

Notes:

1   The pronouns 'nôtre(s)' (ours) and 'vôtre(s)' (yours) take a circumflex accent '^' over the 'o'. This is not the case with the corresponding possessive adjectives:

> Ce n'est pas votre faute, c'est   *It is not your fault, it's ours.*
>   la nôtre.

2   The possessive pronouns can sometimes be replaced by the preposition 'à' (= to) and the relevant prepositional pronoun: 'moi' (me), 'toi' (you fam.), 'lui' (him), 'elle' (her), 'nous' (us), 'vous' (you), 'eux' (them—masc.), 'elles' (them—fem.)

Compare: Cette maison est la vôtre   *Is this house yours or*
                 ou la leur?   *theirs*?
and: Cette maison est à vous   *Does this house belong to*
                 ou à eux?   *you or to them?*

> A la vôtre!
> *Your health!*
> *(lit.: to yours!)*

Exercise 23(i)

Replace the possessive noun phrase in brackets by the appropriate possessive pronoun. The gender and number of the relevant noun has been given to assist you:

1 Vous allez rester dans votre chambre (fem. sing.) et nous dans (notre chambre). **2** Votre femme (fem. sing.) est avec (ma femme). **3** Nous avons écouté vos disques (masc. plur.), maintenant vous allez écouter (nos disques). **4** Mes frites (fem. plur.) étaient infectes. Est-ce que (tes frites) étaient bonnes? **5** Si ton rasoir (masc. sing.) est cassé, je te prêterai (mon rasoir). **6** Est-ce que nous avons notre parapluie (masc. sing.)? Non, mais mes amis ont (leur parapluie). **7** J'ai oublié mes allumettes (fem. plur.), mais Jacques a (ses allumettes). **8** Nous venons d'envoyer nos cartes postales (fem. plur.). Avez-vous envoyé (vos cartes postales)?

Exercise 23(ii)
Translate into English:

1 Ton bifteck était tendre mais le mien était très dur. **2** Est-ce que vous avez votre montre? J'ai perdu la mienne. **3** Cette serviette est à moi; la vôtre est là-bas sur le rocher. **4** Si votre voiture est en panne, prenez la nôtre! **5** Nous allons laisser nos bagages à la réception et nous allons monter les vôtres. **6** Est-ce que tu désires mes lunettes de soleil? Non merci, j'ai les miennes. **7** Moi, j'ai mon visa, mais mon associé n'a pas encore le sien. **8** Je leur ai donné notre adresse et ils m'ont donné la leur.

How to say 'I wash (myself), you shave (yourself)' etc.

We have seen that direct and indirect object noun phrases help us to determine who or what is affected by the action performed by the subject.

Je vois (qui? =) le facteur. *I see (whom? =) the postman.*
Il parlait (à qui? =) à la *He was talking (to whom? =)*
    concierge.   *to the concierge.*

In the above examples the performer of the action and the person 'on the receiving end' are distinct.

Sometimes, however, the performer of the action can also be the person subjected to it:

> *I see myself in the mirror.   He was speaking to himself.*

Such constructions are called reflexive. In English a reflexive construction is generally (but not always) signalled by pronouns such as 'myself', 'yourself', 'himself', etc.

The French equivalents of these pronouns are given below against the corresponding subject ones.

Subject pronoun	Reflexive pronoun	Meaning
je	me	*myself*
tu	te	*yourself (fam.)*
il/elle	se	*him/her/itself*
nous	nous	*ourselves*
vous	vous	*yourself/yourselves*
ils/elles	se	*themselves*

Work it out

Look at the following sentences, then make the appropriate comments about the way French reflexive pronouns function and where they are placed in the sentence. The infinitive of the relevant reflexive verb (which is signalled by 'se' = oneself) is given in brackets at the end of each example:

1 Je me couche tard le soir. (se coucher)

I go to bed late at night (lit.: in the evening).

2 Elle se levait à sept heures du matin. (se lever)

She used to get up at seven in the morning.

3 Il s'est coupé avec son rasoir. (se couper)

He cut himself with his razor.

4 Nous nous laverons avant le dîner. (se laver)

We shall wash before dinner.

5 Ils se sont trompés au dernier croisement. (se tromper)

They made a mistake at the last crossroads.

6 Vous vous souvenez de moi? (se souvenir)

Do you remember me?

7	Vous allez vous perdre dans cette forêt! (se perdre)	*You are going to lose your way in this forest!*
8	Tu viens de te décider à partir? (se décider)	*Have you just made up your mind to leave?*
9	Vite les enfants, cachez-vous sous l'escalier! (se cacher)	*Quick children, hide (yourselves) under the stairs!*

Conclusions

A 'se' (himself, herself, itself, oneself, themselves) loses its 'e' when the next word begins with a vowel or a 'mute' h. This will also be the case with 'me' (myself) and 'te' (yourself).

B In simple (= one-word) tenses, the reflexive pronoun must be placed *between* the subject and the verb (sentences 1, 2, 4, 6).

C In the case of the immediate future (sentence 7) and the immediate past (sentence 8) the reflexive pronoun is placed *after* 'aller' and 'venir de' respectively.

D In the case of the perfect (with 'être') the reflexive goes *before* the auxiliary (sentences 3 and 5).

E In the imperative positive the reflexive pronoun is placed *after* the verb (sentence 9).

Important

(a) Reflexive verbs cannot use 'avoir' as an auxiliary to form their perfect (sentences 3 and 5).

(b) Many verbs can be used either as reflexives or with direct or indirect objects:

Compare:	Je me coupe (je coupe qui? = moi).	*I cut (whom? =) myself.*
and:	Je coupe le pain. (je coupe quoi? = le pain).	*I cut (what? =) the bread.*

Beware: Some verbs which do not appear to be reflexive in English are constructed reflexively in French:

Il se lavait et se rasait avant de prendre son petit déjeuner. — *He used to wash and shave before having his breakfast.*

Ne vous affolez pas.
Don't panic.

Exercise 23(iii)

Translate the sentences overleaf into English:

1 Nous nous sommes couchés à minuit et nous nous sommes endormis tout de suite. **2** Elles vont se faire mal sur ces rochers. **3** Est-ce que vous vous êtes excusés? **4** Il va s'acheter une petite maison à la campagne. **5** Vous vous lèverez à huit heures et vous descendrez prendre votre petit déjeuner avec nous. **6** Je me suis coupé avec le couteau à pain, mais ce n'est pas grave. **7** Ils se sont amusés dans le jardin toute la matinée. **8** La prochaine fois, nous nous adresserons directement à vous. **9** Je me demande si tu t'es regardé dans la glace.

Have a try

—Caroline! Robert! Are you ready? Remember that we are going to the Duponts' to eat. They are expecting (= waiting for) us in an hour for the aperitif . . . . Caroline, have you washed (yourself)?

—Yes, mum, I am nearly ready . . . Where are my glasses?

—On the kitchen table with mine. Don't forget to take a jumper (= a pullover): the Duponts' house is always very cold . . . Where is your father?

—I am in the bathroom, darling! I have just had a wash (= washed myself). I am all wet and there is no towel (in) here.

—Don't panic! Here is mine!

—Thank you, darling . . . Are you ready?

—No! . . . I wanted to have (the) time to get ready (= prepare myself) this morning. But it's always the same (thing) in this house! There is always someone in the bathroom before me! Have you finished?

—Wait a minute! I am shaving . . . Oh, I have cut myself with the razor!

—Is it serious?

—No, not really (= truly) . . . I have finished. I apologize . . . Go (and) get yourself ready now, the bathroom is free.

Ce n'est pas trop tôt!
And about time too!
(lit.: that is not too early!)

24 How to express numbers over one hundred, fractions, percentages and ratios

How to express numbers over one hundred

Having learnt in Chapter 11 how to form numbers up to one hundred in French, we shall now study how to express higher figures.

Numbers between 101 and 999
All that is required to express these is to indicate the correct number of hundreds: 'cent', 'deux cents', 'trois cents' etc., followed by the appropriate number from one to ninety-nine, as seen in chapter 11:

    327 = trois cent vingt-sept
    684 = six cent quatre-vingt-quatre
    800 = huit cents
    999 = neuf cent quatre-vingt-dix-neuf

Numbers over 999
The basic words we require for the purpose are:

mille	*(one thousand)*
un millier	*(approximately one thousand)*
un million	*(one million)*
un milliard	*(one thousand million)*

Notes:
1 Mille is invariable and will not take an 's' regardless of the number of thousands expressed:

   Voici cinquante mille francs.   *Here are fifty thousand francs.*

Beware: Do not use 'mille' after: 'quelques' (some), 'plusieurs' (several), or a phrase expressing an approximate number.

× Il y a quelques mille de
  touristes dans la région.

✓ Il y a quelques milliers de   *There are a few thousand*
  touristes dans la région.   *tourists in the area.*

× J'ai vu plusieurs mille de
  personnes.

✓ J'ai vu plusieurs milliers de   *I saw several thousand people.*
  personnes.

2 Milliers, millions and milliards are masculine nouns.
Consequently, they will take an 's' in the plural.

> Il y avait des milliers de   *There were thousands of young*
> jeunes au festival.   *people at the festival.*
>
> Cette planète est à deux   *This planet is two million*
> millions de kilomètres de   *kilometres (away) from the*
> la terre.   *earth.*
>
> La France produit six à sept   *France produces six to seven*
> milliards de litres de vin   *thousand million litres of*
> par an.   *wine per year.*

3 If dates are written in letters instead of numbers, 'mille' will be
replaced by 'mil'.

> Il est né en mil neuf cent vingt- *He was born in 1927.*
> sept.

4 Numbers between 1100 and 1999 may be expressed in two
different ways:

(*a*) either as 'mille (mil) cent' (one thousand one hundred), 'mille
       (mil) deux cents' (one thousand two hundred), etc. . .

(*b*) or as 'onze cents' (eleven hundred), 'douze cents' (twelve
       hundred), etc. . .

> En mil neuf cent quatre-vingt-   *In 1985, there were*
> cinq/En dix-neuf cent quatre-   *54,800,000 inhabitants*
> vingt-cinq il y avait cinquante- *in France.*
> quatre millions huit cent mille
> habitants en France.

Word list

Nouns

l'Américain	*American*	à l'étranger	*abroad*
	(person)	la capitale	*capital*

le déficit	*deficit*	le passager/	*passenger*
la fortune	*fortune*	la passagère	*(masc./fem.)*
le gouvernement	*government*	la planète	*planet*
la guerre	*war*	la poche	*pocket*
l'habitant (masc.)	*inhabitant*	la rose	*rose*
l'industrie (fem.)	*industry*	le ruban	*ribbon*
le jeune	*young person*	la sardine	*sardine*
la livre	*the pound*	la tour	*tower*
(sterling)	*(sterling)*	le travailleur	*worker*
la marche	*step*	la variété	*variety*
le millionnaire	*millionaire*	la ville	*town*

Adjectives

effrayant	*frightening*	mondial	*world-wide*
(im)possible	*(im)possible*	passionnant	*thrilling/exciting*
impressionnant	*impressive*	serré	*tight*

Verbs

annoncer	*to announce*	habiter	*to live/to dwell*
exporter	*to export*	naître (né)	*to be born*

Other words

exactement	*exactly*	qui	*who/whom*

Important: The basic statement made in Chapter 11 concerning the fact that numbers do not normally change in the plural, now needs to be refined as follows:

1 'Un' (one) changes to 'une' whenever it appears at the end of a number referring to a feminine.

> Nous avons cinquante et une   *We have fifty one varieties of*
> variétés de roses.   *roses*

2 'vingt' takes an 's' in the exact expression 'quatre-vingts' (eighty), but not if followed by a number from one to nineteen or by 'mille'.

Compare: Elle m'a donné quatre-   *She gave me eighty francs.*
           vingts francs.
and: Il a payé quatre-vingt-   *He paid ninety two francs.*
           douze francs.

3   'cent' takes an 's' when it expresses exact multiples of one hundred and is not followed by 'mille'.

J'avais deux cents francs   *I had two hundred francs in*
   dans ma poche.   *my pocket.*
but: Ils ont deux cent mille francs   *They have two hundred*
   à la banque.   *thousand francs in the bank.*

Beware: Whenever *exact* multiples of 'cent' are followed by the words 'milliers' ('approximate' thousands), 'millions' (millions) or 'milliards' (thousand millions), they will take an 's', and the number will be followed by 'de' (of).

Nous exportons deux cents   *We export two hundred million*
   millions de litres de vin.   *litres of wine.*
Le gouvernement a annoncé   *The government announced a*
   un déficit de sept cents   *deficit of seven hundred*
   milliards de francs!   *thousand million francs!*
but: Nous avons transporté deux   *We carried two hundred and*
   cent dix millions de passagers.   *ten million passengers.*

Note: Dates are often written in figures rather than in letters:

Le 6 juin 1944 (for: le six juin   *6th June 1944*
   mil neuf cent quarante-
   quatre)

Fractions

In French, $\frac{1}{2}$, $\frac{1}{3}$ and $\frac{1}{4}$ are expressed by 'un demi','un tiers' and 'un quart' respectively. For all other fractions, a cardinal number will be used at the top (numerator) and an ordinal (= ranking) number at the bottom (denominator):

$\frac{2}{5}$: (les) deux cinquièmes
$\frac{3}{8}$: (les) trois huitièmes
$\frac{9}{10}$: (les) neuf dixièmes.

Les cinq huitièmes de la   *Five eighths of the population*
   population habitent dans   *live in towns.*
   les villes.

In French, a 'decimal comma' is used instead of the English decimal point and the point (or a gap) is used instead of the English comma:

French	*English*
2.384 (or 2 384)	2,384
6,739	6.739

Vérifiez votre monnaie!
Check your change!

Percentages and ratios

The expression used to formulate a percentage is simply: '. . . pour cent':

| Les banques offrent sept pour cent d'intérêt. | *Banks are offering seven per cent interest.* |
| Quarante pour cent des travailleurs sont dans l'industrie. | *Forty per cent of workers are in industry.* |

The expression '. . . out of . . .' is translated by '. . . sur . . .':

| Un Français sur dix va en vacances à l'étranger. | *One French person out of ten goes on holiday abroad.* |

C'est peu!
It's not much!
(lit.: it's little!)

Exercise 24(i)
Translate the following sentences into English:

1 La France produit six milliards deux cent cinquante millions de litres de vin; c'est impressionnant! **2** Cet escalier a exactement trois cent quatre-vingt-dix-neuf marches! Vous êtes sûr? **3** Il est absent les trois quarts du temps. **4** Les deux tiers des Français vont au bord de la mer pour leurs vacances. **5** 'Mil neuf cent quatre-vingt-quatre' de George Orwell est un livre passionnant mais effrayant. **6** Dans cet hôtel un client sur deux est anglais.

Exercise 24(ii)

Translate into French writing figures as words:

1 In 1995 we will work thirty hours a (= per) week. 2 The second world war started in 1939. 3 This tower measures 300 metres. 4 We live 520 kilometres from the capital. 5 I would like 2.50 metres of white ribbon. 6 She stays with us one week out of five.

Have a try

—Vous avez passé de bonnes vacances?

—Pas mauvaises! Nous sommes allés passer quinze jours sur la Côte d'Azur.

—C'était calme?

—Calme? Diable non! Il y avait des millions de personnes dans les magasins, sur la plage, dans les rues, partout! Impossible de bouger! Nous avons fait huit cents kilomètres pour être serrés comme des sardines! Au bord de la mer, impossible de trouver une place! On marchait sur des mains, sur des pieds . . . .

—Quelle horreur!

—Oui, mais à deux cent cinquante mètres du bord, il y avait les bateaux des millionnaires qui étaient là pour le week-end.

—Vous étiez dans un hôtel?

—Oui, à huit cents mètres de la plage. Le matin, on prenait notre petit déjeuner sur le balcon de la chambre et on regardait la mer.

—L'hôtel était cher?

—Oui, très. Mais là-bas tout est cher: les cafés, les restaurants, les magasins . . . Trois mille francs pour un costume!

—Trois mille francs? Ca fait trois cents livres!

—A peu près. . . Nous sommes allés au casino deux ou trois fois. C'est extraordinaire, il y a des gens qui gagnent et qui perdent des fortunes en une nuit! Un soir, j'ai vu un Américain gagner cinq cent mille francs. J'aurais (bien) aimé être à sa place!

Le veinard! (fam.)
The lucky so-and-so!

25 How to say 'who, which, that', and 'against whom, for which' etc.

How to say 'who, which, that'

We have already examined how useful pronouns are to avoid repeating whole sections of sentences. In this chapter, we shall introduce some more words which play a similar role.

The following sentences:

> The man goes to the market. The man is tall.
> The apple is on the table. The apple is ripe.

can all be simplified thus:

> The man who goes to the market is tall.
> The apple which is on the table is ripe.

The words 'who', 'which', 'that' used in the above (and similar) sentences can all be translated by 'qui' in French.

> L'homme qui va au marché est grand.
> La pomme qui est sur la table est mûre.

Similarly, the following sentences:

> The man is charming. I have met the man.
> The meal is excellent. She is eating the meal.
> The house is small. We are going to visit the house.

could be modified in the following way:

> The man (whom) I have met is charming.
> The meal (that) she is eating is excellent.
> The house (which) we are going to visit is small.

In this case, the words 'whom', 'which' and 'that' are translated by 'que' in French:

L'homme que j'ai rencontré est charmant.
Le repas qu'elle mange est excellent.
La maison que nous allons visiter est petite.

Important: 'qui' must be used whenever the subject (= performer) is the same in the two sections which are to be linked; 'que' must be used whenever the subjects (= performers) of the two sections are distinct.

Compare:	Le film qui passe à la télévision ce soir est excellent. (= Le film passe à la télévision ce soir; le film est excellent.)	*The film which is (lit.: passing) on the television this evening is excellent.*
and:	Le film que je regarde est excellent. (= Le film est excellent; je regarde le film.)	*The film (which) I am watching is excellent.*

Note: In several of the above examples, 'which', 'whom' or 'that' have been put in brackets because, in English, they can be omitted. Whenever this is the case, the French pronoun required to translate them will be 'que' and not 'qui'.

A man (that) I know broke the dish (which) I bought.	*Un homme que je connais a cassé le plat que j'ai acheté.*

Beware: In French, such pronouns cannot be omitted.

> Quelle vie!
> *It's a dog's life!*
> *(lit.: What a life!)*

Word list

Nouns

l'affaire (fem.)	*business matter deal*	l'indication (fem.)	*instruction/direction (for use)*
l'Afrique (fem.)	*Africa*	l'insecte (masc.)	*insect*
le banc	*bench*	le lampadaire	*street light/ lamp-post*
le contact	*contact*		
le festival	*festival*	le mensonge	*lie*
la grotte	*cave*	la mesure	*measure*

la montagne	*mountain*	le ruisseau	*brook*
le prix	*price/prize*	la trace	*trace*
la question	*question*	le voleur	*thief*

Adjectives

avare	*mean*	exigeant	*demanding*
blond	*blond*	pittoresque	*picturesque*
déchiré	*torn*	risqué	*risky*
dynamique	*dynamic*	sympathique	*friendly*

Verbs

couvrir (couvert)	*to cover (covered)*	retrouver	*to find (or meet) again*
mettre (mis)	*to put (put)*	taper	*to type/to knock*
passer	*to pass/to cross/ to go over*	voler	*to steal/to fly*

Other Words

| à cause de | *because of* | du moins | *at least* |

Exercise 25(i)

Complete the following sentences, using 'qui' or 'que' as appropriate:

1 Le pull-over *qui* est sur la chaise est déchiré. 2 Les cadeaux *que* j'ai achetés sont très beaux. 3 Les invités *qui* arrivent sont les amis de mon père. 4 Le disque *que* tu aimes est cassé. 5 J'ai l'adresse *que* vous désirez. 6 Mon frère *qui* arrive ce soir a passé six ans à l'étranger. 7 Voici l'agent *qui* a arrêté le voleur. 8 La région *que* nous allons visiter est très pittoresque.

Exercise 25(ii)

Translate the following sentences into French:

1 The man who is ill is my brother's friend. 2 Here is the book (which) I have bought for him. 3 My uncle, who has a farm, is very rich and very mean. 4 The wine (that) we are going to order is expensive. 5 The purse which is over there on the table is empty. 6 I am looking at the passport (which) he left on the bed.

How to say 'against whom', 'for which', etc.

In certain sentences, the pronouns 'whom' and 'which' are used in conjunction with a preposition: 'against, for, behind, to', etc. In such cases, 'whom' and 'which' may be translated differently according to the circumstances:

1   If the noun phrase to be replaced refers to one or more things or beings, one of the following pronouns can be selected, according to the gender (masc. fem.) and number (sing. plur.) required:

lequel	(masc. sing.)
laquelle	(fem. sing.)
lesquels	(masc. plur.)
lesquelles	(fem. plur.)

Note: Each pronoun incorporates the definite article ('le, la, les') appropriate to the gender and number of the noun phrase it represents.

L'homme pour lequel elle travaille est très aimable.	*The man she works for (lit.: for whom she works) is very pleasant.*
Est-ce que vous avez lu la lettre dans laquelle il explique son départ?	*Have you read the letter in which he explains his departure?*
Voici les amis avec lesquels je vais partir en vacances.	*Here are the friends with whom I am going to go on holiday.*
N'oubliez pas ces indications sans lesquelles vous ne trouverez jamais notre villa.	*Don't forget these directions, without which you will never find our villa.*

If the preposition used before 'lequel', 'lesquels' or 'lesquelles' ends with the word 'de' (of/from): 'autour de' (around), 'au-dessous de' (below), 'au-dessus de' (above) . . . , 'de' will combine with the article 'le' or 'les' contained in the pronoun (in the usual way) to form 'duquel', 'desquels' and 'desquelles':

Voici le rocher au-dessous duquel nous avons passé la nuit.	*Here is the rock below which we spent the night.*
Il regardait les lampadaires autour desquels volaient des insectes.	*He looked at the street lights around which insects were flying.*

Les montagnes au-dessus desquelles nous venons de passer sont couvertes de neige.

The mountains over which we have just flown (lit.: passed) are covered with snow.

2   If the noun phrase replaced by 'whom' or 'which' refers to one or more human beings, 'qui' will be used after the required preposition:

La dame avec qui je parlais est la propriétaire du magasin.

The lady with whom I was talk-ing is the owner of the shop.

Les clients pour qui nous travaillons sont très exigeants.

The customers (whom) we are working for are very demanding.

Note: The combination of the preposition 'de' (of/from) placed immediately after a noun and any of the above pronouns (including 'qui'), is normally avoided and replaced by a single word: 'dont', whatever the gender and number of the noun phrase to be replaced:

Voici le livre dont (= duquel) je t'ai parlé.

Here is the book I talked to you about (lit.: of which . . .)

L'affaire dont (= de laquelle) vous me parlez est très risquée.

The business matter you are talking to me about (lit.: about which . . .) is very risky.

Exercise 25(iii)

Complete the following sentences using lequel, laquelle, lesquels, lesquelles as appropriate:

1 La compagnie pour . . . il travaille est très dynamique.   2 Les jeunes filles avec . . . nous voyageons sont étudiantes.   3 Est-ce que tu as vu le sac dans . . . j'ai mis les sandwichs?   4 Voici les arbres derrière . . . vous avez laissé la voiture.   5 Je vais vous expliquer les raisons à cause (de) . . . je suis parti.   6 Nous avons visité un village près (de) . . . il y a des grottes magnifiques.   7 Voilà la maison dans . . . je suis né.   8 Ils ont abandonné les mesures contre . . . j'ai protesté.

Exercise 25(iv)

Translate the following sentences into French using 'qui' and 'dont' whenever possible:

1 The employee with whom she arrived this morning is a good worker. **2** Where is the corkscrew with which I am going to open the bottle? **3** The house in which we live is not big, but it is very beautiful. **4** Over there, there is a brook beside which there are some benches. **5** Here is the machine on which this letter has been typed. **6** The people with whom I came are my neighbours. **7** The problem I speak of (= of which I speak) is not new, but it is becoming more and more serious. **8** The film you are talking about (= of which you talk) won (the) first prize at the festival.

Have a try (Use the 'familiar' question form)

—Good morning. Police! Do you know the people who live in that house?

—The Dubois family? Yes, why?

—Do you know them well?

—No, not really; the Dubois are people with whom we have few contacts. . . . Why?

—Just a minute! It is I who ask the questions here! Do they have any children?

—Yes, they have a son, who is abroad, in the United States I think, and a daughter who lives with them. The daughter is here, but the parents are on holiday in Spain.

—The girl you are talking about (= of whom), have you seen her recently?

—Two or three days ago . . . No, wait, I'm telling a lie! I saw her yesterday morning!

—Was she alone?

—No, she was with a friend. At least, I suppose he's her friend . . .

—Can you give me some details about (= on) him?

—Not a great deal . . . Somebody whom she works with and who comes to fetch her every morning in an old car which makes a lot of noise . . . A red Volkswagen. . . A charming young man: blond, tall, very friendly . . . But I would like to know why you are asking me all those questions!

—This morning, we found the car you were talking about, against a lamp-post. It was empty. No trace of the young man. We would like to find him (again) to ask him a few questions . . .

C'est louche!
It's suspicious!

26 How to express days of the week, months, seasons

How to express days of the week

In French, the days of the week are all masculine:

(le) lundi	*Monday*
(le) mardi	*Tuesday*
(le) mercredi	*Wednesday*
(le) jeudi	*Thursday*
(le) vendredi	*Friday*
(le) samedi	*Saturday*
(le) dimanche	*Sunday*

Important:

1 In French, days of the week do not begin with a capital letter (except, of course, at the start of a sentence).

2 'On Monday, Tuesday . . .' (next or last) is simply translated by 'lundi', 'mardi' . . . The tense of the verb will normally clarify whether you are talking about next or last Monday, Tuesday etc. . .

Ils arriveront mardi soir.	*They will arrive on Tuesday night.*
Dimanche nous sommes allés au bord de la mer.	*On Sunday we went to the seaside.*

If you want to emphasize the idea of 'next' (or last), the word 'prochain' (or 'dernier'/'passé') can be placed after the name of the day:

Jeudi prochain c'est mon anniversaire!	*Next Thursday is my birthday!*
Vendredi dernier nous avons vu ta sœur.	*Last Friday we saw your sister.*

3 'On Sundays' (or 'every Sunday'), etc., expressing a repetition or habitual state of affairs, is simply translated by 'le dimanche' etc. . .

> Le samedi nous travaillons jusqu'à midi.
> *On Saturdays we work until noon (=midday).*
>
> Le mercredi les enfants ne vont pas à l'école.
> *On Wednesdays children do not go to school.*

Beware: Do not use 'les lundis', etc. . . to express the repetition or habitual occurrence of an event:

> × Les vendredis et les samedis nous fermons le magasin à huit heures.
>
> ✓ Le vendredi et le samedi nous fermons le magasin à huit heures.
> *On Fridays and Saturdays we close (the shop) at eight o'clock.*

When the words 'matin' (morning) or 'soir' (evening) are used in conjunction with the name of a day, they will be placed immediately after it:

> Venez me voir jeudi soir ou vendredi matin.
> *Come and see me on Thursday evening or Friday morning.*

If they are used alone, the following remarks will apply:

(a) If you wish to translate 'this morning' or 'this evening', 'ce' will be placed before both. The tense of the verb will indicate the relevant time-zone:

> Ce matin il est descendu à sept heures.
> *This morning he came down at seven o'clock.*
>
> Ce soir après le dîner, nous ferons une petite promenade à pied.
> *This evening after dinner, we will go for a little walk.*

(b) If you wish to express a habitual or recurring event, 'le' (and not 'les') must be used:

> Le matin je me lève à l'aube, et le soir je me couche à dix heures.
> *In the mornings I get up at dawn and in the evenings I go to bed at ten.*

Word list

Nouns

l'anniversaire (masc.)	*birthday/ anniversary*	la nouvelle	*(piece of) news*
l'aube (fem.)	*dawn*	le pays	*country*
le fiancé/la fiancée	*fiance(e)*	la pluie	*rain*
le fil	*thread*	le ski	*skiing*
l'hirondelle (fem.)	*swallow*	la température	*temperature*
le jouet	*toy*	le temps	*weather/time*

Adjectives

bas (basse)	*low*	libre	*free/available*
calme	*calm/quiet*	seul	*alone/lonely*
général	*general*		

Verbs

(se) découvrir (découvert)	*to uncover (oneself)*	durer	*to last*

Other words

à pied	*on foot*	jusqu'à	*up to/until*
généralement	*generally*	seulement	*only*

Exercise 26(i)

Put the following sentences into English, avoiding clumsy translations:

1 Lundi soir nous sommes allés voir un film policier au cinéma. **2** Le vendredi, après son travail, il va au café prendre un verre. **3** Dimanche prochain, nous irons faire un pique-nique s'il fait beau. **4** Mardi dernier, ton frère est venu avec sa fiancée. **5** Le mercredi matin et le jeudi après-midi, nous allons en ville faire les commissions. **6** Samedi, nous appellerons ta mère pour lui annoncer la nouvelle. **7** Le magasin est ouvert du lundi au samedi.

Exercise 26(ii)

Translate into French, using the standard form of question when necessary:

1 On Saturdays I go to my parents' for lunch. **2** Last Tuesday evening we telephoned you but you did not answer. **3** Will you go to the bank for me on Friday morning? **4** This shop is closed on

Sundays.   **5** Will she be in her office on Monday morning at nine?   **6** The doctor came on Monday. He will be back on Thursday before noon.   **7** He works for us on Tuesdays, Thursdays and Saturdays but only in the morning.

Vivement dimanche!
Roll on Sunday!

Months

In French, the word for 'month' is 'le mois'. It is masculine, as are all the following:

janvier	*January*
février	*February*
mars	*March*
avril	*April*
mai	*May*
juin	*June*
juillet	*July*
août	*August*
septembre	*September*
octobre	*October*
novembre	*November*
décembre	*December*

En avril ne te découvre pas d'un fil. (proverb)
Don't cast a clout till May is out
(lit.: In April do not uncover yourself of a thread).
Les grandes vacances commencent en juillet.
The summer holiday begins in July.

Important:
1   In French, months do not begin with a capital letter (except of course if they start a sentence).

Nous arriverons le mardi dix-sept juillet à huit heures du soir.	*We shall arrive on Tuesday 17th July at 8 p.m.* *(lit.: 8 of the evening)*

2 'In January' etc . . . can be translated either as 'en janvier' or as
'au mois de janvier' (in the month of January).

Compare: En juin, le temps est   *In June, the weather is*
                généralement beau.   *generally nice.*
            Quelquefois il y a des   *Sometimes there are storms*
                orages au mois de juillet.   *in July.*

3 Although the tense used in a given sentence is normally sufficient
to indicate the time-zone of the action, it is possible to use the words:
'prochain' (next) and 'dernier' (last) if desired.

Compare: En février, ils sont allés en
                Allemagne; en septembre
                ils iront passer quinze
                jours en Espagne.
and: En février dernier, ils sont   *In (or last) February, they*
                allés en Allemagne; en   *went to Germany; in (or*
                septembre prochain ils   *next) September they will*
                iront passer quinze   *go and spend a fortnight*
                jours en Espagne.   *in Spain.*

Note: 'All the year round' is translated in French by 'Du 1er
(premier) janvier au 31 (trente et un) décembre'. (lit.: from January
1st to December 31st)

Seasons

Seasons are masculine in French:

    le printemps   *spring*
    l'été   *summer*
    l'automne   *autumn*
    l'hiver   *winter*

    L'été dernier nous avons passé   *Last summer we spent a month*
        un mois en Corse.   *in Corsica.*
    L'hiver prochain nous irons   *Next winter we will go skiing.*
        faire du ski.   *(lit.: do some skiing).*

Important:
1 'In spring' is translated by 'au printemps'; for the other seasons
'en' is used instead of 'au' (to avoid a vowel-clash).

En hiver les températures sont   *In (the) winter temperatures*
très basses, mais au printemps   *are very low, but in (the)*
et en été le temps est chaud et   *spring and summer the*
sec.   *weather is hot and dry.*

2   It is possible to convey the idea of a past or forthcoming season
without using 'dernier' (past) or 'prochain' (next). All you need is 'ce'
(or 'cet' before a vowel or a 'mute' h) and the appropriate tense to
situate the action clearly in a given time-zone:

Cet été ils iront probablement   *This summer they will probably*
au Portugal.   *go to Portugal.*
Cet automne j'ai passé huit   *This autumn I spent eight days in*
jours en Ecosse.   *Scotland.*

Il n'y a plus de saisons!
There is no good weather these days!
(lit.: There are no seasons any more!)

Exercise 26(iii)
Translate into English:

1 Au mois de mai, la campagne est très belle.   **2** En septembre, nous
irons passer quelques jours dans les Pyrénées.   **3** En février, les
enfants ont une semaine de vacances.   **4** Au mois de décembre, les
magasins sont pleins de jouets.   **5** Le printemps commence le vingt
et un mars.   **6** Cet hiver, nous resterons à la maison.   **7** L'été
dernier nous avons passé des vacances formidables.   **8** Une
hirondelle ne fait pas le printemps. (proverb)

Exercise 26(iv)
Translate into French:

1 In May, June and July, we have a great deal of work.   **2** Autumn
is the quietest season for us.   **3** We are going to spend the winter in a
warm (= hot) country.   **4** In autumn and in winter, the hotel is
closed because there are no visitors.   **5** This spring, the weather will
be mild and there will be no rain.   **6** This summer, we had ten days
of sunshine (= sun), that's all!   **7** When I was young, I used to hate
the autumn. Now I think it's the best season.

There are two words to express the word 'year':

(*a*)   One, 'l'an', is masculine and is used when you merely wish to state a precise number of years without any subjective overtones:

> Elle a eu vingt ans la semaine   *She was twenty (years of age)*
>   dernière.   *last week.*
> La guerre a duré six ans.   *The war lasted six years.*

(*b*)   the other, 'l'année', is feminine and is used:

(i)   when the number of years is not precisely fixed, particularly after: 'beaucoup de' (many), 'plusieurs' (several), 'quelques' (some), 'un certain nombre de. . . ' (a number of).

> Dans quelques années je   *In a few years I will be free.*
>   serai libre.
> Nous avons attendu plu-   *We waited several years.*
>   sieurs années.

(ii)   in the expression 'last year', 'next year' as an alternative to 'an'. You can say 'l'an dernier' or 'l'année dernière' (last year), and 'l'an prochain' or 'l'année prochaine' (next year); but for 'this year' you must say 'cette année' and not 'cet an!'.

(iii)   when you wish to introduce subjective overtones (happiness, (boredom . . .) into your statement.

Compare: Nous avons passé trois   *We spent three years in*
>   ans en Afrique.   *Africa.(objective state-*
>   *ment)*
and: Nous avons passé trois   *We spent three (long or*
>   années en Afrique.   *happy) years in Africa.*
>   *(subjective statement)*

> A l'an prochain!
> *See you next year!*
> *(lit.: to the next year!)*

Have a try

—Taxi, taxi! . . . Vous êtes libre?

— Oui, monsieur . . . Où désirez-vous aller?

— Est-ce que vous pouvez me conduire 135 Boulevard de la République?

—Bien sûr! Attendez, je vais mettre vos valises dans la malle! Voilà, montez . . . Bienvenue dans notre ville! C'est votre première visite?

—Non, je suis déjà venu l'année dernière, mais je suis resté un jour seulement.

—Et cette fois-ci?

—Je suis ici jusqu'à vendredi prochain!

—Oh, alors vous avez toute une semaine pour découvrir la ville . . . Vous venez en vacances ou pour affaires?

—Les deux! . . . Il y a des choses intéressantes à faire?

—Vous savez, notre ville est très sympathique et très dynamique! C'est un grand centre industriel, mais nous recevons aussi beaucoup de touristes, surtout l'hiver! La station de ski est à dix kilomètres du centre-ville. L'été, on peut faire des promenades dans la montagne . . . Il y a des centres de sports qui sont ouverts tous les jours de huit heures à vingt-deux heures . . . Des théâtres . . . Des musées. Ceux-ci sont gratuits mais ils sont fermés le mardi. Nous avons aussi beaucoup de cinémas et le lundi l'entrée est moins chère.

—Vous n'êtes pas un peu loin de la capitale?

—Pas du tout! Il y a un service de trains à grande vitesse vers Paris et Marseille. L'été, vous pouvez être à la plage en deux heures et demie . . . Ah, nous voilà arrivés! Le 135 est là . . . J'espère que vous passerez une agréable semaine!

—Merci. Combien est-ce que je vous dois?

—Ca fait vingt-cinq francs.

—Voilà! Gardez la monnaie! Au revoir!

A la prochaine!
See you sometime!
(lit.: to the next (time)!)

27 How to say: 'I must, I do, I can, I know, I want . . . ' and 'I will have to, I should,' etc.

We have so far examined the behaviour of a variety of French verbs in each of the three time-zones (past, present, future). We shall now have a close look at five verbs which are among the most frequently used in French:

'devoir'	to have to/must
'faire'	to do/make
'pouvoir'	to be able to/can
'savoir'	to know
'vouloir'	to want to

All belong to the third group (infinitive ending in 'oir/re'). Their present and past participles, as well as their other tenses, will be presented after the Word list.

Word list

Nouns

l'ascenseur (masc.)	lift (= elevator)	le plombier	plumber
le beurre	butter	la poêle	frying pan
le chalet	chalet	le projet	project
le détour	detour	le transistor (familiar)	transistor radio
l'œuf (masc.)	egg	la vaisselle	washing up

Adjectives

| humide | wet/damp |

Verbs

abandonner	to abandon/leave	chauffer	to heat up
avoir l'air	to seem	déranger	to disturb
avoir raison	to be right	disparaître (disparu)	to disappear (disappeared)
baisser	to turn down/ lower	envoyer	to send
(se) calmer	to calm (oneself) down	nager	to swim
		perdre (perdu)	to lose (lost)

Other words

alors	*then (= in that case/at that time)*	d'ailleurs	*besides*
		de bonne heure	*early*
à partir de	*from*	un peu	*a little*
au moins	*at least*		

The present and past participles of the five verbs presented at the beginning of this chapter are listed below against their infinitives.

Infinitive	Present participle	Past participle
devoir	devant	dû
faire	faisant	fait
pouvoir	pouvant	pu
savoir	sachant	su
vouloir	voulant	voulu

The present, perfect, imperfect, future and conditional tense of these five verbs are as follows:

Present

devoir	*to have to*	faire	*to do/make*
je dois	*I have to*	je fais	*I do*
tu dois	*you have to (fam.)*	tu fais	*you do (fam.)*
il/elle doit	*he/she/it has to*	il/elle fait	*he/she/it does*
nous devons	*we have to*	nous faisons	*we do*
vous devez	*you have to*	vous faites	*you do*
ils/elles doivent	*they have to*	ils/elles font	*they do*

pouvoir	*to be able to/can*	savoir	*to know*
je peux	*I am able to*	je sais	*I know*
tu peux	*you are able to (fam.)*	tu sais	*you know (fam.)*
il/elle peut	*he/she/it is able to*	il/elle sait	*he/she/it knows*
nous pouvons	*we are able to*	nous savons	*we know*
vous pouvez	*you are able to*	vous savez	*you know*
ils/elles peuvent	*they are able to*	ils/elles savent	*they know*

vouloir	*to want*
je veux	*I want*
tu veux	*you want (fam.)*
il/elle veut	*he/she/it wants*
nous voulons	*we want*
vous voulez	*you want*
ils/elles veulent	*they want*

Imperfect

The imperfect of French verbs is a simple (= one-word) tense composed of a stem + an ending. The endings required for the above five verbs are the same as for all others; you can refresh your memory by referring to page 132 (Chapter 20). The stems used to form their imperfect tense are:

devoir	→	dev-
faire	→	fais-
pouvoir	→	pouv-
savoir	→	sav-
vouloir	→	voul-

Note: With the exception of 'faire', these stems are all predictable (= infinitive minus ending).

Future

In French, the future is, as we have seen, a simple (= one-word) tense made up of a stem + endings. You will also remember that the endings are the same as those of the present of 'avoir' (to have) (see p. 143 in Chapter 22).

The stems of the five verbs, on the other hand, do not follow the normal pattern for that tense (i.e. infinitive *minus* ending). They are:

devoir	→	devr-
faire	→	fer-
pouvoir	→	pourr-
savoir	→	saur-
vouloir	→	voudr-

Note: If, in a French sentence, the word 'quand' (when) is used to express an action which has not yet taken place, it must be followed by a verb in the future tense, whereas in English a present will suffice.

Compare: Vous pourrez me téléphoner quand vous voudrez.
and: *You will be able to telephone me when(ever) you want.*

Conditional

We already know that, in French, the conditional is a simple (= one-word) tense made up of a stem + endings. We also know that:

(a) the endings are the same as those of the imperfect and are identical for all verbs; and
(b) the stems are the same as those of the future and that this applies to all verbs. In consequence, this tense is very easy to form and to remember:

> Nous devrions abandonner ce projet. *We should abandon this project.*
>
> Vous pourriez au moins vous excuser! *You could at least apologize!*

Important:

1 The conditional of 'pouvoir', 'savoir' and 'vouloir' can be used to turn a forceful demand into a polite request:

Compare: Nous voulons une chambre pour deux personnes. *We want a double room. (lit.: a room for two persons)*
and: Nous voudrions une chambre pour deux personnes. *We would like a double room.*

2 'Devoir' can sometimes be used, particularly in the present, to express great probability.

> Il n'est pas là? Alors, il doit être malade. *Isn't he here? Then (= in that case) he must be ill.*

3 'Faire' followed by an infinitive often has the meaning of 'to have something done' or 'to cause something to be done'. It is frequently used in cooking recipes or 'care' labels:

> Faire revenir dans une poêle. (recipe) *Brown (lightly) in a frying pan. (lit.: to cause to come back in a frying pan).*
>
> Faites cuire à feu doux. *Cook on a low light. (lit.: cause to cook on soft fire)*

4 'Devoir', 'faire', 'pouvoir', 'savoir' and 'vouloir' can be followed by an infinitive *without* a preposition.

> Je voudrais vous envoyer   *I would like to send you a letter.*
> une lettre.
> Il ne peut plus parler.   *He can no longer speak.*

5 In French, 'savoir' and *not* 'pouvoir' is used to express the idea of 'to know how to':

Compare: Est-ce que tu sais nager?   *Can you swim? (lit.: Do you know how to swim?)*

and: Est-ce que tu peux nager?   *Are you able (or allowed) to swim?*

> Vouloir c'est pouvoir!
> *Where there's a will, there's a way!*
> *(lit.: To want to is to be able to.)*

Exercise 27(i)
Translate into English:

1 Nous voudrions trouver un petit restaurant pas cher. 2 Tous les matins il devait préparer le petit déjeuner. 3 Nous ferons tout ce que nous pourrons pour retrouver votre bague. 4 Est-ce que vous pourriez vous calmer un peu s'il vous plaît? 5 Vous devriez savoir que le client a toujours raison. 6 Nous saurons tout quand il nous appellera. 7 Est-ce que vous savez faire cuire les œufs? 8 Tu pourrais baisser ton transistor s'il te plaît?

Exercise 27(ii)
Translate the following sentences into French, giving two versions when required: (*a*) forceful statement; (*b*) polite request (use 'est-ce que' to formulate questions):

1 We	(*a*) want (*b*) would like	} a thousand francs.
2 We	(*a*) have to (*b*) should	} telephone him.
3	(*a*) Can you (*b*) Could you	} do the washing up?
4 I	(*a*) must (*b*) should	} pay my bill.

5 She

- (a) wants
- (b) would like

} a bottle of mineral water.

6 The children

- (a) must
- (b) should

} go to bed before midnight.

7 Can you dance? I can, but I am not allowed to!

8 Heat the butter slowly in a frying pan. (Recipe)

Have a try (use the familiar style in statements and questions)

— Hello John! You seem sad today. Are you ill?

— No, not exactly . . . I have (some) problems.

— Is it serious?

— Yes and no . . . I am unhappy . . . I am always unable to take decisions . . . I never know what (= that which) I have to do . . . At work I am too shy and at home I have no energy . . . I am always tired . . .

— Have you been (= gone) to see your doctor?

— No, I don't want to tell him my problems and besides I don't like him . . . No, I must make an effort. I would like to become more sure of myself, to take my own decisions . . . You are my friend, you must help me . . . I want to be full of confidence like you. I have decided to make a big effort. As from today, I am going to do what I want! I shall go where I want, when I want. Things are going to change. I am going to travel, meet people . . . To begin (with), I want to learn to drive!

— That's wonderful!

— Yes, thank you for your help!

— My help? But I haven't done anything!

— You have given me a great deal of confidence!

— Do you think (= believe) so? . . . Well then, come (on)! Let's go for a drink!

— Oh, I don't know . . . I would like to, but my mother is waiting for me at home . . . I don't want to be late . . .

Ca ne pouvait pas durer!
It (lit.: that) couldn't last!

**28   How to tell the time   How to say
'I had done (been doing)' etc.   How
to translate 'only' and to express
duration**

How to tell the time

Most learners find the prospect of working out how to tell the time in French rather daunting. It is in fact quite simple, once the numbers have been learned. Although, in some cases, the twenty-four hour and the sixty-minute system are used (as they are in English), particularly for official time-tables and public announcements, most people tend to use the twelve hour system:

Compare:	Le train arrivera en gare à dix-huit heures. (official announcement)	
and:	Le train arrivera en gare à six heures (du soir). (normal speech)	*The train will arrive at the station at 18.00 or 6 p.m.*

Important:
1   The word 'heure(s)' (hour(s)) must be used when telling the time. It cannot be omitted as is the case in English. The word 'minutes' (minutes), however, is almost always omitted!

    Deux heures trente (minutes)   *Two-thirty.*

2   The standard phrase for asking the time is:

    Quelle heure est-il?   *What time (lit.: hour) is it?*

And the reply:

    Il est . . .   *It is . . .*

Note: Although you may hear native French speakers say 'Quelle heure il est?' rather than 'Quelle heure est-il?' when asking the time, you should at this stage avoid the former — more colloquial — expression and use the latter.

3   When the twelve-hour system is used, 'midi' (midday) and 'minuit' (midnight) will replace 12.00 hrs and 24.00 hrs respectively.

4   'Quarter past' will be expressed by 'et quart', 'half past' by 'et demie' and 'quarter to' by 'moins le quart'.

> La course commencera à   *The race will start at half past*
>   deux heures et demie.   *two.*

5   When expressing minutes from 01 to 29 past the hour, you simply need to state the required number after the hours:

> Il est trois heures douze.   *It is twelve minutes past three.*
>   (3.12)

Don't forget that 'quarter past' is 'et quart':

> Ils rentreront à quatre heures   *They will come back at 4.15*
>   et quart ou quatre heures   *or 4.20.*
>   vingt.

6   When expressing minutes from 29 to 01 before the hour, you simply need to use the word 'moins' between the hours and the minutes.

> Le film finit à onze heures   *The film finishes at twenty to*
>   moins vingt.   *eleven.*

7   The words 'juste' (precisely), 'précise(s)' (sharp) or 'exactement' (exactly) can be used to translate '. . . o'clock sharp'.

> Je serai là à deux heures   *I will be there at two o'clock*
>   précises.   *sharp.*

> Il est l'heure de plier bagages!
> *It is time to pack up and go!*
> *(lit.: It is the hour to fold luggage!)*

Word list

Nouns

l'aéroport (masc.)	*airport*	l'heure (fem.)	*hour/time*
les Alpes (fem. plur.)	*Alps*	l'hypermarché (masc.)	*hypermarket*

le journal	*newspaper*	la réunion	*meeting/reunion*
la journée	*day (time-span)*	le sol	*floor/ground*
la liste	*list*	la terrasse	*terrace*
le piano	*piano*	le vol	*flight/theft*

Adjectives

| juste | *just/precise/sharp (time)* | précis | *precise/accurate* |

Verbs

| glisser | *to slip/slide* | protester | *to protest* |
| plier | *to fold* | (se) sentir | *to feel (reflexive)* |

Exercise 28(i)
Translate into English:

1 Quelle heure est-il? Il est exactement trois heures dix-huit.   **2** Elles sont descendues à sept heures et demie et elles ont pris leur petit déjeuner sur la terrasse.   **3** Est-ce que l'avion arrive à vingt heures trente ou à vingt heures quarante?   **4** Il y a une heure dix que je suis ici.   **5** Est-ce que vous avez l'heure s'il vous plaît? Oui, il est midi moins cinq.   **6** Le magasin est ouvert de huit heures du matin à sept heures et demie du soir.   **7** La réunion a commencé à trois heures précises et elle a fini à six heures et quart.

Exercise 28(ii)
Translate into French:

1 She will call you at eight o'clock sharp. (polite form).   **2** He takes his lunch between one and two.   **3** I would like to go (= leave) before nine-thirty.   **4** What time is it? I have forgotten my watch!   **5** This hypermarket is open until 10 p.m. (official notice).   **6** I have an appointment at the dentist's at half past four.   **7** Flight No. 203, departure 19.07, gate (= porte) No. 10. (official announcement)

'A tout à l'heure'
See you soon/in a little while.

How to say 'I had done (been doing),' etc.

When you need to state the fact that an action took place in the past, you have two tenses at your disposal:

(*a*)   The perfect, if you merely want to say that the action occurred (without any other shade of meaning):

> Ils ont acheté un chalet dans   *They bought a chalet in the*
> les Alpes.   *Alps.*

(*b*)   The imperfect, if you wish to express the fact that an action occurred regularly, was in progress when another one began, or happened every time another took place:

> Il écoutait la radio tous   *He used to listen to the radio*
> les matins à sept heures.   *every morning at seven.*
> Tu dormais quand je suis   *You were asleep (lit.: sleeping)*
> arrivé.   *when I arrived.*

If you need to express actions which happened *before* those indicated by either the perfect or the imperfect, you need a new tense which, in English, is formed with the imperfect of 'to have' and the relevant past participle:

> Suddenly, she stopped; she *had forgotten* her key!
> When the child arrived in the shop, he *had lost* the list.

It is called the *pluperfect*. A similar tense also exists in French. There are, however, significant differences between the two.

Work it out

Study the following sentences carefully, then state the way the pluperfect tense functions in French:

1   Ce jour-là nous étions partis   *That day we had left early and*
    de bonne heure et nous étions   *come back home very late.*
    rentrés à la maison très tard.

2   J'ai retrouvé ta montre: elle   *I have found your watch*
    était tombée derrière le piano.   *(again): it had fallen behind*
    the piano.

3   Ils l'ont trouvée là: elle avait   *They found her there: she had*
    glissé sur les rochers et elle   *slipped on the rocks and*
    s'était blessée.   *(she had) hurt herself.*

4   Ce matin, nous avons fini la   *This morning, we finished the*
    discussion que nous avions   *discussion (which) we had*
    commencée hier.   *begun yesterday.*

5 Quand elle est entrée, ils avaient déjà fait leurs valises.	*When she went in, they had already packed their cases.*

Conclusions

A The pluperfect tense is used to indicate an action which was over before the one expressed by the perfect — or the imperfect — took place.

B It is a compound tense (auxiliary + past participle) in which the imperfect of 'avoir' or 'être' (as appropriate) is used as the auxiliary.

C The normal rules of agreement of the past participle stated in Chapter 13 apply:

1 After 'être', past participles agree like adjectives. Sentences 1, 2 and 3 (reflexive verb).

2 After 'avoir' the past participle agrees *only* if the answer to the question 'qui/quoi?' (who/what?), formulated after the past participle, occurs before it. Sentences 3 and 5: no agreement; sentence 4: agreement.

Ah, si j'avais su!
Oh, if (only) I had known!

Exercise 28(iii)
Translate into English:

1 Je suis allé à l'aéroport à six heures. Elle était arrivée à cinq heures et quart. 2 Toutes les fois qu'il m'invitait, il avait oublié son portefeuille. 3 Quand elle a voulu lire le journal il avait disparu! 4 Il nous a raconté qu'il avait habité en Afrique. 5 Le client a dit qu'il n'avait pas utilisé l'ascenseur. 6 Nous avons protesté parce que le plombier avait mal fait son travail.

Exercise 28(iv)
Translate into French:

1 When he looked in his pocket, the wallet had disappeared. 2 I went out alone; my wife had decided to stay at home. 3 She was very red: she had stayed in the (= au) sun all day. 4 We had thought (that) he would like his birthday present! 5 Ah, if only I had waited a moment! 6 She said (that) he had slipped on the wet floor!

How to translate 'only'

The word 'only' can be expressed in French in two distinct ways:

(*a*) as 'ne . . . que', placed on either side of the verb group:

Cet enfant n'a que dix ans. *This child is only ten (years old).*

Je ne vais prendre qu'un apéritif. *I am going to have only one aperitif.*

(*b*) As 'seulement' (adverb). This word will normally be placed according to the rules governing the position of adverbs (chapter 19), but it can also be positioned at the end of the sentence.

Elle vient seulement le vendredi. *She only comes on Fridays.*

Nous les avons entendus une fois seulement. *We only heard them once.*

Exercise 28(v)
Translate into English:

1 Elle avait trois ans seulement quand ses parents sont partis.   **2** Le repas ne coûte que quarante francs.   **3** Le docteur ne viendra qu'à six heures.   **4** J'ai seulement demandé si le directeur était là!   **5** Nous n'avons rencontré qu'un touriste anglais.   **6** Vous ne partirez qu'après le dîner.

How to express duration

In French, duration can be expressed by the following:

(*a*) 'pendant' ('for' or 'during'), to indicate a time-span with no fixed starting point:

Il a dormi pendant trois jours. *He slept for three days.*

Tu resteras avec nous pendant les vacances. *You will stay with us during the holiday.*

(*b*) 'pour' ('for'), to express anticipated duration:

Nous allons à Paris pour trois semaines. *We are going to Paris for three weeks.*

(*c*) 'il y a . . . que' ('for' or 'ago'), for an event which started in the past, and the effects of which have endured to the present:

> Il y a trois ans que je ne l'ai *I haven't seen him for three*
>   pas vu. *years.*

(*d*) 'depuis' ('for/since'), for an action which began in the past, and the duration or starting point of which is known. It is used with the present:

> J'habite en Angleterre depuis *I have been living in England*
>   des années. *for years.*
> Ils sont en Italie depuis le *They have been in Italy since*
>   trois octobre. *3rd October.*

Note: 'il y a', when used with a past tense (i.e. perfect), can be translated by 'ago'.

> Je leur ai parlé il y a quinze *I talked to them a fortnight*
>   jours. *(= fifteen days) ago.*

Exercise 28(vi)
Translate into French:

1 The children are going to my parents' for the weekend. **2** During the winter, we have a great deal of snow. **3** We have been walking since dawn. **4** His wife came to see me three weeks ago. **5** We would like the house for a month this summer. **6** Stay in bed for a day or two and you will feel better.

Have a try

—Chéri, tu te rappelles les Smith?

—Qui?

—Les Smith que nous avons rencontrés il y a quatre ou cinq ans dans un hôtel au bord de la mer!

—Non, je ne me souviens pas!

—Mais si, rappelle-toi! Lui était docteur à Brighton et elle était directrice d'école!

—Ah oui, ça me revient . . . Et alors?

—Eh bien, ils nous ont envoyé une carte postale.

—De Brighton?

—Mais non! . . . Ils sont allés en vacances en Allemagne et ils

viennent pour quelques jours en France. Ils se demandent s'ils
pourraient passer nous voir.

—Ah oui?

—Oui; nous leur avions donné notre adresse et tu leur avais dit: "Si
vous passez près de chez nous, venez nous voir".

—Moi, j'avais dit ça?

—Mais oui, chéri. Tu as oublié? C'étaient des gens absolument
charmants!

—Oui, c'est vrai . . . Ils étaient très sympathiques et nous avions bien
ri avec eux . . . Et quand passeront-ils dans la région?

—Euh . . . Ce soir.

—Ce soir? Mais nous ne pouvons pas les recevoir ce soir! J'ai une
réunion de travail organisée depuis trois semaines . . . Je suis
obligé d'y aller! . . . .

—Pas de problème. Pendant que tu seras à la réunion, je leur offrirai
l'apéritif et quand tu rentreras nous irons au restaurant! Il y a des
mois que tu me dis que nous irons manger au restaurant . . . Je
pourrai mettre ma nouvelle robe!

—Oui, bien sûr, avec toi c'est toujours la même chose! Toutes les
occasions sont bonnes pour sortir et dépenser de l'argent!

Tu me coûtes les yeux de la tête!
You cost me a fortune!
(lit.: . . . the eyes of the head!)

Cette fois-ci, c'est bien fini!
This time, it's well and truly over!

Key to the exercises

Chapter 1

Exercise 1(i)
1 f, 2 f, 3 m, 4 f, 5 m, 6 f, 7 m, 8 f, 9 f, 10 f.

Exercise 1(ii)
1 la, 2 la, 3 le, 4 la, 5 le, 6 la, 7 la, 8 la, 9 le, 10 la.

Exercise 1(iii)
1 les tulipes, 2 les pins, 3 les fraises, 4 les éléments, 5 les palmiers, 6 les actions, 7 les chênes, 8 les moments.

Chapter 2

Exercise 2(i)
1 The bag is black. 2 The house is small. 3 The door is closed. 4 The boys are pleased. 5 The flowers are pretty. 6 The girls are tall. 7 The black cat is tired. 8 The small café is closed. 9 The big red car is old. 10 The black dresses are dirty.

Exercise 2(ii)
1 grande, 2 petites, 3 vieille, contente, 4 verts, fermés, 5 jolie, petit, noir, 6 nouvelles, belles, 7 noirs, fatigués, 8 jeune, malade, 9 grands, forts, 10 rouges, jolies, grandes.

Exercise 2(iii)
1 un, 2 la, 3 une, 4 le, 5 la, 6 un, 7 des, 8 les, 9 des, 10 les.

Have a try
The little girls are sad: the black cat is ill. The man is young and he is strong. The lady is in the house. She is pleased. The night is black and the boy is tired. The green car is dirty. The roses and the tulips are in the vase. They are pretty. The door is closed. The green apples are in the bag.

Chapter 3

Exercise 3(i)
1 The old lady is behind the bar. 2 The chair is against the wall. 3 The menu is outside the restaurant. 4 The little girl is behind the big red car. 5 The customers are in the green room. 6 The aperitifs are on the table in the café. 7 The pretty yellow flowers are in the big blue vase. 8 The black cat is in front of the door. 9 The empty bottles are under the table in a bag. 10 The house is between the café and the cinema.

Exercise 3(ii)
1 Le client est devant le bar. 2 La pomme est sur la table derrière la bouteille. 3 La petite fille et la vieille dame sont dans la chambre. 4 Nous sommes dans un petit restaurant entre le café et le cinéma. 5 Elle a une belle petite maison derrière la gare.

Exercise 3(iii)
1 Elles sont dans le vase. 2 Il est sous la table. 3 Il est devant la bouteille. 4 Elle est entre le verre et

le livre. 5 Il est derrière la
bouteille. 6 Ils sont sur la table.

Have a try

Chers amis,
Nous sommes dans un petit hôtel
entre la gare et le cinéma. Les
chambres sont petites mais elles sont
jolies. Les menus sont bons. Le
garçon est un ami. L'hôtel est
presque vide. Il a un jardin avec des
arbres et des fleurs. Nous sommes
fatigués mais les enfants sont
contents.
A bientôt.
Jean et Marie.

Chapter 4

Exercise 4(i)

1 Est-ce que la dame est fatiguée?
2 Est-ce que vous avez un garçon?
3 Est-ce que les clients sont
contents? 4 Est-ce que la porte est
fermée? 5 Est-ce que le potage est
chaud? 6 Est-ce que les fleurs sont
dans le vase?

Exercise 4(ii)

1 Are the boys sad? No, they are
pleased. 2 Is the soup good? Yes, it
is good but it is cold. 3 Do you
have a menu, waiter? Yes, it is on the
table outside the door. 4 Are they
rich? No, they are poor but they are
happy. 5 Do you have the bag?
No, it is in the bedroom behind the
door. 6 Is the policeman outside
the station? No, he is in the small
café. 7 Where is the passport? It is
in the blue bag. Is the bag open? No,
it is closed. 8 Is the manager in the
restaurant? No, he is in the
bedroom. Is he ill? No, he is tired.

Exercise 4(iii)

1 Elle a une petite voiture noire dans

le garage. 2 Le vieux monsieur a
une fille dans le village. 3 J'ai un
sac vert dans la chambre. 4 La
maison a un grand jardin. 5 Les
filles ont des robes rouges.

Exercise 4(iv)

1 Est-ce qu'il y a des magasins dans
le village? 2 Est-ce qu'il y a un
garage derrière l'hôtel? 3 Il y a une
pauvre femme devant la porte. 4 Il
y a des clients dans le café. 5 Est-ce
qu'il y a un homme dans la voiture?
Non, mais il y a une jeune femme.

Have a try

—Hello! Is the hotel closed?
—No sir, it is open. —Do you have
a room? —Yes, of course. —Is it
big? —No, it is small but it is very
pretty. —Is there a restaurant in the
hotel? —No sir, but there is a little
inn behind the station. —Are the
menus expensive? —Yes, but the
meals are very good. Do you have
any suitcases? —Yes. —Where are
they? —In the car, outside the
hotel... Is there a bar in the hotel?
—Yes, but it is closed.

Chapter 5

Exercise 5(i)

1 à l', 2 au, 3 au, 4 aux, 5 aux,
6 à l', 7 à la, 8 à l'.

Exercise 5(ii)

1 The boy is going to the market. He
has a big bag. 2 The little girl is in
bed. She is tired. 3 The tourists are
at the door, but it is closed. 4 We
are going shopping with the car.
5 Are you going to the hotel?
Impossible, it is full. 6 The
manager is going to the workshop.
He is furious. 7 Are you going to
school? No, I am ill. 8 Are the

children at the cinema? No, they are at home.

Exercise 5(iii)

1 Oui, nous allons rester à la maison. 2 Oui, ils vont aller au restaurant. 3 Oui, je vais visiter l'église. 4 Oui, elles vont entrer dans le magasin. 5 Oui, tu vas aller à la gare. 6 Oui, il va arriver à l'hôtel. 7 Oui, elle va manger la pomme. 8 Oui, vous allez acheter des fleurs.

Have a try

Je vais aller au village. Il y a un marché et je vais acheter des fruits. Est-ce que vous allez visiter l'église et le château, ou rester à la maison pour regarder la télévision ou écouter la radio? Le repas est sur la table. Il y a des pommes dans le sac jaune derrière la porte. L'autobus va arriver dans un moment... A plus tard!

Chapter 6

Exercise 6(i)

1 The tourists have just arrived in front of the castle. They are in the coach. 2 We have just watched a beautiful film on the television. 3 The manager has just telephoned. The taxi is about to arrive. 4 Have you just visited the church? No, we have just been looking at the sea. 5 I have just eaten the dessert. I am going to order a coffee. 6 The young boy has just bought a watch. It is beautiful but it is very dear.

Exercise 6(ii)

1 Le car vient d'arriver devant la gare. 2 Je viens de commander un apéritif au bar. 3 Elle vient d'acheter une valise neuve dans le

magasin. 4 Vous venez de parler au directeur. 5 Nous venons de manger un repas froid. 6 Un homme vient d'entrer dans la banque avec un grand sac noir.

Exercise 6(iii)

1 As-tu une belle maison? 2 Est-il content? 3 A-t-elle une jolie montre? 4 Ai-je un bon livre dans la voiture? 5 Les petites filles sont-elles sur la route? 6 La jeune dame va-t-elle téléphoner? 7 L'hôtel a-t-il un restaurant? 8 Les magasins sont-ils vides? 9 Le chauffeur est-il dans la banque? 10 Le car va-t-il arriver?

Exercise 6(iv)

1 Le directeur de la banque vient d'entrer dans le restaurant. 2 Le chauffeur du car va fermer la porte. 3 La valise de la dame est vide. 4 Le père des enfants va commander le dessert. 5 Le repas des clients va être froid. 6 Le fils de l'agent (de police) vient de parler au petit garçon.

Have a try

—Have you just arrived? —Yes, we have just got out of the car! —Are you going to stay (a) long (time)? —No, just a (= one) night. Are there any problems? —No, that's alright (= OK)! Do you have a passport? —Yes, there you are. —Thank you! Do you have (any) children? —Yes, a boy and a girl. —Are they old (= big)? —No, they are very young. —Do you have any animals? —No. —Good, that's alright... You are going to put the caravan behind the trees between the blue tent and the yellow tent. Alright? —Alright!

Chapter 7

Exercise 7(i)
1 visitez, 2 prépare, 3 regardent,
4 appelons,   5 jette,   6 casses,
7 demande, 8 visitent.

Exercise 7(ii)
1 We are buying (some) books in the
shop. 2 The little girl is playing in
the garden. 3 The guests are danc-
ing on the terrace. 4 Are you
listening to the new record? 5 I am
refusing the neighbours' invitation.
6 You are switching the bedroom
light on. 7 The manager is clos-
ing the bar. 8 The waiter is
asking for the tip.

Exercise 7(iii)
1 Où sont les fleurs? Là, dans le
vase. 2 Le taxi est ici et l'autobus est
là-bas devant la gare. 3 Où est la
carte? Là, sur la table, sous le sac!
4 Allô! Est-ce que Robert est là?
Oui, il vient d'arriver. 5 Est-ce
que vous êtes là, Madame? Oui, je
suis dans la cuisine.   6 Il va
venir ici et je vais aller là-bas.

Have a try
Je viens d'arriver à la gare avec mon
père. Nous attendons le train de
Paris. Je regarde la montre de mon
père. Le train va arriver bientôt.
Voilà le train et voilà monsieur
Dupont. Il est grand et élégant. Il
porte une grosse valise noire. Il
vient vers mon père. — Bonjour
Robert! — Bonjour Jean. Ca va?
— Oui, mais je suis très fatigué. Est-
ce qu'il y a un porteur dans la gare?
— Non, mais je vais porter ta
valise . . . La voiture est juste
devant la gare; nous allons aller à la
maison. Marie vient de préparer un
repas délicieux. — Excellent. Où est
la sortie? — Là-bas!

Chapter 8

Exercise 8(i)
1 pneus.   2 châteaux.   3 yeux.
4 chapeaux. 5 chevaux. 6 bals.
7 oiseaux. 8 feux

Exercise 8(ii)
1 La serveuse espagnole est avec les
clients anglais. 2 Il y a une histoire
intéressante dans les journaux ce
matin. 3 Il va acheter les chapeaux
noirs dans le petit magasin. 4 Elle
va manger de la crème fraîche. 5 Le
vieil   homme   est   un   touriste
américain. 6 Ma propre voiture est
très sale.

Exercise 8(iii)
1 The   inspector   has   a   false
moustache. 2 The manager has a
very harsh voice. 3 There is (some)
soft music on the radio. 4 Your
shirt is clean but my own suit is
dirty. 5 The young lady is an
Italian singer.   6 I have an
astonishing story but you are in a
hurry. 7 They have a new house in
the old town. 8 We are going to
buy a small Japanese motorbike.

Have a try
The weather forecast is excellent.
The sea and the sky are blue. We are
going to have a wonderful carnival.
The shops are closed and the streets
are already full of people: French,
but also English, Italian, Spanish
and even Japanese! There are also
policemen and inspectors, but the
atmosphere is excellent. The costumes are very beautiful. The children are happy. They have red, blue
and green balloons and adorable hats.
Ah, there is a lost little boy . . . No,
here is the mother. And there is the
queen of the carnival. She is beautiful and very elegant . . . This even-

ing, rich and poor people are going to dance, sing and eat together and they are going to light fires on the beach . . . I adore the carnival.

Chapter 9

Exercise 9(i)
1 Robert's watch fell into the water. 2 The travellers climbed onto the train. 3 The waitress brought the tray. 4 Mr Dupont asked for the bill. 5 We left the house during the night. 6 Have you closed the suitcases? 7 I bought some peaches in the market. 8 The friends ordered an aperitif. 9 The children left yesterday morning. 10 We spent a wonderful evening.

Exercise 9(ii)
1 J'ai regardé le film. 2 Nous avons mangé au restaurant. 3 Ils ont eu un petit accident. 4 Le train est arrivé à la gare. 5 Les voyageurs sont descendus du car. 6 Les touristes ont admiré le tableau.

Exercise 9(iii)
1 La femme a fermé la porte. 2 Le client a parlé au directeur. 3 Elle est descendue dans la salle à manger et elle a commandé le vin. 4 Le chat est monté sur la chaise et a mangé le poulet. 5 La valise est tombée sur la tête du voyageur. 6 Nous sommes arrivés devant le magasin avant le directeur.

Have a try
Quand nous sommes arrivés à la villa, nous avons trouvé la porte fermée. J'ai téléphoné au propriétaire et nous avons attendu une heure dans la voiture, sous le soleil. Enfin, le propriétaire est arrivé

avec la clé. Il a ouvert la porte et il a dit: 'Voilà! Bonnes vacances!' Puis il est parti. Nous avons mis les valises dans les chambres et j'ai demandé: 'Est-ce que vous désirez manger ou aller à la plage?' Les enfants ont crié: 'A la plage!' J'ai mis les serviettes et les maillots de bain dans un sac et nous sommes allés vers la mer. Nous avons marché longtemps. Enfin nous sommes arrivés sur la plage. Les enfants ont demandé: 'Où sont les gens? La plage est vide. Ah! Il y a un écriteau là-bas.' Nous sommes allés vers l'écriteau et nous avons lu: 'Attention pollution. Défense de nager.'

Chapter 10

Exercise 10(i)
1 Nous aimons cette maison. 2 Je déteste cette robe, mais j'aime ce pull-over. 3 Cette petite fille est adorable. 4 Il va manger cette viande! 5 Ce tableau est formidable, mais cette sculpture est abominable. 6 Ces enfants-ci sont très intelligents. 7 Cette énorme pierre va tomber sur la route. 8 Est-ce que vous avez regardé ce film? 9 Cette chambre-ci est trop chère. 10 Ces chiens sont toujours dans le jardin.

Exercise 10(ii)
1 Le vieux monsieur ne monte pas dans le taxi. 2 La serveuse n'est pas dans la salle à manger. 3 Nous n'allons pas visiter la cathédrale. 4 Est-ce que les magasins ne vont pas fermer demain? 5 Ils n'ont pas commandé le champagne. 6 Les voyageurs ne sont pas restés dans le car. 7 Le garçon n'a-t-il

pas apporté l'apéritif? 8 Tu ne viens pas de téléphoner au docteur?

Exercise 10(iii)

1 Nous ne mangeons pas là! 2 Est-ce que les touristes ne sont pas fatigués? 3 Il ne va pas rester dans le magasin. 4 Les repas ne sont pas très bons dans ce restaurant. 5 Les visiteurs ne sont pas arrivés. 6 Je n'ai pas acheté ce pull-over noir. 7 Les enfants ne sont pas dans la maison. 8 Elle ne va pas aller dans cet hôtel.

Have a try

—Have you been here long? —Since this morning. —Did you see the accident? —Yes, did you? —No, I have just arrived. —This is how the accident happened: at the crossroads, the young man with the motorcycle came out of the small road; he did not see the stop sign and he crossed the main road. The driver of the car braked, but he did not avoid the collision. The young man is injured and the motorcycle and the car are badly damaged! I have telephoned the ambulance and the police . . . Ah, here comes the ambulance; but the police are not here yet! —Are you going to wait? —Of course, I am the only witness!

Chapter 11

Exercise 11(i)

1 I called my sister on the phone. 2 You are going to break my bike! 3 Robert is happy; his brother and sister arrived yesterday. 4 I have just seen your children on the beach. 5 She bought her jumper in my new shop. 6 I hate your (girl)friend; her ideas are ridiculous.

Exercise 11(ii)

1 Je vais aller dans ma chambre. 2 Est-ce que vous avez vu sa nouvelle maison? 3 Elle regarde sa fille. 4 Le garçon apporte notre vin. 5 Où sont vos sacs, mes amis? 6 J'ai mis mon pull-over dans sa valise. 7 Ma sœur et son mari sont là-bas! 8 La fille a cassé mon beau vase avec sa balle.

Exercise 11(iii)

1 She is going to be twenty-one. 2 Waiter, three beers and two lemonades please! 3 Your father was fifty-seven yesterday. 4 We watched twelve films in one week. 5 This horse came ninth in the third race. 6 One second, please!

Exercise 11(iv)

1 Je viens d'acheter douze belles pommes dans ce petit magasin. 2 Ce vieux monsieur a cent ans demain. 3 Il y a soixante-quinze tableaux dans ce château. 4 Il a mangé onze biscuits ce matin. 5 Elle a trente-sept disques dans sa chambre. 6 Je vais commander six croissants pour le petit déjeuner.

Have a try

—Vite, le taxi est devant la porte! Nous allons être en retard à l'aéroport! —Non, nous avons le temps . . . Est-ce que les valises sont prêtes? —Oui, elles sont en bas . . . Est-ce que tu as les passeports? —Ils sont sur la table, dans la cuisine, mais j'ai perdu les billets . . . Où sont-ils? —Reste calme! Ils sont dans mon sac à main! N'oublie pas l'enveloppe avec l'argent! —Elle est dans ma poche . . . C'est curieux! . . . Je viens de poser ma montre là . . . Où est-elle? —Regarde, elle est là. Elle est tombée sous le lit! —Vite, ou nous allons manquer l'avion . . . Et alors, adieu notre weekend à Paris!

Chapter 12

Exercise 12(i)

1 réfléchis, 2 investit, 3 accomplissent, 4 garantissez, 5 nourris, 6 réussissent, 7 saisit, 8 remplissons.

Exercise 12(ii)

1 I am thinking about your proposal. 2 She invests her money with care. 3 Today, doctors accomplish miracles. 4 Do you guarantee the repair? 5 Do you feed the neighbour's cat? 6 They manage to finish the work on time. 7 The small boy catches the beautiful red balloon. 8 We fill up the tank.

Exercise 12(iii)

1 descends, attends, 2 sort, prend, 3 mourons, 4 rit, ouvre, 5 recevez, 6 croyons, entendons.

Exercise 12(iv)

1 I think I understand his attitude. 2 Do you take the car to go to the office? 3 We do not believe your story. 4 We are going to find a café: the children are dying of thirst. 5 Did you open my letter? 6 He took the precaution of telephoning before leaving.

Have a try

— Mum, where are you? — I'm here in the kitchen, I'm preparing dinner. — Is it ready? — It is going to be ready in a little while. Are you in a hurry? — Yes, I think I am going to go to the pictures with John and Robert. — Again? But you already went out last night! What about your work? Is it finished? — No, I'm going to finish it before I go out.

— No, my boy! This evening, you are going to stay at home. You are going to come and eat and afterwards you are going to go up to your room to work! — Oh, mum! . . . It's a fantastic film, and it's the last night! — I said no! You go out too much; and you do not work at school! Your father is not pleased!   — Mum, please . . . — No! . . . I speak in your interest. Your attitude is not good. You are intelligent,   but   you   are lazy . . . Does the neighbours' son go to the cinema three or four times in the week? No! he stays at home and (he) works. — He is stupid! — Not at all! He is first in French, in English, in History. . You're always last!   — You are horrible!   — Too bad! It's for your own good! — I am going to ask dad about the cinema!

Chapter 13

Exercise 13(i)

1 Je l'ai mangé.   2 Tu vas la fermer.   3 Nous venons de le voir. 4 Nous ne l'avons pas accepté. 5 Il l'achète?   6 Elle les voit?

Exercise 13(ii)

1 Have you seen Robert? Yes, I saw him yesterday morning. 2 Are you going to visit the exhibition? No, I have just visited it. 3 Do you like television? Yes, I watch it often. 4 You are going to put your cases here. The customs officer is going to check them. 5 Did the manager listen to you? No, he dismissed me! 6 The waiter is going to serve you in a minute. 7 Are you calling us? No, we are not calling you! 8 Here are the dishes; the waitress is

bringing them.
Exercise 13(iii)
1 Nous avons acheté un beau bifteck et votre chien l'a mangé. 2 Voilà le chauffeur de taxi; je vais le payer. 3 Est-ce que vous avez la note? Non, je ne l'ai pas. 4 Est-ce que vous allez les inviter? Non, ils me détestent. 5 Je t'écoute mon garçon. 6 Elle vient de le trouver dans le garage.
Exercise 13(iv)
1 vu, 2 appelés, 3 invitée, 4 remerciées, 5 arrêtés, 6 écoutée.

Have a try
Nous avons de charmants voisins. Ils travaillent dans une banque. La femme est belle, jeune et élégante. Le mari est très amical et il est excellent cuisinier. Hier soir, ils nous ont invités pour le dîner. Nous sommes arrivés à la tombée de la nuit. La femme a ouvert la porte:
— Je suis désolée, mon mari est dans la cuisine, il prépare le repas. Il va nous rejoindre dans une minute. Est-ce que vous allez prendre un apéritif? — Oui, s'il vous plaît. — Nous avons du whisky, du sherry et de la bière. — Je vais prendre une bière. — Et vous, Anne? — Un petit sherry, s'il vous plaît... — Voilà! Une bière pour vous Jean, et un sherry pour vous Anne... Ah, voici mon mari! Est-ce que tu as fini dans la cuisine chéri? — Oui, tout est prêt, mais je vais boire un petit whisky.

Après l'apéritif, nous sommes allés dans la salle à manger et nous avons mangé un merveilleux repas. Nous avons parlé des enfants, de la politique, de la situation économique, de la mode, de la musique, dans une atmosphère excellente et très décontractée. Nous sommes rentrés très tard à la maison.

Chapter 14

Exercise 14(i)
1 Do you like these dresses? No, I prefer those. 2 We have two menus today: that one is dear, but this one is cheap. 3 I am going to reserve four seats. These? No, those. 4 This restaurant is full; we are going to that one! 5 The theatre is not in this street, it is in that one! 6 Denise and Christine have eaten my chocolate! Oh, those two...!
Exercise 14(ii)
1 celle-là, 2 celui-là, 3 ceux-ci, ceux-là, 4 celle-ci, celle-là, 5 celle-là, 6 celui-ci, celui-là.
Exercise 14(iii)
1 You are lucky: I have just bought some petrol. 2 Do your parents have any luggage? 3 We bought chocolate and mineral water at the supermarket. 4 You have energy but you have no class. 5 Do you have much work this week? 6 She does not have children but she has a crowd of friends.
Exercise 14(iv)
1 Est-ce que vous avez eu de la chance aux courses? 2 Je suis désolé(e), je n'ai pas de monnaie. 3 Elle a du courage mais elle n'a pas d'expérience. 4 Nous venons de commander du fromage et des fruits. 5 Nous allons avoir de l'organisation dans ce bureau! 6 Garçon, est-ce que vous pouvez apporter du café et des croissants s'il vous plaît? Désolé monsieur, nous n'avons pas de croissants, mais je vais vous apporter du café dans une minute.

Have a try

— Bonjour! — Bonjour. Est-ce que vous avez des salades s'il vous plaît? — Oui, bien sûr! Elles viennent juste d'arriver et elles sont belles. Est-ce que vous voulez celle-ci ou celle-là? — Celle-là s'il vous plaît. — Une seconde. Je vais la mettre dans une poche en papier. — Merci... Je vais prendre un kilo de poires. — Celles-ci? — Non, elles ne sont pas très mûres! Je préfère celles-là. — Voilà! Un kilo de poires. — Merci. — C'est tout? — Non, je crois que j'ai oublié quelque chose... Ah oui, un kilo de tomates! — Mûres? — Non, pas trop. — Ça va? — Oui, parfait. Combien? — Quinze francs vingt-cinq. — Voilà. Au revoir...

Chapter 15

Exercise 15(i)

1 Haven't you found anything under the bed? 2 We didn't meet anybody in the street. 3 They are going to say nothing to their parents. 4 I have no more money to pay (for) the hotel. 5 I'm sorry but Mr Dubois no longer lives here. 6 Your secretary is never late. 7 Please do not touch. 8 Please do not feed the animals (lit.: request to give nothing to the animals).

Exercise 15(ii)

1 je n'ai vu personne, 2 ils n'ont rien mangé, 3 elle ne travaille plus, 4 ils ne viennent jamais le voir, 5 je ne vais pas répondre.

Exercise 15(iii)

1 en, au, 2 en, aux, 3 au, en, 4 de, à, 5 en, 6 d', de, 7 du, 8 de, à.

Exercise 15(iv)

1 The Dubois family have a house in Caen, in Normandy. 2 We are going to go on holiday to Greece and Italy this summer. 3 My parents are arriving from the Netherlands this evening, by plane. 4 I am going to go and spend a week in Provence. 5 Do you come from Spain? Yes, from Madrid. 6 The manager has organised an exhibition in Japan. 7 Are you going to France for the holidays? No, we are staying here. We have no money left!

Have a try

"Ladies and Gentlemen,
Welcome aboard this ferry. You can now put your handbrake on, get out of your vehicle and lock the doors. Do not leave valuables, handbags, wallets, cameras etc, inside. You are going to follow the yellow arrows to go up to the passenger deck, where you are going to find comfortable seats, an excellent cafeteria and a restaurant. There is also a television lounge for children. The film begins in thirty minutes. On the passenger deck there is a duty-free shop where you are going to find drinks, cigarettes, cigars and gifts at attractive prices. The journey is going to last approximately two hours.

It is forbidden to return to the car deck before the end of the crossing. Thank you."

Chapter 16

Exercise 16(i)

1 ayez, 2 sois, 3 réfléchissons, 4 attendez, partez, 5 sors, reviens, 6 prenez, 7 perdons, soyons, 8 finis, rentre.

Exercise 16(ii)

1 Stop the car over there, under the trees. 2 Quick, telephone the

doctor. 3 Listen to this song. It's fantastic. 4 Do not come tonight, we are going out with (some) friends. 5 Let's get down, the taxi has arrived. 6 Place in a saucepan and cook on a low light. 7 Look for the key and close the door. 8 If the television does not work properly, switch it off!

Exercise 16(iii)

1 Paul, ne mange pas cette pêche, garde-la pour ta sœur. 2 Allons demander une chambre. 3 Ne criez pas, votre père n'est pas sourd! 4 Ecoutez le bulletin météo: il y a des orages en Bretagne. 5 N'écoutez pas ce garçon; il est bête. 6 Rincer avec soin et sécher à plat. Ne pas tordre. 7 Ne pas laver à la main.

Have a try

— Peter, where are you? — I am here, darling. I'm coming! — Good! Carry those bags please. They are very heavy. — Yes, darling... — Let's cross the street... No, wait, the lights are red! Ah, now they are green! Let's go!... Well then, what are you waiting for? You are dreaming again!... You never listen to me! — Sorry darling. — It doesn't matter... I'm used to it!... I am going to go into that shop. There are some splendid dresses in there! Wait for me here. — Alright! —... Peter! Come here. Look! I have found a lovely dress... and cheap! Do you like it? — Yes, it's pretty! — Well then, I'm going to buy it... Blast! I've left my purse at home, in my old handbag. Do you have any money? — Yes, I think so... Wait, I'm going to pay with my credit card. — Good idea!... There you are... Carry the dress with the rest... No, not in the big bag, it's going to be all crumpled! — Listen, don't shout, I am not deaf! — I'm not sure (about that)!

Chapter 17

Exercise 17(i)

1 Have you sent the letter to Michael? Yes, I sent it to him this morning. 2 The Duponts did not leave us the key. I asked them for it three times. 3 My ball! You are going to give it (back) to me or I'll call my father! 4 Yes, we have your ladder; just a second, we are going to give it back to you. 5 We would like breakfast. Are you going to bring it up to us? 6 Here are John's books! Good, you are going to give them to me and I'm going to send them to him. 7 Do you have my suitcase? No, I don't have it. You did not lend it to me.

Exercise 17(ii)

1 Est-ce que ma valise est dans la chambre? Non, madame; je vous l'ai descendue. 2 Si cette histoire est très triste, ne me la racontez pas. 3 Le repas est prêt. Je vais vous l'apporter. 4 Voici la note, donnez-la lui. 5 C'est un secret; ne le leur répétez pas! 6 Est-ce que mon journal est arrivé? Apportez-le moi sur le balcon. 7 Nous avons les résultats; vous nous les avez envoyés le mois dernier. 8 Je désire parler au directeur! Je suis désolé vous ne pouvez pas lui parler. Il n'est pas là.

Exercise 17(iii)

1 eux, 2 vous, 3 toi, 4 moi, 5 lui, 6 elle, 7 nous, 8 toi.

Have a try

— Bonsoir Monsieur Dame... Vos passeports s'il vous plaît...

Merci . . . Est-ce que vous rentrez de vacances? —Oui. —Quels pays avez-vous visités? —Nous sommes restés en France tout le temps. —Vous n'êtes pas allés en Espagne? —Non! —Est-ce que vous avez lu ce document? —Oui! —Est-ce que vous avez quelque chose à déclarer? —Non, juste les quantités normales de cigarettes, de vin et d'alcool. —Est-ce que vous avez acheté des cadeaux? —Oui, deux ou trois disques, un livre de cuisine, une douzaine de verres . . . —Où sont ces choses? —Dans une valise, dans la malle de la voiture. —Descendez de la voiture s'il vous plaît et ouvrez la malle . . . Merci! —Je suis désolé, la malle n'est pas très propre . . . —Ouvrez cette valise s'il vous plaît! —Celle-là? —Non, pas celle-là, celle-ci. —D'accord . . . Voilà. —Tiens, tiens! Vous avez plusieurs bouteilles d'alcool espagnol dans cette valise, Monsieur . . . Je suis désolé mais vous allez venir avec moi; et demandez à votre femme de venir aussi . . .

Chapter 18

Exercise 18(i)

1 Here are the ruins of the castle, and there is the church, over there, behind the trees. 2 Ah, there you are at last! The director wishes to see you at once. 3 Here comes the storm. We are going to stay here a while. 4 Waiter, the bill please! There you are Madam! 5 Have you found my watch? Yes, here it is. 6 The visitors are going to arrive in a minute. Ah, there they are!

Exercise 18(ii)

1 Nous attendons l'autobus. . . Le voilà enfin! 2 Un kilo de pommes et un melon . . . Voilà Monsieur.

3 Est-ce que vous avez acheté le pain? Oui, le voici. 4 Voici le facteur. . . Il porte un colis. 5 Voici l'appareil-photo. Bon, nous allons prendre des photos. 6 Vous désirez me parler? Me voici.

(*Note*: in ordinary spoken French 'voilà' could be used in all the above examples.)

Exercise 18(iii)

1 toute, 2 tous, 3 toutes, 4 tout, 5 toute.

Exercise 18(iv)

1 Elle n'est pas très contente: Son bébé a pleuré toute la nuit. 2 Toute la famille arrive dans une heure. 3 L'orage a cassé tous les arbres. 4 Tout est fini entre nous. 5 Rien n'est prêt pour le pique-nique. 6 Nous avons vu les photographies du mariage. Elles sont toutes superbes. 7 Je pardonne tout mais je n'oublie rien. 8 Nous avons rencontré ses amis. Ils sont tous charmants.

Exercise 18(v)

1 j'y vais, 2 ils en ont parlé, 3 il n'en vient pas, 4 il n'y va pas, 5 elle en descend, 6 je ne vais pas en acheter.

Exercise 18(vi)

1 Ce problème n'est pas important! Nous n'y pensons pas! 2 Est-ce que vos parents vont à l'hôtel? Oui, ils y vont. 3 Ils ne sont pas dans la maison. J'en viens. 4 Est-ce que votre mari va au match ce week-end? Non il n'y va pas, il a trop de travail. 5 La situation est mauvaise. J'en ai parlé au directeur. 6 L'exposition est ouverte. Est-ce que vous y êtes allé? Non, je vais y aller cet après-midi.

Have a try

—Hello! —Hello! —Are you

waiting for the bus? —Yes . . . —
So am I. We are going to wait for it
together . . . It's late this morning!
—Is it often late? —Rarely! One or
two minutes sometimes. . . I catch it
every day of the week . . The driver is
a friend of mine. —Really? —Yes
he is! . . . Travelling is always a
problem when one doesn't have a
car. Do you have one? —Yes, but it
is at the garage for repairs. What
about you? —No! I am not rich
enough . . . Is that bus coming or
not? —There's a lot of traffic. Be
patient! —Be patient, be patient! I
have an important appointment in
twenty minutes! . . . It's a scandal! . . .
I'm going to write a letter to . . . Ah,
here it comes, at last! —Yes, but it's
full! There isn't a single space
available (on it). —That's awful!
And the next one is in an hour. I am
going to be late . . . Come with me!
We are going to take a taxi!

Chapter 19

Exercise 19(i)

1 simplement,　　2 agréablement,
3 calmement,　　4 prudemment,
5 absolument,　　6 récemment,
7 extraordinairement,　　8 furieuse-
ment,　9 terriblement.

Exercise 19(ii)

1 I simply ask you to accept my
apologies. 2 I hope you are going
to spend the evening pleasantly
with them. 3 We are going to
think calmly about this problem.
4 Let's proceed cautiously. There is
no light. 5 John is absolutely
furious. His trousers are torn.
6 They recently had a visit from my
uncle. 7 He is extraordinarily
dynamic for his age. 8 She is
knocking furiously at the door.

9 Our society is terribly violent.

Exercise 19(iii)

1 Je vais rentrer. Je commence à
avoir froid. 2 Il a peur d'être en
retard pour le dîner. 3 Nous avons
besoin de repos. Partons en
vacances. 4 Elle n'a pas honte de
ses opinions. 5 Votre mari a raison,
n'écoutez pas les voisins. 6 J'espère
que les enfants ne sont pas malades.
7 Il a de la chance. Il gagne
toujours. 8 Nous n'avons pas
l'habitude de conduire à droite.

Have a try

—Bonjour, jeune homme! Vous
allez loin? —A Bordeaux. Est-ce
que vous pouvez m'emmener avec
vous? —Vous avez de la chance. Je
vais en Espagne, mais je vais
traverser Bordeaux. Donnez-moi
votre sac et montez vite . . . La
circulation est terrible aujourd'hui.
—Oui . . . Merci beaucoup! —D'où
venez-vous? —De Paris. Je suis
parti ce matin très tôt . . . Qu'est-ce
que vous transportez dans votre
camion? —Des machines pour le
marché espagnol. —Vous traversez
la frontière régulièrement? —A peu
près une fois par semaine . . . Vous
êtes étudiant? —Oui. Je rentre chez
moi pour les vacances. —Vous
habitez à Bordeaux? —Pas
exactement; mes parents ont une
maison près de la ville. —Vous
faites souvent de l'auto-stop? —
Non, pas très souvent; à peu près une
fois par mois . . . Je ne suis pas assez
riche pour avoir ma propre voiture.
—Pauvre étudiant! Je suis désolé
pour vous! . . . Ecoutez, il est
presque midi. Je vais manger dans un
restaurant routier dans quelques
minutes. Vous avez faim? —Je ne

suis pas sûr, j'ai mal à la tête. —
C'est parce que vous avez faim!
Allez, venez, je vous invite. — Vous
êtes sûr? — Pas de problème. J'ai de
l'argent. Je ne suis pas étudiant! —
Merci beaucoup!

Chapter 20

Exercise 20(i)

1 étions, allions, 2 mangeais, re-
gardais, 3 arrivaient, refusait,
4 écoutiez, 5 travaillait, allait,
6 sortaient, rentraient, 7 offrais,
refusait.

Exercise 20(ii)

1 After dinner, he used to smoke a
cigar on the terrace. 2 When(ever)
his parents went to see him, he used
to take them out to the concert or the
theatre. 3 She was washing the
jumper when we came home.
4 Every week, his father gave him a
hundred francs. 5 If he arrived late,
he always invented an incredible
excuse. 6 When(ever) it rained too
hard, he did not go out. 7 While he
was cleaning the car she prepared
lunch.

Exercise 20(iii)

1 Chaque fois que je le rencontrais,
il me parlait. 2 Nous allions au
marché quand nous avons trouvé le
portefeuille. 3 Quand notre père
venait ici, il nous apportait des
cadeaux. 4 Il était grand et il
marchait vite. 5 Chaque matin la
serveuse apportait mon petit
déjeuner dans ma chambre.
6 Quand elle était fatiguée, elle
pleurait et appelait sa mère.

Have a try

—Today life is very complicated.
When I was young (small), things
were simple. — Is that true? — Of
course! We didn't have (any)

television. — Why? — Because it
did not exist! Cinema was rare and
the car was a luxury: few people had
one. — Did you take the bus to go to
school? Goodness gracious no! We
used to go to school on foot: four
kilometres in the morning and four
in the evening. We used to leave early
and come home late. — And when it
rained? — Well, we arrived wet.
—It was dreadful! — Not at all!
We were used to being outside summer and winter. Nowadays, to go a
hundred metres, people need their
car. — And did you stay at home on
Sundays? — No, we often went for a
walk in the forest and for a picnic, if
the weather was fine . . . Today you
have everything and you are
unhappy!

Chapter 21

Exercise 21(i)

1 Paris is bigger than Marseilles.
2 In France, mineral water is almost
as expensive as table wine.
3 Madame Dubois is going to wait a
minute; she is less in a hurry than I
am. 4 With his sports car he drives
like a madman. 5 I am not as rich
as you (are) but I often go to the
restaurant. 6 The storm is
(becoming) more and more violent
and we do not have an umbrella.
7 We go out less and less in the
evening, we prefer to stay at home.
8 The louder you shout the less the
children listen to you.

Exercise 21(ii)

1 Cette plage est plus tranquille que
celle-ci. 2 Plus je mange, plus j'ai
faim. 3 Les pêches sont plus
grosses que les abricots mais elles ne
sont pas aussi bonnes. 4 Il est
moins préoccupé que moi parce qu'il

est plus optimiste. 5 Il est fort comme un bœuf et il devient de plus en plus grand. 6 Paul est plus petit que son frère mais il court plus vite. 7 Vous n'êtes pas aussi heureux que ce matin. 8 Ces machines sont de plus en plus compliquées et de moins en moins fiables.

Exercise 21(iii)

1 The critics think that this film is the best of the season. 2 We climbed the highest mountain. 3 François was the best behaved child in the class. 4 We did not have the slightest problem during the journey. 5 This is the least interesting part of our visit. 6 The director is going to reward the secretary who works the best. 7 Yesterday the pound fell to its lowest level. 8 I am sure that this solution is the most acceptable.

Exercise 21(iv)

1 La partie la plus difficile du voyage est terminée. 2 Voici le plus grand leader politique de notre époque. 3 Je vais vous raconter l'histoire la plus amusante. 4 Il cherche toujours les meilleurs restaurants. 5 Acceptez mes vœux les plus sincères pour Noël. 6 C'est le week-end qui passe le plus vite. 7 Nous allons prendre le menu le plus cher: nous avons faim. 8 Le travail le plus dangereux est le mieux payé.

Have a try

— Come in Dupont. — Do you wish to talk to me, sir? — Yes, one second; I'm finishing this letter. . . There we are. . . Dupont, I have asked you to come because I am not pleased with you! — Why (sir)? — Listen, Dupont. . . I am no more stupid than you are. Your attitude to work is getting worse and worse. — But (sir). . . — No buts: you arrive late every morning, you leave before the other workers and you are absent more and more frequently. And your work is deplorable. Don't protest. You are very slovenly in your work. (You work like a pig.) — But, Sir, I have problems at home . . . — I am sorry for you, but that is not (a) sufficient reason to botch up the job. You are no longer reliable: Yesterday, I was forced to ask your colleague Lemercier to check all your work. This is your last chance. Next time, you're out!

Chapter 22

Exercise 22(i)

1 arriverons, 2 finirez, 3 irons, 4 achèteras, 5 seront, 6 verrai, 7 pourra, 8 viendra.

Exercise 22(ii)

1 Hallo Mary! We will arrive this evening at nine o'clock. 2 You will finish your work tomorrow morning before going out. 3 Next year we will go on holiday to France. 4 You'll buy a litre of wine and a kilo of tomatoes at the grocer's. 5 His friends will be pleased to see him again. 6 I will not see you before I go (= before my departure). 7 My father will never be able to pay for the repair(s). 8 She will come to fetch us at the station.

Exercise 22(iii)

1 prendrais, 2 désirerions, 3 pourriez, 4 voudrais, 5 aimerais, 6 devriez.

Have a try

— Are you (day-)dreaming? — Yes, I'm thinking of what I'll do when I am rich ... —Oh yes? What will you do? —Well, I'll travel. I'll go everywhere: Japan, China, Peru ... I will meet all sorts of interesting people ... What about you? —Oh, (personally) I hate travelling. When I am on a boat I'm sea-sick. In a plane I'm air-sick. I'm even ill in a car ... But I would like (= be happy) to have a big house. —Where? In Paris? —No! On the Côte d'Azur, by the seaside, with a huge garden. —But you hate working in the garden! —Yes, but I'd have a professional gardener, a cook and a dozen servants to do all the work! —And you'd eat caviar and drink champagne from morning till night, I suppose! —Why not? —Don't you think you are a little ambitious for a secretary? —And what about you, then? .. Listen, you'll carry on with your dream some other time; let's go and fetch our sandwiches.

Chapter 23

Exercise 23(i)
1 la nôtre, 2 la mienne, 3 les nôtres, 4 les tiennes, 5 le mien, 6 le leur, 7 les siennes, 8 les vôtres.

Exercise 23(ii)
1 Your steak was tender but mine was very tough (= hard). 2 Do you have your watch? I have lost mine. 3 This towel is mine; yours is over there on the rock. 4 If your car has broken down, take ours. 5 We are going to leave our luggage at the reception and we are going to take yours upstairs. 6 Do you want my sunglasses? No thank you, I have (got) mine. 7 I have my visa, but my colleague doesn't have his yet. 8 I gave them our address and they gave me theirs.

Exercise 23(iii)
1 We went to bed at midnight and we fell asleep at once. 2 They are going to hurt themselves on those rocks. 3 Did you apologize? 4 He is going to buy (himself) a small house in the country. 5 You'll get up at eight o'clock and you will come down to have your breakfast with us. 6 I've cut myself with the bread knife, but it's not serious. 7 They played in the garden all morning. 8 Next time, we will contact you directly. 9 I wonder if you have looked at yourself in the mirror.

Have a try
—Caroline, Robert! Vous êtes prêts? Rappelez-vous que nous allons manger chez les Dupont. Ils nous attendent dans une heure pour l'apéritif ... Caroline, tu t'es lavée? —Oui maman, je suis presque prête ... Où sont mes lunettes? —Sur la table de la cuisine avec les miennes. N'oublie pas de prendre un pull-over: il fait toujours très froid chez les Dupont ... Où est ton père? —Je suis dans la salle de bains, chérie! Je viens de me laver. Je suis tout mouillé et il n'y a pas de serviette ici. —Ne t'affole pas. Voilà la mienne! —Merci chérie ... Tu es prête? —Non! .. Je voulais avoir le temps de me préparer ce matin. Mais c'est toujours la même chose dans cette maison! Il y a toujours quelqu'un dans la salle de bains avant moi! Tu as fini? —Attends une minute! Je me rase ... Oh, je me suis coupé avec le rasoir! —C'est grave? —Non, pas vraiment ... J'ai fini. Je

m'excuse . . . Va te préparer maintenant, la salle de bains est libre!

Chapter 24

Exercise 24(i)
1 France produces six thousand two hundred and fifty million litres of wine; it's impressive.   2 This staircase has exactly three hundred and ninety-nine steps! Are you sure?   3 He is away (= absent) three quarters of the time.   4 Two thirds of the French population (= French people) go to the seaside for their holidays.   5 'Nineteen eighty-four' by George Orwell is a thrilling but frightening book.   6 In this hotel one customer out of two is English.

Exercise 24(ii)
1 En mil neuf cent quatre-vingt-quinze nous travaillerons trente heures par semaine.   2 La seconde guerre mondiale a commencé en mil neuf cent trente-neuf.   3 Cette tour mesure trois cents mètres.   4 Nous habitons (= vivons) à cinq cent vingt kilomètres de la capitale.   5 Je voudrais deux mètres cinquante de ruban blanc.   6 Elle reste avec nous une semaine sur cinq.

Have a try
— Did you have a good holiday? — Not bad! We went and spent a fortnight on the Côte d'Azur. — Was it quiet? — Quiet? Goodness no! There were millions of people in the shops, on the beach, in the streets, everywhere! It was impossible to move. We drove eight hundred kilometres to be packed like sardines! At the seaside it was impossible to find a place. We were

stepping on hands, on feet . . . — How dreadful! — Yes, but two hundred and fifty metres from the beach (= the edge) there were the boats of the millionaires who were there for the weekend. — Were you in a hotel? — Yes, eight hundred metres from the beach. In the morning, we used to eat our breakfast on the balcony of the bedroom and we looked at the sea. — Was the hotel expensive? — Yes, very. But everything is dear over there: cafés, restaurants, shops . . . Three thousand francs for a suit! — Three thousand francs? That's three hundred pounds! — Approximately . . . We went to the casino two or three times. It's extraordinary, there are people who win and lose (whole) fortunes in one night! One evening, I saw an American win five hundred thousand francs. I would have liked to have been in his place!

Chapter 25

Exercise 25(i)
1 qui, 2 que, 3 qui, 4 que, 5 que, 6 qui, 7 qui, 8 que.

Exercise 25(ii)
1 L'homme qui est malade est l'ami de mon frère.   2 Voilà le livre que j'ai acheté pour lui.   3 Mon oncle, qui a une ferme, est très riche et très avare.   4 Le vin que nous allons commander est cher.   5 Le porte-monnaie qui est là-bas sur la table est vide.   6 Je regarde le passeport qu'il a laissé sur le lit.

Exercise 25(iii)
1 laquelle, 2 lesquelles, 3 lequel, 4 lesquels, 5 desquelles, 6 duquel, 7 laquelle, 8 lesquelles.

Exercise 25(iv)

1 L'employé avec qui elle est arrivée ce matin est un bon ouvrier. 2 Où est le tire-bouchon avec lequel je vais ouvrir la bouteille? 3 La maison dans laquelle nous vivons n'est pas grande, mais elle est très belle. 4 Là-bas il y a un ruisseau à côté duquel il y a des bancs. 5 Voici la machine sur laquelle cette lettre a été tapée. 6 Les gens avec qui je suis venu sont mes voisins. 7 Le problème dont je parle n'est pas nouveau, mais il devient de plus en plus grave. 8 Le film dont vous parlez a gagné le premier prix au festival.

Have a try

— Bonjour. Police! Vous connaissez les gens qui habitent dans cette maison? — Les Dubois? Oui, pourquoi? — Vous les connaissez bien? — Non, pas vraiment; les Dubois sont des gens avec qui nous avons peu de contacts . . . Pourquoi? — Une seconde! C'est moi qui pose les questions ici! Ils ont des enfants? — Oui, ils ont un fils qui est à l'étranger, aux Etats-unis je crois, et une fille qui habite avec eux. La fille est là, mais les parents sont en vacances en Espagne. — La fille dont vous parlez, vous l'avez vue récemment? — Il y a deux ou trois jours . . . Non, attendez je dis un mensonge! Je l'ai vue hier matin! — Elle était seule? — Non, elle était avec un ami. Du moins, je suppose qu'il est son ami. — Vous pouvez me donner quelques détails sur lui? — Pas beaucoup . . . Quelqu'un avec qui elle travaille et qui vient la chercher tous les matins dans une vieille voiture qui fait beaucoup de bruit . . . Une Volkswagen rouge . . . Un charmant garçon (= jeune homme): blond, grand, très sympathique . . . Mais je voudrais savoir pourquoi vous me posez toutes ces questions! — Ce matin, nous avons trouvé la voiture dont vous parlez contre un lampadaire. Elle était vide. Pas de trace du jeune homme. Nous aimerions le retrouver pour lui poser quelques questions . . .

Chapter 26

Exercise 26(i)

1 On Monday evening we went to the cinema to see a thriller. 2 On a Friday, after work, he goes to the café for a drink. 3 Next Sunday we will go on a picnic if the weather is good. 4 Last Tuesday, your brother came with his fiancée. 5 On Wednesday mornings and Thursday afternoons, we go into town to do our shopping. 6 On Saturday, we will call your mother to tell her the news. 7 The shop is open Monday to Friday.

Exercise 26(ii)

1 Le samedi je vais déjeuner chez mes parents. 2 Mardi soir nous vous avons téléphoné mais vous n'avez pas répondu. 3 Est-ce que vous irez à la banque pour moi vendredi matin? 4 Ce magasin est fermé le dimanche. 5 Est-ce qu'elle sera dans son bureau lundi matin à neuf heures? 6 Le docteur est venu lundi. Il reviendra jeudi avant midi. 7 Il travaille pour nous le mardi, le jeudi et le samedi mais seulement le matin.

Exercise 26(iii)

1 In May, the countryside is very beautiful. 2 In September, we will go and spend a few days in the

Pyrenees. 3 In February, the children have a week's holiday. 4 In December, the shops are full of toys. 5 Spring begins on March 21st. 6 This winter, we will stay at home. 7 Last summer, we had a wonderful holiday. 8 One swallow does not make a summer.

Exercise 26(iv)

1 En mai, juin et juillet, nous avons beaucoup de travail. 2 L'automne est la saison la plus calme pour nous. 3 Nous allons passer l'hiver dans un pays chaud. 4 En automne et en hiver, l'hôtel est fermé parce qu'il n'y a pas de visiteurs. 5 Au printemps, il fera doux et il n'y aura pas de pluie. 6 Cet été, nous avons eu dix jours de soleil, c'est tout! 7 Quand j'étais jeune, je détestais l'automne. Maintenant je pense que c'est la meilleure saison.

Have a try

—Taxi, taxi!... Are you free? —Yes, sir ... Where do you want to go? —Can you take me to 135 Boulevard de la République? —Of course! Just a second, I'm going to put your cases in the boot! There we are, climb in ... Welcome to our town! Is this your first visit? —No, I came last year, but I only stayed for one day. —And this time? —I'm here until next Friday! —Well, in that case, you have a whole week to discover the town ... Are you here on holiday or on business? —Both! ... Are there interesting things to do? — Our town is very friendly and very dynamic, you know! It's a big industrial centre, but we also welcome a great many tourists, especially in winter! The skiing resort is ten kilometres away from the town centre. In the summer, you can go for walks in the mountain ... There are some sports centres which are open every day from eight o'clock in the morning till ten o'clock at night ... And theatres ... And museums. The latter are free but they are closed on Tuesdays. We also have many cinemas and on Mondays it costs less to go in. — Aren't you a bit far from the capital? — Not at all! There is a high-speed train service to Paris and Marseilles. In the summer, you can be on the beach in two and a half hours ... Ah, here we are! This is number 135 ... I hope you'll have a pleasant week! — Thank you. How much do I owe you? — Twenty-five francs. — There you are! Keep the change! Goodbye!

Chapter 27

Exercise 27(i)

1 We would like to find a small, inexpensive restaurant. 2 Every morning he had to prepare breakfast. 3 We will do everything we can to find your ring. 4 Could you please calm down a little? 5 You should know that the customer is always right. 6 We will know everything when he calls us. 7 Do you know how to cook eggs? 8 Could you turn your transistor radio down please?

Exercise 27(ii)

1 (a) Nous voulons mille francs. (b) Nous voudrions mille francs. 2 (a) Nous devons lui téléphoner. (b) Nous devrions lui téléphoner. 3 (a) Est-ce que vous pouvez faire la vaisselle? (b) Est-ce que vous pourriez faire la vaisselle?

4 (*a*) Je dois payer ma note.
(*b*) Je devrais payer ma note.
5 (*a*) Elle veut une bouteille d'eau
minérale. (*b*) Elle voudrait une
bouteille d'eau minérale.
6 (*a*) Les enfants doivent aller au lit
avant minuit. (*b*) Les enfants
devraient aller au lit avant minuit.
7 Est-ce que vous savez danser?
Je sais, mais je ne peux pas!
8 Faire chauffer le beurre douce-
ment dans une poêle.

Have a try

—Bonjour Jean! Tu as l'air triste
aujourd'hui. Tu es malade? —Non,
pas   exactement . . . J'ai   des
problèmes. —C'est grave? —Oui et
non . . . Je suis malheureux . . . Je
ne peux jamais prendre de
décisions . . . Je ne sais jamais ce
que je dois faire . . . Au travail je
suis trop timide et à la maison je n'ai
pas d'énergie . . . Je suis toujours
fatigué . . . —Tu es allé voir ton
docteur? —Non, je ne veux pas lui
raconter mes problèmes et d'ailleurs
je ne l'aime pas . . . Non, je dois
faire un effort. Je voudrais devenir
plus sûr de moi, prendre mes propres
décisions . . . Tu es mon ami, tu dois
m'aider. Je veux être plein de
confiance comme toi. J'ai décidé de
faire un gros effort. A partir
d'aujourd'hui je vais faire ce que je
veux. J'irai où je voudrai, quand je
voudrai! Les choses vont changer. Je
vais   voyager,   rencontrer   des
gens . . . Pour commencer, je vais
apprendre   à   conduire!   —C'est
formidable! —Oui, merci de ton
aide! —Mon aide? Mais je n'ai
rien   fait!   —Tu   m'as   donné
beaucoup de confiance! —Tu crois?
Eh bien, viens! Allons prendre un
verre! —Oh, je ne sais pas . . . Je

voudrais bien, mais ma mère
m'attend à la maison . . . Je ne veux
pas être en retard . . .

Chapter 28

Exercise 28(i)

1 What time is it? It's exactly
eighteen   minutes   past   three.
2 They came down at half past seven
and they had their breakfast on the
terrace. 3 Does the plane arrive at
8.30 or 8.40 pm? 4 I have been
here for one hour and ten minutes.
5 Do you have the time please? Yes,
it's five to twelve (midday). 6 The
shop is open from 8 am till
7.30 pm. 7 The meeting began at
three o'clock sharp and ended at a
quarter past six.

Exercise 28(ii)

1   Elle vous appellera à huit heures
juste (or précises). 2 Il prend son
déjeuner entre une heure et deux
heures. 3 Je voudrais partir avant
neuf heures et demie. 4 Quelle
heure est-il? J'ai oublié ma montre!
5 Cet hypermarché est ouvert
jusqu'à vingt-deux heures. 6 J'ai
rendez-vous chez le dentiste à quatre
heures et demie. 7 Vol numéro
deux cent trois, départ dix-neuf
heures sept, porte numéro dix.

Exercise 28(iii)

1 I went to the airport at six o'clock.
She had arrived at a quarter past
five. 2 Every time he invited me, he
had forgotten his wallet. 3 When
she wanted to read the (news)paper,
it had vanished (= disappeared).
4 He told us (that) he had lived in
Africa. 5 The customer said (that)
he had not used the lift. 6 We
complained because the plumber
had done his work badly.

Exercise 28(iv)

1 Quand il a regardé dans sa poche, le portefeuille avait disparu. 2 Je suis sorti seul; ma femme avait décidé de rester à la maison. 3 Elle était très rouge: elle était restée au soleil toute la journée. 4 Nous avions pensé qu'il aimerait son cadeau d'anniversaire. 5 Ah, si (seulement) j'avais attendu un moment! 6 Elle a dit qu'il avait glissé sur le sol mouillé.

Exercise 28(v)

1 She was only three (years old) when her parents left. 2 The meal only costs forty francs. 3 The doctor will only come at six (o'clock). 4 I only asked if the director (manager) was here! 5 We only met one English tourist. 6 You will not leave till after dinner.

Exercise 28(vi)

1 Les enfants vont chez mes parents pour le week-end. 2 Pendant l'hiver, nous avons beaucoup de neige. 3 Nous marchons depuis l'aube. 4 Sa femme est venue me voir il y a trois semaines. 5 Nous voudrions la maison pour un mois cet été. 6 Restez au lit un jour ou deux et vous vous sentirez mieux (or: et ça ira mieux).

Have a try

— Darling, do you remember the Smiths? — Who? — The Smiths we met four or five years ago in a hotel at the seaside! — No, I don't recall. — Yes, think back! He was a doctor in Brighton and she was a headmistress. — Oh yes, it's coming back to me . . . So? — Well, they have sent us a postcard. — From Brighton? — No! . . . They have been on holiday in Germany and they are coming to France for a few days. They are wondering if they could come and see us. — Oh yes? — Yes; we had given them our address and you had told them: "if you come our way, pop in and see us". — I said that? — Of course, darling. Have you forgotten? They were absolutely delightful (people). — Yes, that's true. . . They were very friendly and we had a good laugh with them . . . When are they coming this way? — . . . Er . . . This evening. — This evening? But we can't have them here this evening! I have a business meeting which has been organised for three weeks . . . I have to go! . . . — No problem. While you are at the meeting, I'll give them an aperitif and when you come back we will go to a restaurant (for a meal). You have been telling me for months that we will go to eat in a restaurant. I'll be able to wear my new dress! — Yes, of course, it's always the same with you! Every excuse is good enough to go out and spend money!

French-English vocabulary

The vocabulary list includes most of the words which have been used in the examples and the exercises. It does not, however, include items appearing in lists since, in such cases, the individual translation has already been given. The meanings chosen are applicable in the context of the sentences presented. Irregular forms (adjectives, nouns or past participles) are included after the relevant item.

Abbreviations

f = feminine   s = singular
m = masculine   pl. = plural
s.o. = someone

à *at/to*
abandonner *to abandon/leave*
abominable *abominable*
absolu *absolute*
accepter *to accept*
accident (m) *accident*
accomplir *to accomplish/achieve*
d'accord *alright/o.k./agreed*
acheter *to buy*
acteur (m) *actor*
actrice (f) *actress*
addition (f) *bill (in restaurant/ hotel)*
adieu *goodbye*
admiration (f) *admiration*
adorable *adorable*
adorer *to adore*
s'adresser à *to contact/speak to*
aéroport (m) *airport*
affaire (f) *business matter/deal*
affreux, -euse *ugly/awful*
affronter *to face*
Afrique (f) *Africa*
âge (m) *age*
âgé *old*

agent de police (m) *policeman*
agile *agile/nimble*
agir *to act*
agneau (m) *lamb*
agréable *pleasant*
aider *to help*
d'ailleurs *besides*
alcool (m) *alcohol*
Allemagne *Germany*
allemand *German*
aller *to go*
allô! *Hallo!*
allumer *to light/switch on*
allumette (f) *match*
alors *then/in that case*
Alpes (f. pl.) *Alps*
ambitieux, -ieuse *ambitious*
ambulance (f) *ambulance*
amener *to bring*
Américain (m) *American (person)*
américain *American*
ami, e (m, f) *friend*
amical *friendly*
amusant *amusing*
an (m) *year*
Angleterre *England*
Anglais (m) *Englishman*
anglais *English*
animal, animaux (m) *animal(s)*
année (f) *year*

anniversaire   (m)   *birthday/anniversary*

annoncer   *to announce*

apéritif (m)   *aperitif*

appareil-photo (m)   *camera*

appartement (m)   *apartment*

appeler   *to call*

apporter   *to bring*

après   *after*

après-midi (m)   *afternoon*

arbre (m)   *tree*

argent (m)   *money*

arriver   *to arrive*

ascenseur (m)   *lift (= elevator)*

assez   *enough*

associé (m)   *partner/associate*

atelier (m)   *workshop*

attention!   *caution/beware!*

attitude (f)   *behaviour*

aube (f)   *dawn*

auberge (f)   *inn*

aujourd'hui   *today*

aussi   *as well/also*

aussitôt   *immediately*

auto (f)   *car*

autobus (m)   *bus*

auto-stop (m)   *hitch-hiking*

avaler   *to swallow*

en avance   *early*

avancer   *to advance/move forward*

avant   *before*

avare   *mean*

avec   *with*

par avion   *by air/plane*

avoir (eu)   *to have*

avoir l'air   *to seem*

avoir raison   *to be right*

avoir faim   *to be hungry*

bagage (m)   *luggage*

baisser   *to turn down/lower*

bal (m)   *ball/dance*

balcon (m)   *balcony*

balle (f)   *ball*

ballon (m)   *balloon/ball*

banc (m)   *bench*

banque (f)   *bank*

bar (m)   *bar*

bas, basse   *low*

bateau (m)   *boat*

beau, belle   *beautiful*

besoin (m)   *need*

bête   *silly/stupid*

beurre (m)   *butter*

bien (m)   *good*

bientôt   *soon*

bienvenue (f)   *welcome*

bière (f)   *beer*

bifteck (m)   *(beef)steak*

billet (m)   *ticket/note*

biscuit (m)   *biscuit*

blessé   *wounded/hurt*

bleu   *blue*

blond   *blond*

bœuf (m)   *ox*

boire (bu)   *to drink*

boisson (f)   *drink*

bon, bonne   *good*

bon marché   *cheap*

bord (m)   *edge/side*

à bord   *on board/aboard*

bouchon (m)   *cork*

bouger   *to move/stir*

boulanger, -ère (m, f)   *baker*

boulot (m)   *job (fam.)*

bouquet (m)   *bunch/bouquet*

bouteille (f)   *bottle*

boutique (f)   *shop*

Bretagne (f)   *Brittany*

bruit (m)   *noise*

bulletin (m)   *bulletin*

bureau (m)   *office/desk*

cabinet de travail (m)   *study*

cacher   *to hide (something)*

(se) cacher   *to hide (oneself)*

cadeau (m)   *present/gift*

cafétéria (f)   *cafeteria*

calme   *quiet*

(se) calmer   *to calm down*

camion (m) *lorry*
campagne (f) *country(side)*
capitale (f) *capital*
car (m) *coach*
carte (f) *card/map*
carte postale (f) *postcard*
carnaval (m) *carnival*
casino (m) *casino*
cassé *broken*
casser *to break*
casserole (f) *pan*
cathédrale (f) *cathedral*
à cause de *because of*
caviar (m) *caviar*
chaise (f) *chair*
chalet (m) *chalet*
chambre (f) *bedroom*
champ (m) *field*
champagne (m) *champagne*
chance (f) *luck/chance*
changer *to change*
chanson (f) *song*
chanter *to sing*
chanteur, -euse (m, f) *singer*
chapeau (m) *hat*
chaque *each*
charcuterie (f) *pork-butcher's*
charcutier, -ière (m, f) *pork-butcher*
charger *to load*
charmant *charming*
chasseur (m) *hunter*
chat (m) *cat*
château (m) *castle*
chaud *hot*
chauffer *to heat up*
chauffeur (m) *driver/chauffeur*
chaussure (f) *shoe*
chemin (m) *lane/path/way*
cher, chère *dear/expensive*
pas cher *cheap*
chéri *darling/dearest*
chercher *to look for/search*
cheval, chevaux (m, pl.) *horse(s)*
chien (m) *dog*
chocolat (m) *chocolate*

choisir *to choose*
chose (f) *thing*
ciel (m) *sky*
cigare (m) *cigar*
cigarette (f) *cigarette*
cinéma (m) *cinema*
classe (f) *class*
clé (or clef) (f) *key*
client, -e (m, f) *customer*
cochon (m) *pig/slovenly person*
coffre (m) *(car)boot*
colis (m) *parcel*
collègue (m, f) *colleague*
collision (f) *collision*
commander *to order*
comme *as/like*
commencer *to begin*
comment *how*
commissions (f pl.) *errands/shopping*
complet, -ète *full/complete*
compliqué *complicated*
compter (sur) *to count (on)*
concierge (m, f) *concierge/caretaker*
conduire *to drive/lead*
confortable *comfortable*
congé (m) *holiday*
conserver *to keep*
considérable *considerable*
contact (m) *contact*
content *pleased/glad*
contre *against*
costume (m) *costume*
se coucher *to lie down/go to bed*
(se) couper *to cut (oneself)*
courrier (m) *mail*
course (f) *race/errand*
cousin, e (m, f) *cousin*
couteau à pain (m) *bread-knife*
cravate (f) *tie*
crédit (m) *credit*
crème (f) *cream*
crier *to shout*
croire (cru) *to believe*
croisement (m) *crossroad/crossing*

croissant (m)   *croissant*
cuire (cuit)   *to cook*
cuisine (f)   *kitchen*
curieux, -ieuse   *strange/curious*

dame (f)   *lady/woman*
dangereux, -euse   *dangerous*
dans   *in*
danser   *to dance*
déchiré   *torn*
déchirer   *to tear*
décider   *to decide*
(se) décider   *to make up one's mind/
  decide*
déclarer   *to declare/say*
décontracté   *relaxed*
(se) découvrir   *to uncover (oneself)*
défaut (m)   *fault/defect*
défense de (+ infin.)   *it is forbidden
  to*
déficit (m)   *deficit*
dégoûtant   *disgusting/awful*
dehors   *outside*
déjà   *already*
délicieux, -ieuse   *delicious*
demain   *tomorrow*
demander   *to ask (for)*
se demander   *to wonder*
demoiselle (f)   *young lady*
départ (m)   *departure*
depuis   *since/for*
déranger   *to disturb*
dernier, -ière   *last*
derrière   *behind*
désolé   *sorry*
dessert (m)   *dessert*
détail (m)   *detail*
détester   *to hate/detest*
détour (m)   *detour*
devant   *in front of*
devenir   *to become*
diable (m)   *devil*
diable!   *goodness gracious!*
difficile   *difficult*
dîner (m)   *dinner*

dire (dit)   *to say/tell*
directement   *directly*
directeur, -trice (m, f)   *director/
  manager*
discuter   *to discuss/talk*
disparaître (disparu)   *to disappear*
disque (m)   *record*
docteur (m)   *doctor*
document (m)   *document*
domestique (m)   *servant*
donner   *to give*
douanier (m)   *customs officer*
doux, douce   *soft*
à droite   *on the right*
durer   *to last*

eau (f)   *water*
école (f)   *school*
économique   *economic/economical*
écouter   *to listen (to)*
écriteau (m)   *sign/notice*
effrayant   *appalling/frightening*
eh bien!   *well then!*
église (f)   *church*
élégant   *smart/elegant*
elle (f. sg.)   *she, her*
elles (f. pl.)   *they, them*
emmener   *to take (s.o.) away*
employé, e (m, f)   *employee*
encore   *still/yet/again*
énergie (f)   *energy*
énerver   *to irritate (s.o.)*
enfant (m, f)   *child*
enfin   *at last/finally*
énorme   *enormous*
ensemble   *together*
ensuite   *then/afterwards*
entendre   *to hear*
entre   *between*
entrée (f)   *entrance*
entrer   *to enter/go in*
environ   *approximately*
envoyer   *to send*
épicier, -ière (m, f)   *grocer*
époque (f)   *era*

épuisé *exhausted*
escalader *to climb*
escalier (m) *staircase*
Espagne *Spain*
espagnol *Spanish*
essayer *to try*
et *and*
Etats-Unis (m. pl.) *United States*
été (m) *summer*
étonnant *astonishing*
à l'étranger *abroad*
éviter *to avoid*
exact *exact*
exactement *exactly*
excellent *excellent*
excuse (f) *excuse*
s'excuser *to apologize*
exigeant *demanding*
exister *to exist*
expérience (f) *experience*
exporter *to export*
exposition (f) *exhibition*
extraordinaire *extraordinary*
extrême *extreme*

fâché *angry/cross/annoyed*
facile *easy*
facteur (m) *postman*
facture (f) *bill (to pay)*
faim (f) *hunger*
faire *to do/make*
se faire mal *to hurt oneself*
falloir *to be necessary*
fatigué *tired*
fauteuil (m) *armchair*
femme (f) *wife/woman*
ferme (f) *farm*
fermé *closed*
ferry (m) *ferry*
festival (m) *festival*
feu, feux (m pl.) *fire(s)/light(s)*
feu rouge (m) *traffic lights*
fiable *reliable*
fiancé, -ée (m, f) *fiancé(e)*
fil (m) *thread*

fillette (f) *little girl*
film (m) *film*
film policier (m) *thriller (film)*
fils (m) *son*
finir *to finish*
fleur (f) *flower*
fois (f) *time*
une fois *once*
forêt (f) *forest*
formidable *wonderful/formidable/ fantastic*
fort *strong/loudly*
fortune (f) *fortune*
fou, folle (m, f) *madman, mad-woman*
fouiller *to search*
Français (m) *Frenchman*
français *French*
frapper *to knock/strike (a blow)*
frein (à main) (m) *(hand)brake*
freiner *to brake*
fréquent *frequent*
frère (m) *brother*
frite (f) *chip (= potato)*
froid *cold*
froissé *creased/crumpled*
fromage (m) *cheese*
fruit (m) *(piece of) fruit*
fumer *to smoke*
furieux, -euse *furious*

gagner *to win/earn*
garage (m) *garage*
garagiste (m) *mechanic/garage owner*
garantir *to guarantee*
garder *to keep*
gardien (m) *keeper/warden*
gare (f) *station*
gâteau (m) *cake*
général *general*
généralement *generally*
généreux -euse *generous*
gens (m pl.) *people*
glace (f) *ice/ice-cream/mirror*

glisser *to slip/slide*
gouvernement (m) *government*
grand *tall/high/big*
grandir *to grow (in size)*
grave *grave/serious*
grogner *to grumble*
gros, grosse *big/fat*
grotte (f) *cave*
guerre (f) *war*
guide (m) *guide*

habitant (m) *inhabitant*
habiter *to live/dwell*
habitude (f) *habit*
d'habitude *usually*
hélas! *alas!*
heure (f) *hour/time*
à l'heure *on time*
de bonne heure *early*
heureux, -euse *happy*
hier *yesterday*
hirondelle (f) *swallow*
histoire (f) *story/history*
hiver (m) *winter*
homme (m) *man*
horrible *horrible/awful*
hors-taxes *duty-free*
hôtel (m) *hotel*
humide *wet/damp*
hypermarché (m) *hypermarket*

idée (f) *idea*
il *he/it (m, s.)*
ils *they (m, pl.)*
immédiat *immediate*
impossible *impossible*
impressionnant *impressive*
inciter *to urge/incite*
incroyable *incredible*
indication (f) *indication*
industrie (f) *industry*
infect *stinking/foul*
insecte (m) *insect*
inspecter *to inspect*
inspecteur, -trice (m, f) *inspector*

intelligent *intelligent*
interdit *forbidden*
intérêt (m) *interest*
intéressant *interesting*
intérieur (m) *inside/interior*
inventer *to invent*
investir *to invest*
invitation (f) *invitation*
invité (m) *guest*
inviter *to invite*
Italie *Italy*
italien, -ienne *Italian*

jamais *never*
Japon (m) *Japan*
japonais *Japanese*
jardin (m) *garden*
jardinier (m) *gardener*
jaune *yellow*
jeter *to throw*
jeune (m) *young person*
jeune *young*
joli *pretty*
jouer *to play*
jouet (m) *toy*
jour (m) *day*
journal (m) *newspaper*
journée (f) *day (time-span)*
jusqu'à *until*
juste *just/precise/sharp (time)*

kilo(gramme) (m) *kilo(gram)*

la (f) *the*
là *there*
lac (m) *lake*
laisser *to leave (behind)*
lampadaire (m) *street light/lamp-post*
lampe (f) *lamp*
(se) laver *to wash (oneself)*
le (m) *the*
leader (m) *leader (political)*
les (m, f. pl.) *the*
lettre (f) *letter*

se lever *to get up*
libre *free/available*
limonade (f) *lemonade*
lire (lu) *to read*
liste (f) *list*
lit (m) *bed*
litre (m) *litre*
livre (m) *book*
livre de cuisine (m) *cookery book*
livre (sterling) (f) *pound (sterling)*
loin (de) *far (from)*
Londres *London*
longtemps *(a) long (time)*
lourd *heavy*
lumière (f) *light*
lunettes (f. pl.) *glasses (= spectacles)*
lunettes de soleil (f. pl.) *sunglasses*
luxe (m) *luxury*

machine (f) *machine*
magasin (m) *shop*
maillot de bain (m) *swimsuit*
main (f) *hand*
à la main *by hand*
maintenant *now*
mais *but*
maison (f) *house*
mal (m) *evil/ache*
mal *badly*
mal à la tête (m) *headache*
malade (m, f.) *sick person/patient*
malade *ill/sick/badly damaged*
malheureux, -euse *unhappy*
malle (f) *(car)boot*
maman *mum(my)*
manger *to eat*
marche (f) *step*
marché (m) *market*
marcher *to walk/work (for a machine)*
mari (m) *husband*
Maroc (m) *Morocco*
matin (m) *morning*
matinée (f) *morning (time-span)*

mauvais *bad*
melon (m) *melon*
même *even/same*
mensonge (m) *lie*
menu (m) *menu*
mer (f) *sea*
merci *thank you*
mère (f) *mother*
mesure (f) *measure*
météo (f) *weather forecast*
mettre (mis) *to put*
merveilleux, -euse *wonderful*
millionnaire (m) *millionaire*
minéral, -aux *mineral*
minuit *midnight*
minute (f) *minute*
miracle (m) *miracle*
mode (f) *fashion*
au/du moins *at least*
moins *less*
mois (m) *month*
mondial *worldwide*
moment (m) *moment*
monnaie (f) *change*
montagne (f) *mountain*
monter *to go up/take something up*
montre (f) *watch*
moto(cyclette) (f) *motorbike*
mouchoir (m) *handkerchief*
mouillé *wet*
moustache (f) *moustache*
mur (m) *wall*
mûr *ripe*
musicien (m) *musician*
musique (f) *music*

nager *to swim*
naître (né) *to be born*
nécessaire *necessary*
nettoyer *to clean*
neuf (neuve) *new*
nez (m) *nose*
noir *black*
non *no*
non alors! *most definitely not!*

note (f)   *bill*
nouvelle (f)   *(piece of) news*
nuage (m)   *cloud*
nuit (f)   *night*
numéro (de téléphone) (m)   *(phone) number*

obliger   *to oblige/force/compel*
œil, yeux (m)   *eye(s)*
œuf (m)   *egg*
offrir   *to offer*
oncle (m)   *uncle*
orage (m)   *storm*
organiser   *to organize*
ou   *or*
où   *where*
oublier   *to forget*
oui   *yes*
ouvert   *open*
ouvrier, -ière (m, f)   *worker*
ouvrir (ouvert)   *to open*

pain (m)   *bread*
pâlir   *to turn pale*
en panne   *out of order/broken down*
panneau (m)   *(road)sign*
papa   *dad(dy)*
par   *through/by*
parapluie (m)   *umbrella*
parce que   *because*
pardonner   *to forgive*
paresseux, -euse   *lazy*
parler (à)   *to talk/speak (to)*
partenaire (m, f)   *partner*
partir   *to go away/leave*
à partir de   *from*
partout   *everywhere*
pas du tout   *not at all*
passager, -ère (m, f)   *passenger*
passer   *to spend/pass (time)*
passeport (m)   *passport*
passionnant   *exciting*
patron, -onne (m, f)   *manager/ owner*
pauvre   *poor*
payer   *to pay*

pays (m)   *country*
paysage (m)   *scenery*
pêche (f)   *peach*
pendant   *during/for*
penser   *to think*
perdre (perdu)   *to lose*
se perdre   *to lose one's way/get lost*
perdu   *lost*
père (m)   *father*
personne (f)   *person*
personne   *nobody*
petit   *small*
petit déjeuner   *breakfast*
un peu   *a little*
à peu près   *approximately*
photo(graphie) (f)   *photo(graph)*
pièce (f)   *room/coin/play*
pied (m)   *foot*
à pied   *on foot*
pierre (f)   *stone*
pique-nique (m)   *picnic*
pittoresque   *picturesque*
placer   *to place/put*
s'il vous/te plaît   *please*
planète (f)   *planet*
plat (m)   *dish*
à plat   *flat*
plateau (m)   *tray*
plein   *full*
pleuvoir   *to rain*
plier   *to fold*
plombier (m)   *plumber*
pluie (f)   *rain*
plusieurs   *several*
pneu (m)   *tyre*
poche (f)   *pocket*
poche en papier (f)   *paperbag*
poêle (f)   *pan*
poire (f)   *pear*
politique (f)   *politics*
pont (m)   *bridge*
porte (f)   *door*
porte-monnaie (m)   *purse*
porteur (m)   *porter*
poser   *to put down/lay down*
potage (m)   *soup*

poulet (m) *chicken*
pour *for/in order to*
pourboire (m) *tip*
pourquoi *why*
précaution (f) *precaution*
précis *precise/accurate*
préférer *to prefer*
prendre (pris) *to take*
se préparer *to get ready*
près (de) *near*
presque *almost/nearly*
pressé *in a hurry*
prêt *ready*
prêter *to lend*
prière de (+ inf.) *please/you are requested to*
prix (m) *price/prize*
prochain *next*
profondeur (f) *depth*
programme (m) *programme*
projet (m) *plan*
promenade (f) *trip/walk*
propriétaire (m, f) *owner/proprietor*
protester *to protest*
prudence (f) *care*
pull-over (m) *pullover*

quand *when*
que *that/whom/which*
quelques *some*
quelque chose *something*
quelquefois *sometimes*
quelqu'un *someone*
qu'est-ce que . . . ? *what . . ?*
question (f) *question*
qui *who/whom*

raconter *to tell (a story)*
radio (f) *radio*
rapide *quick/fast*
rare *rare/unusual*
rasoir (m) *razor*
récent *recent*
récompenser *to reward*

redescendre *to go down again*
refermer *to re-seal/close again*
réfléchir *to think/ponder*
réfrigérateur (m) *refrigerator*
refuser *to refuse*
regarder *to look at/watch*
région (f) *region/area*
règne (m) *reign*
regretter *to regret*
rejoindre *to rejoin*
remplir *to fill up*
rencontrer *to meet*
rendez-vous (m) *appointment*
renvoyer *to fire/send back*
réparation (f) *repair*
réparer *to repair*
reparler *to talk again*
repas (m) *meal*
répondre *to reply*
repos (m) *rest*
réserver *to reserve/book*
réservoir (m) *tank*
reste (m) *rest/remainder*
rester *to stay/remain*
en retard *late*
retour (m) *return*
de retour *back (again)*
retrouver *to find (or meet) again*
réussir *to succeed*
revenir *to come back/return*
rêver *to (day)dream*
revoir *to see (meet) again*
riche *rich*
rien *nothing*
rincer *to rinse*
rire (ri) *to laugh*
risqué *risky*
robe (f) *dress*
rocher (m) *rock*
rond *round*
rose (f) *rose*
route (f) *road*
royal, royaux *royal*
ruban (m) *ribbon*
rue (f) *street*
ruisseau (m) *brook*

sable (m)   *sand*
saboter   *to botch up/sabotage*
sac (m)   *bag*
sac à main (m)   *handbag*
sage   *wise/well-behaved*
saisir   *to seize/catch*
saison (f)   *season*
salade (f)   *salad/lettuce*
sale   *dirty*
salle à manger (f)   *dining-room*
salle de bains (f)   *bathroom*
salon (m)   *living-room*
sandwich (m)   *sandwich*
sans   *without*
sardine (f)   *sardine*
scandale (m)   *scandal*
sculpture (f)   *sculpture*
sec, sèche   *dry*
sécher   *to dry*
seconde (f)   *second*
secrétaire (m, f)   *secretary*
semaine (f)   *week*
(se) sentir   *to feel*
serré   *tight*
serveuse (f)   *waitress*
serviette (f)   *towel/serviette/napkin*
servir   *to serve*
seul   *alone*
seulement   *only*
sherry (m)   *sherry*
si   *if*
simple   *simple*
sincère   *sincere*
situation (f)   *situation*
ski (m)   *ski(ing)*
société (f)   *society*
sœur (f)   *sister*
soif (f)   *thirst*
soin (m)   *care*
soir (m)   *evening*
solution (f)   *solution*
sorte (f)   *kind*
sortie (f)   *exist*
sortir   *to go out*
soudain   *suddenly*
souffrir   *to suffer*

sourd   *deaf*
sous   *under*
souvenir (m)   *souvenir/memory*
se souvenir   *to remember*
souvent   *often/frequently*
stationner   *to park*
stop (m)   *stop (road sign)*
stupide   *foolish/stupid*
stupidité (f)   *foolishness/stupidity*
stylo (à bille) (m)   *(ball-point)pen*
suffisant   *sufficient*
suivre   *to follow*
superbe   *superb*
supermarché (m)   *supermarket*
sur   *on*
sûr   *sure/reliable/safe*
surpris   *surprised*
s'il te plaît   *(if you) please (fam. form)*
s'il vous plaît   *(if you) please (pol. or plur. form)*
sympathique   *friendly*

tableau (m)   *painting*
tant pis!   *too bad!*
tante (f)   *aunt*
taper   *to type/knock*
tard   *late*
trop tard   *too late*
taxi (m)   *taxi*
téléphoner à   *to telephone s.o.*
télévision (f)   *television*
température (f)   *temperature*
temps (m)   *weather/time*
tendre   *tender*
tenir (tenu)   *to hold*
terminer   *to finish*
terrasse (f)   *terrace*
terre (f)   *ground/earth*
terrible   *terrible/dreadful*
tête (f)   *head*
théâtre (m)   *theatre*
timbre (m)   *stamp*
timide   *shy*
tire-bouchon (m)   *corkscrew*
tomate (f)   *tomato*

tombée de la nuit (f) *nightfall*
tomber *to fall*
tordre *to wring/twist*
toucher *to touch*
toujours *always/still*
tour (f) *tower*
touriste (m, f) *tourist*
tout *everything*
tout de suite *at once/immediately*
tout le temps *all the time*
trace (f) *trace*
train (m) *train*
transistor (m) *transistor (radio)*
transporter *to carry (in a vehicle)*
travail (m) *work*
travailler *to work*
travailleur (m) *worker*
travailleùr, -euse *hard-working*
traversée (f) *crossing*
traverser *to go through/cross*
très *very*
triste *sad*
trop *too much*
trouver *to find*

un, une (m, f) *a/an/one*
usage (m) *use/usage*

vacances (f. pl.) *holidays*
vache (f) *cow*
vaisselle (f) *washing up*
valise (f) *suitcase*
variété (f) *variety*
vase (m) *vase*
vélo (m) *bicycle*

vendre *to sell*
vérifier *to check*
verre (m) *glass*
vert *green*
viande (f) *meat*
vide *empty*
vie (f) *life*
vieux, vieille *old*
villa (f) *villa/(detached) house*
village (m) *village*
ville (f) *town*
vin (m) *wine*
visite (f) *visit*
visiter *to visit*
visiteur, -euse (m, f) *visitor*
vite *quickly*
vivre *to live*
voie (f) *track/way*
voir (vu) *to see*
voisin, voisine (m, f) *neighbour*
voiture (f) *car*
vol (m) *flight/theft*
voler *to steal*
voleur (m) *thief*
voyage (m) *journey*
voyager *to travel*
voyageur, -euse (m, f) *traveller*
vrai *true/right*

week-end (m) *weekend*

y *there*

zéro *nought/zero*
zut! *blast!*